Awakening

Also by Rodney Smith

*Stepping Out of Self-Deception: The Buddha's Liberating
 Teaching of No-Self*

Lessons from the Dying

Awakening

*A Paradigm Shift
of the Heart*

RODNEY SMITH

Shambhala • *Boston & London* • 2014

Shambhala Publications, Inc.
Horticultural Hall
300 Massachusetts Avenue
Boston, Massachusetts 02115
www.shambhala.com

9 8 7 6 5 4 3 2 1

First Edition
Printed in the United States of America

♾ This edition is printed on acid-free paper that meets
the American National Standards Institute z39.48 Standard.
♻ This book is printed on 30% postconsumer recycled paper.
For more information please visit www.shambhala.com.

Distributed in the United States by Penguin Random House LLC
and in Canada by Random House of Canada Ltd

Designed by James D. Skatges

Library of Congress Cataloging-in-Publication Data

Smith, Rodney (Teacher)
Awakening: a paradigm shift of the heart / Rodney Smith.
pages cm
ISBN 978-1-61180-126-2 (paperback)
1. Spiritual life. 2. Spiritual life—Buddhism. 3. Spirituality.
4. Enlightenment (Buddhism) I. Title.
BL624.S59485 2014
204'.2—dc23
2013022309

I have a feeling that my boat
Has struck, down there in the depths,
Against a great thing.
And nothing
Happens! Nothing . . . silence . . . waves . . .
—Nothing happens? Or has everything happened
and are we standing now, quietly in the new life?

—JUAN RAMON JIMENEZ

Contents

Acknowledgments

This book is dedicated to everyone who explores their curiosity to complete satisfaction, and a deep bow to my teachers who did just that.

A special thanks to Nancy Burnett and Parker Huey for their editing, both of whom have the power to transform words into an understandable narrative, and to Ellen McCown, who skillfully drew the diagrams and encouraged me throughout the process. Heartfelt appreciation to Joseph Goldstein and Ajahn Sucitto for their comments and suggestions.

Introduction

You that come to birth and bring the mysteries,
Your voice-thunder awakens us.
Roar, lion of the heart,
And tear me open.

—RUMI

Many of us do not understand what spiritual transformation requires. We may think of it as a slight alteration or deviation from our normal routines or perhaps merely an inconvenience. Life after this adjustment will go on pretty much as before, though we will be wiser and more judicious in our actions of body, speech, and thought. If we follow the Buddhist path, we may have a more penetrating understanding of the causes of our conflicts and torments. We may perceive our motivations and thoughts with more subtlety and generally live in a lighter, more joyous manner. These are the adaptations that occur when anyone allows the dharma[1] to affect his or her consciousness, but they are not the full story. The transformation that I am referring to in this book is a complete shift of paradigms, a total reorganization of perception. It is not an adaptation but a merging with and an abiding within reality.

This book attempts to explain genuine spiritual realization. When we speak of enlightenment and awakening, what do we

mean? What actually occurs when we slip beyond consensus or conventional reality,[2] and why would we undertake such a journey?
This book looks at the topography of the journey from beginning to
end, the multiple ways we undermine the very growth we seek, the
shift in consciousness that does occur, and the life that arises out of
that shift. The book was written to unmask the process of awakening, to expose it completely and free it from cultural and arcane language. When Buddhist references are appropriate, they are used, but
for the most part this journey is unique to each traveler and therefore
difficult to categorically map within any spiritual structure.

What inspired this book was the dearth of information on the
radical shift of paradigms that occurs when moving through and beyond our current perceptions of reality. There are spiritual books
that speak eloquently on the process of awakening, and books that
prepare the student for awakening, but few that actually describe the
alterations in perception and the accompanying mental reorganization in awakening. Many books seem to work around the adaptive
spiritual changes that occur by explaining how spiritual practice im-
proves our lives and increases our fulfillment, but the central issue in
spiritual growth is not self-enhancement but self-understanding.
The movement through the isolated objects of the world into the
wonderment of interconnection is the spiritual journey. But are
there causal conditions that facilitate this movement, and what, if
anything, does that process need from us? Where does this shift ultimately take us, and what happens to "me" during the process?

Buddhism is my spiritual home, but it is not the only guide
available. I will frequently reference Buddhism because that is what I
know, but I call upon the reader to find verses from his or her own
system to lead him or her forward. Every tradition offers the reassurance of those who have safely gone before, but that does little to diminish the fear and trepidation almost all of us feel as we journey the
path alone. This is ultimately a path through our aloneness that ends
within the unifying stillness of all things. This book is not only a
companion guide through that journey but equally a workbook toward its completion. Sidebar exercises are offered throughout the
chapters to experientially bring some of the more abstract points into

concrete realizations. Genuine transformation is governed by realization, by how much we truly allow in and how much we actually open and ingest the principles mentioned.

The book is divided into three loosely organized sections with considerable overlap among them. The first four chapters are an attempt to understand the transformative qualities of this paradigm shift of the heart while offering an overview of the problems intrinsic within consensus reality. We see how the perception of separation arose over time to secure a habitat for our species. We look at the value of seeing the world as separate and the limitations that are inherent within that perception. We also examine how the mind has arranged its internal processes to support the perception of separation, and the way that life lines up within that distortion. We explore mentally created laws like time and distance that are true only within the consensus paradigm and the principles that accompany the holistic nature of mind once freed of its internal division.

The next section of the book investigates the passageway between the conventional and formless paradigms. How does this work and what is needed? This section also deals with the various spiritual pathways that set our course and direction from beginning to end. This is the heart of the book, and the first continuum we follow to completion is the Buddhist perspective of suffering to the end of suffering. Other continua are explored that may be more suitable to different temperaments, but each pathway is rigorously defined and thoroughly examined for authenticity.[3] The common elements of every pathway, including counterinfluences, the false nirvanas, and the shifts in consciousness, are explored and explained, and guidelines are offered for choosing methods that will not undermine the authentic direction for each continuum.

The final chapters of the book work with the qualities of the heart that arise naturally as the paradigm shifts beyond conventional reality. Qualities like love can have powerful motivating effects upon us, but as soon as we make love an objective goal, we lose sight of the formless nature of love that surrounds us at every point. What does a life look like when it is lived within love rather than for love?

Finally, I wanted to write a book that would not only be a

description of the radical transformation that occurs but encourage a participation in the process as well. The sole prerequisite for joining this adventure is an enthusiasm and curiosity to know what is true rather than living with what is convenient and easy. But this single requirement seems to vastly limit the number of participants. The intended audience of this book is anyone who is hungry enough to question conventional assumptions and allow the truth to take us wherever it will. If we are motivated to know what is true, then let us dive into the mystery of life together and relish this joyful journey to fulfillment.

Awakening

I

In Search of the Essence

Ultimately, we are merely observing the act of creation.

—AJAHN CHAH

No one knows what a single thing is. For example, we can describe a leaf's green appearance derived from chlorophyll and the interaction of chlorophyll and light in photosynthesis. We can explain our experiences of the leaf, our thoughts and feelings about it, and how we receive it through our senses; we can discuss how the leaf interacts with CO_2 and sunlight to produce sugars and organic compounds, but what it is in its essence is unknowable. We can discover its composition and probe its molecular and atomic structure, but in so doing we are merely breaking down something unknowable into smaller and smaller unknowable parts. Nothing is known or can be known in essence. This is an amazing statement, because after our prolonged history of scientific investigation probing the nature of matter, we have come up empty-handed, and perhaps even more disconcerting, after a lifetime of collecting objects of worth and value, we are left wondering what we have actually gathered around us.

Pursue this inquiry into essence a little further. Lift your hand and ask, "What is this?" Do not stop asking the question until you have sifted through what you call the object: what you can say about it, what it looks like, its color, its weight and dimensions, and the object's use and utility. Keep asking the question deeply until your mind simply stops answering and has come to the end of its descriptions and knowledge. How close have you now come to what "hand" is? Calling the object something, naming it, doesn't make it "something," it only makes it what the mind says it is, though something seems to remain in the silence after the words have faded away. "Hand" now floats free of the mooring to definition and becomes empty and almost translucent yet somehow silently connected with the rest of the muted world. The silence we now find ourselves in may be a clue to the object's true nature, but let's keep this inquiry alive and see where it takes us.

If we searched on a grand scale, we might be able to place an object in context to something larger and, in doing so, approach its essence. Perhaps by opening our awareness to the vastness of space and time, we could come closer to its true existence. If we panned out beyond the earth, our solar system, the Milky Way galaxy, and continued to move outward even farther, beyond the beyond, we would bear witness to a universe of 100 billion galaxies with 100 billion stars in each galaxy, a size and reach incomprehensible to our minds. We would behold billions of stars being born into the cosmos within nurseries formed by the gas and nebulae of space, and the clustering of primordial galaxies as gravity pulls matter into itself. Because light has been journeying billions of years to reach our eyes, as we stare back into this vast dimensionless void, we are actually seeing back in time, as the universe existed in its youthful formative stage. And if we could see back far enough and therefore early enough, some 13.8 billion years ago, we would witness the moment of creation, known as the Big Bang in cosmology.

Where did that burst of creativity come from? Who or what was behind it, and who or what is now in control of this unfolding, this miraculous display? What is guiding the expansion of the universe in its wonder and mystery? Quoting Mark Whittle, a cosmologist from the University of Virginia, "Within the first second of the Big Bang, all the subatomic particles and all the laws of physics were created. But what determined those laws and the configuration the universe took? How does nature know to produce a quark and an anti-quark pair, for instance, instead of two quarks? Where does that knowledge reside? Our best guess is that the knowledge is somehow embedded in the vacuum (the nothing) of space itself. This knowledge is located within every point of space. The vacuum gives life to the universe and informs it how to behave."[1]

There is something even more astounding, and we do not need to understand the math or science to get the point. Cosmologists have calculated the total mass of the universe by knowing that there are an average of 5.8 hydrogen atom masses per cubic meter within the universe. Taking the radius of the visible universe at 14 billion years, they have calculated the total mass of the universe to be 10^{53} kilograms. To figure accurately the total mass, the scientists have to add the negative effect of gravity upon this positive sum of mass. This negative impact turns out to exactly equal to the positive weight of the total mass, a negative 10^{53} kilograms. The astrophysicists have calculated that "the total mass of the universe sums to nothing. *The universe sums to zero*."[2] This is certainly one of the most amazing conclusions offered by science.

Let us explore this mystery a little further and ask the question, "Into what does the universe expand?" Is there a preexisting region or vacuum outside that is filled as the cosmos expands? Not according to the cosmologists, who say that the expanding universe itself is creating the very space it expands into. There is not a preexisting region that the expansion fills; it creates the space into which it inflates. Furthermore, scientists tell us that the heavier elements that compose our bodies were birthed from exploding stars that spewed their contents outward and were eventually re-collected by gravity into newly born stars, solar systems, planets, and the people that inhabit them. We are literally the "stuff of stars."

Ontologic
mat

Suppose we went the other way and narrowed down our vision to the very small, down to the microscopic cellular level, and gazed upon the living wonders of one of the 50 trillion cells[3] of the human body. We enter a kingdom of unparalleled complexity with a myriad of materials flowing in and out of a million cellular openings, each opening guarded for false entry. We move through the cellular membrane, bypassing the mitochondria, the golgi apparatus, the ribosomes and lysosomes, passing through the cytoplasm, and enter the cell's nucleus.[4] There is orchestrated movement throughout the entirety of the cell as each cell of the body engages in more than 6 trillion functions per second and somehow instantly knows what all the other cells are doing. Each cell had its origin within the DNA molecule that held the instructions for the entire organism. It divided just fifty times to form the human being, creating trillions of cells from those divisions.[5] But who or what is in charge of this vast network of intricacy? Where is all of this going, and who is controlling it?

To answer these questions, we may have to look with more subtlety; perhaps we need to refine our focus, zooming down many thousands of times into much smaller regions. Maybe this level of reality will reveal what is behind this creation. We are now peering into the world of the very small, beyond the microscopic to the subatomic dimension of reality, where if a proton in the nucleus of a hydrogen atom were enlarged to the size of a basketball, the electron would be some twenty miles away.

empty space

If it were possible to observe directly at this magnification, we would see sheer chaos. Forms would arise and spontaneously pass away; the same form might be at two different locations in the same moment. This quantum foam[6] moves occasionally like waves and sometimes like discrete lumps of matter. The way we perceive cannot intuit this process, but scientists interpret quantum matter as simultaneously being a wave and a particle, and in its latent form, existing as a potential state in between the two. The Nobel Prize–winning physicist Richard Feynman has said, "Quantum mechanics deals with nature as she is . . . absurd."[7] Absurd as it may be, some scientists now believe that "quantum mechanics applies to everything in the universe, even to us. Quantum behavior eludes visualization and common sense. It forces us to rethink how we look at the universe and accept a new and unfamiliar picture of the world."[8]

No one knows what a single thing is.

We could keep increasing the magnification until we ran into an absolute limit known as Planck's constant. Planck's constant is meaninglessly small. If an atom were magnified to the size of the solar system, this unit of measurement would be the size of a tree.[9] But what is truly fascinating is that roughly halfway between the size of the very large known universe (10^{27} meters) and this very small quantum limitation (10^{-35} meters) are the dimensions of our world as we know it. The human species is approximately equally distant from the largest and grandest and the smallest and most diminutive expressions of forms.

Looking in either direction, toward the immense or the minute, we see vast displays of matter and energy in complex and intricate interrelationships, all in movement, seemingly without a controller, creating the universe in the perfection of its total display. It is only here, in the middle, within the perceptual reality of our day-to-day experience, that we attempt to impose a planned, organized, and well-controlled life. We have lost faith that the assumed disorder of the universe could actually hold its own order that we are unable to comprehend. To compensate, we use our thoughts and concepts to smooth the erratic and unpredictable edges of the quantum world into a system of known confidence and assurance. The order we create from our thoughts is mental invested order not systemic order. It seems impossible to be intellectually certain about something that is unknowable, but we have placed names and ideas upon objects that substitute for knowing their true essence. We have formed a certain world from our abstract ideas about each object, even though *abstract* and *certainty* are contradictory terms.

Mystery is above us in the large, mystery is below in the small, and our self-possessed assuredness is in the middle, where we claim our existence. Could it be that this middle section, composed of our mind's conclusions, may be missing the mystery that unites the large with the small? In whatever way we turn, <u>certainty does not seem to be a principle of nature</u>. Nature does not seem to hold the world one

way as opposed to another. It would make sense that if the fundamental elements that form us are utterly unknowable, we too must
be similarly composed.

If we exclude the human species, this middle dimension we
called nature is without self-centeredness and has no governance.
But when we add our species back into the equation, suddenly there
is an egocentric perception that forces the world into an unnatural
rigidity and separation. All of us have had the experience of dropping
our guard when engrossed in the natural world and living for a brief
moment free of our mental discursiveness and language. We suddenly feel "at home," relaxed, and connected to the sights, sounds,
smells, and sensations around us. In fact, this loss of self-centeredness
and the accompanying sense of connectedness may be one of the
reasons we appreciate being in nature. With this experience as a
guide, we can begin to question whether this self-center is authentic
or whether it is keeping us from something natural. Could our mental need to label and fix experiences into a rigidly certain world be
the only inauthentic aspect of nature?

It is within this paradox that we begin the real inquiry into the
essence of life. It is a journey far deeper and richer than has yet been
traveled by science. What we believe ourselves to be is what we make
the world to be, so inevitably we must begin with self-exploration.
Scientists seem to be proclaiming the absolute wonder on which everything rests and into which everything evolves. Perhaps we have
kept ourselves from this wonder far too long, and by questioning our
perceived reality we can return to the mystery of the universe.

A FIXED WAY OF SEEING

What science is now demonstrating is that the fixed way we perceive
the world is misinformed. Science is saying the world is much more
of an enigma than our eyes recognize and is much more alive and
interactive than the frozen way we perceive it. It will probably take
many years before our frozen view of life thaws to include the disclo-
sures of modern science, but just as in medieval times we believed
the earth was the center of the universe and now know otherwise,

our current perceptual beliefs will eventually evolve to accommodate the mysteries now being revealed.

Most modern scientists who are actively exploring these new
realities base their lives and perceptions within the truths of classical
physics that existed prior to the twentieth century. Sir Isaac Newton,
the spokesperson for this classical approach, declared that time and
space "were absolute and immutable entities . . . and supplied the
invisible scaffolding that gave the universe shape and structure."[10]
The world of classical physics, with its dependability of time, space,
and distance, is the home we all recognize and understand. It provides the stable conventional reality that we teach our children. But
the "universe according to quantum mechanics is not etched into
the present; the universe according to [modern physics] participates
in a game of chance."[11]

Some of us have struck out on our own, intuitively feeling the
truth of these anomalies and sensing their spiritual potential. We no
longer want to be held within an antiquated and constricted reality,
and we sense a greater freedom through questioning the boundaries
of our old perceptions. Many of us usually start by studying the sci-
ences or the perennial spiritual philosophies, but study alone does
not seem to satisfy our deepest yearning, nor bring us closer to these
revelations. The question that haunts us is how to live those perceptions so that the world becomes that perspective rather than an
overlaid philosophy upon conventional realty. As Brian Greene, a
physics and mathematics professor at Columbia University, states,
"The overarching lesson that has emerged from scientific inquiry
over the last century is that human experience is often a misleading
guide to the true nature of reality. Lying just beneath the surface of
the everyday is a world we would hardly recognize."[12] Many of us
seek to live beneath the "surface of the everyday" and discover its
rewards. All authentic methods seem to form around the central
intention of experiencing reality as it is, the essence that lies just
below our thoughts. Thoughts may have their value, but they also
hold a limitation that confines us to the conditioned way we have
always perceived. Forming our reality out of our thoughts misses
where science is now pointing.

When we look out of our eyes, we see the world as we have been taught to see it, our eyes organizing reality as objects distant from the subject of "me." The force of our conditioning holds us within this duality, and that conditioning acts as a substantial authority unleashing our doubt if we stray too far away from what we have learned. Here is where science can help. It supersedes the educational imprint that has kept us confined within the logic of consensual reality. We were educated under the logic of the old science, and the new science is showing us a new perception that can arrest our doubt. We can now look out of our eyes and understand that though we perceive in a dualistic way, it is not the truth regardless of what we have been taught to believe.

When I was young, perhaps in my early teens, I began feeling confined by my consciousness. It was as if I could not get away from myself. Everywhere I turned, there I was; my thoughts were always mine, and I was unable to hold any other perspective than the one I was thinking. I was trapped within the content of my mind, as if my perceptions only mirrored back my own ideas. I remember asking my friends if they shared this dilemma. None did. I could not understand why I was feeling this way when no one else seemed to be bothered by it. When I asked my parents, they looked at me quizzically but offered little help. I decided that I must have been sensing something that was not true for others, so I gave up the inquiry, though the sense of being constrained within my consciousness persisted.

It took years to flesh out the details of my psychological confinement. These youthful questions led to a growing disquietude in adulthood that I could not avoid. The questions penetrated much deeper than I had supposed in my youth. Initially I found it difficult to investigate my consciousness because the inquiry inevitably led to a sense of aloneness and distance from others, who seemed to be enjoying the very boundaries I was exploring. Few of us want to follow a line of questioning that upsets the applecart and undermines the very structure of reality, questions that are central to our assumed place in the world. It is hard to be alone, yet when we start asking questions about the nature of existence, that is where the exploration takes us.

The percentage of Americans who report having had "a religious or mystical experience" climbed from 22 percent in 1962 to a remarkable 48 percent in 2009.[13] A mystical experience is defined as an "otherworldly feeling of union with the divine." A little less than half the population surveyed said they had such an experience, but the more interesting fact was that most of the roughly half who acknowledged having such a revelation said they never wanted to have another. I can only assume that this experience had taken them too far away from conventional reality without an obvious way to return.

There is a mystery in quantum physics known as quantum entanglement that seems to provide ample proof of nonseparation. In quantum entanglement a separated pair of electrons with opposite spins are placed far apart, and the rotation of the spin of one of the electrons is reversed. When this occurs, the partner of the electron whose rotation has been altered immediately self-corrects and begins to spin in the opposite direction. It does not do this at the speed of light, which might indicate communication between the two—which would be strange enough—it does this instantaneously, unaffected by distance, as if the two were actually one and the same particle/wave.[14]

Facts such as these suggest a universe that is much more open and accessible than we conceive within our isolated position. We may be more porous and available to life as a whole than we could ever imagine. Perhaps our moment-to-moment presentation is part of the creative expression of the whole, no more separate from the planets than the paired electrons are from each other. Life can and does get through our formidable defenses, revealing a wonder that far exceeds our professed limitations. Here is the physicist Brian Greene stating the obvious: "We are forced to conclude that our view of reality is but one among many—an infinite number, in fact—which all fit together within the seamless whole of space-time."[15] In less guarded moments we may sense this possibility, only to be drawn back to the mundane by our conditioned perceptions, and it is usually this conditioned way of seeing that has the final word on how we move forward.

Our current paradigm has an all-encompassing logic that is based

{ upon the premise of separation: that I, the subject, am having the experience of distinctly separate objects and the universe is divided into a multitude of isolated forms. We rarely challenge this premise because our direction within life rests upon its certainty, <u>and everyone seems to be acting as if it were true.</u> But just because everyone seems to be acting in accordance with this premise does not make it true, and science is showing us that we need an updated paradigm.

{ This book proposes that we do just that, update our paradigm. For a variety of logistical reasons, from political domination, population expansion, and resource diminishment to climate devastation, the time is right for a new paradigm. But beyond the human drama and need, science is proving our current reality false. It is revealing truths that are new only to us but have been present and active since time immemorial, and we have simply been unable or unwilling to experience them. It is like fish suddenly perceiving the water they swim in: as shocking as that might be when first understood, it really changes nothing. The fish go on swimming within a medium that is now made conscious to them. Discovering the mutability of time, space, knowledge, and separation does not change the underlying reality of what has always been; it simply opens a new potential and configuration within that reality.

The crossing over into this new paradigm is the subject of mythology from every culture since the dawn of humankind and is rarely an even and uneventful passage. It is more than a simple perceptual transformation of moving from separation to unity. This involves every facet of our body, speech, and mind. It is a complete and thorough reorganization of thought, sensation, and experience, including the release of every conceptual boundary, inside and out. We would like to keep this transformation safe and expose only the components we would like to change, but the shift of paradigms requires everything from us, and holding anything back keeps it all arrested within conventional logic. We have to proceed without any guarantees, for as we have seen, the universe works best without manual control, and the assurance of security keeps us within our old { mental frame of reference. <u>To change paradigms</u>, we have to live as the universe actually is, not the way we want it to be.

Why are we unable to perceive nonseparation within our existing paradigm? Why do our eyes betray this truth and cast the world as a subjective experience of external objects? Consider that the brain has the ability to convince us of anything. Optical illusions and paradoxes abound. Take a very simple perceptual illusion: the size of the moon when seen rising vertically next to the horizon compared to its size when the moon is overhead. We are convinced the moon is larger when rising in perspective to the earth, but of course intellectually we know that it is not. Try as we might, we cannot shake the perception that it is larger closer to the earth, because the brain is convincing us of that perception. In another experiment revealing the brain's perceptual inflexibility, a pair of unusual goggles that inverted the top half of an image but not the bottom half were placed on subjects. Within a few moments the brain reconverted the image back to its normal perception even though the glasses remained on.[16]

We will explore in the next chapter the history of our species that may have led to this "rearrangement of reality," but for now let's just assume that the brain sees what it wants to see, not necessarily the truth of the situation. On a National Public Radio program called *Radiolab,* an episode explored the question of "how the brain makes me."[17] One neurologist stated that there are literally a billion neurons in our brain that fire simultaneously every second, each carrying a small bit of information about "me." The brain somehow instantly organizes all the data, and an image of "me" is formed. He said it is truer to say there are a billion me's than to say there is one.

Over the years we have learned to ignore the evidence of nonseparation and continued to engage the world as if we were isolated and alone. Occasionally, dedicated pursuers of truth like the Buddha seem to speak from a place of interconnectedness that often affirms the sense of our own nonseparation. Our hearts respond with complete acknowledgment because the sense of unity touches the part of us that is alive beyond the deception of self. Listen to how the Buddha describes his reality: "There is a place of non-possession, a place of nonattachment. It is the total end of death and decay, and is why I call it extinguished and cooled."[18] As we look out from our tired and stressful lives, we know this has to be true. We know there has to be another way to live that is balanced and at ease with all things, and we know that the center of the difficulty lies in how we perceive the world of self and other.

Why would we do this, we might ask? Why would we uproot every assumption we live with and willingly move beyond them? Why? Because it is the true nature of reality, and anything less is living an imaginary existence. How long can we fool ourselves before we concede the truth? Whenever the truth is being circumvented, there will always be a glitch. When the sense of self is deemed true, there arises a nagging feeling of incompletion, as if something had been omitted, and we have no idea how or where to find it. This feeling of incompletion is the defect, the flaw, inherent in separation. This makes sense, of course, because something *has* been left out when we subdivide into parts what is intrinsically whole.

> Try this exercise: Do not authenticate the perception of separation but simply try to feel what comes forth when you believe in this way of seeing. Feel the pain inherent in seeing the world as outside you—being cut off and isolated. Thinking the world is separate forces you to use the world to satisfy your desires, so a tension comes into play. You must also shore up your defenses and security so the world will not overwhelm you, and therefore fear arises. On and on the layers of pain accrue until you are willing to seek a true and natural relationship with reality. You will discover that many of the emotions you take for granted originate from thoughts of separation.

To compensate we seek to offset this sense of incompletion by searching for experiences that offer momentary gratification. We maintain the sense of an external world because it gives us an opportunity to compensate for the flaw of our own making—a flaw created by assuming separation. Much of our action becomes an attempt to remedy the stress of our misperceptions and thereby regain an innate ease and well-being. This works as long as we ignore what is driving our actions and refuse to question the assumptions behind them.

The simple solution is to release the need to be separate, allowing the whole to reemerge; then the struggle would naturally resolve itself, but we have so much at stake in being separate that we forgo the obvious. We have lived with this deficiency for so long, we think it is our natural condition and no longer understand it as a self-generated problem. Living within the view of separation requires us to project the pain of incompletion back onto the world so that we can be free of the consequences. We have developed an elaborate system of defenses to ward off the implication that there is anything wrong with the way we observe other than unwanted and interfering circumstances that keep us from our goals. This has led to a culture that is very good at blaming and accusing others but very poor at assuming any personal accountability.

Isolated objects in movement inevitably collide, causing the predictable conflicts that fill our lives. Life can never be completely satisfactory living within this flawed perception, but most of us equate this discomfort as simply "the way life is." When multiplied by the 7 billion people on earth, all with their own personal demands, special interests, neediness, and longing to alleviate their pain, we realize why our species continually feels at war with itself. The pain inherent in separation prevents us from feeling completely nourished no matter how we try to compensate.

This subtle sense of lacking, which I am calling the flaw of separation, can also be advantageous when it motivates us toward self-advancement, and we learn the skills and knowledge necessary to meet our human and professional needs. This felt limitation incites us to try and improve ourselves and offers the future reward of personal betterment, and as long as we are moving forward, adding skills and becoming more proficient, we seem to be fulfilling our purpose. When we look closer we see this activity is entirely motivated by unconscious and conditioned forces whose real intention is to feed our egoic center with an enhanced self-image.[19] This is not wrong, but it is limiting because the egoic center is insatiably restless, forever moving forward. Any prominence gained can never bring us to complete rest because the insufficiency we feel is not caused by a personal deficiency but by the very view we hold within separation. The methods we apply to compensate for our personal incompleteness end up reinforcing the view of division and further complicate the problem by increasing our discomfort.

If we look at our lives right now, we will sense that we are on shaky ground and feel the stress fractures and struggles of this mode of perception. It is not somewhere else or in some other time, it is here and now that we keep conceding to this misperception. Perhaps we can feel a haunting sense of something missing, a subtle awareness of being fragmented, or a compelling need to acquire something not present. Rather than seeing this as a flaw of perception, we internalize it as a personal defect, something missing in us or something insufficient about us. That assumption keeps us pursuing a remedy, never realizing it is the perception of separation that is causing the pain, and the pursuit to cover over the pain maintains the misperception.

If no one knows what a single thing is, why do we go around acting as if we do? That question, as rhetorical as it may sound, is actually a deep spiritual inquiry. The continuity of knowing held within our neurological patterns gives us a sense that the "I" is a continuous ongoing living reality, not a momentary firing of neurons. Said slightly differently, the sense of I is literally held together by memory. Our perceptions hold the neurological recognition of all the ingredients of the moment, giving us a complete worldview we can relate to. The brain goes backward into its memory to progress forward through the present into its future. For reasons of safety and security, we walk through the present hand in hand with the past, summoning our history to accompany us on our journey through life.

In the next chapter we will learn the value and limitation of past memory on present circumstances. In our ancient history as a species, thinking was not only a unique privilege but also a necessity for survival. The reason it is so difficult to question the assumptions that thoughts are based upon is that thinking is a survival mechanism that is deeply imbedded within our genetic structure. By questioning our thoughts, we question our security.

We seem to have come full circle in this chapter and are no closer in understanding what anything actually is, and we have seen that science is also unable to fully answer the question. We may have to concede the point that we will never intellectually know the essence of life, but that is not to imply that the source itself is unknowable. The essence of life may well be ineffable but still knowable to our hearts. As we venture into this book, let us remain open to this paradox. Many words will be used, but the words cannot reach within the new paradigm for orientation or adequate explanation. That is a journey silent to the heart.

Languages
d different
worldviews

2

Consensus Paradigm
and Abstract Thought

Man has such a predilection for systems and abstract deductions that he is ready to distort the truth intentionally, he is ready to deny the evidence of his senses only to justify his logic.

—FYODOR DOSTOYEVSKY

Now that we have some sense of how the brain denies the inherent wonder of life and misconstrues the naturally aligned view of unity to construct a reality of separation, we might ask how this illusory perception developed. The infinite and infinitesimal are obviously joined in ways that contradict our perceptions of separation, yet our mind stubbornly continues to organize a reality that is disparate and unrelated. It may be helpful to understand how this division occurred in evolution and the dynamics that were at play that made the perception of separation a survival mechanism. Perhaps when properly understood, we can directly address the fear for our survival rather than continuing a distortion that has its roots in ancient times.

Around 1.5 million years ago in what is modern-day Kenya, a species of *Homo erectus* (from the Latin, "to set upright") appeared on the scene.[1] Anthropologists believe this species was capable of primitive tool making and hunting and was perhaps the first hominid to use symbolic communication. They probably lived in a hunter-gatherer society, forming in groups and caring for the infirm or weaker companions. Though controversial, it is possible that they were the first to speak an abstract language though not the first to walk on two legs.[2]

It seems probable that this species, as ape-like as human, wandered away from the protective forest of their ancestors onto the plains of Africa, where they were vulnerable to beasts of prey. They did not have claws or fangs, were not fast or ferocious, and did not hold any other edge that would have allowed them to flourish. Though they appear to have been endurance runners, their survival demanded an evolution of some trait that would give them an advantage over predatory animals. The facility that evolved was their intelligence and cunning. As their brains grew in size, they developed the capacity to see an object as an abstraction, as more than what it was in and of itself. For instance, instead of seeing only a dead branch or an inert rock, they could envision the wood being shaped into a spear or the rock being sculptured into a spearhead. They began to see not what was but what could be, and this imaginative leap freed them from their lack of bodily strength and allowed them to form hunting excursions.

The ability to reason abstractly had enormous consequences not only for their survival, which was paramount, but also for the development of the community and its capacity to expand and improve. Language allowed images to be converted into ideas and reflected upon, ultimately enabling these hominids to surmount the limitations of a situation. But the greatest immediate reward for abstract thought was the entrapment and killing of wild animals that until this point had hunted them, and with this newly evolved ability, our prehistoric ancestors leaped to the top of the food chain.

For most of the 1.5 million years, symbolic communication has served our species well. A glance around demonstrates its effectiveness. The various constructions and buildings we see, the relative ease of living, technological advances, scientific discoveries, the arts, philosophies, and virtually everything human made—all have their origins within abstract thought. The brain has created a world of

Ladder of Abstraction + Inference

complex and consequential objects with an infinite range of possibilities, and its potential has barely been tapped.

{ The range of what symbolic language can create is endless, but it is not always to our advantage. Like any adaptive skill, abstract thought can work for or against us. The imagined world does not stop with the possibilities of what an object can be (a stick can be a spear); it can also enhance or diminish experiences, deny they ever occurred, and refuse any accountability. At first glance, this seems to give us a way out of difficulties: if we feel bored or restless, we can simply imagine ourselves somewhere else that is more interesting; if the problem is overwhelming, we can fantasize it does not exist and move on. But unfortunately, the shortcomings are exactly equal to { the advantages (remember the universe sums to zero).

The ability of abstract thought to conjure alternatives, find loopholes, deceive, defend, and project onto others is infinite. It wiggles and squirms and wants and protests endlessly. It has learned that it can think its way out of any situation, if not through the alternatives available, then through fantasy or denial. This would not necessarily be a problem if objective reality were pliable and could adapt to our demands, but this immediate moment is inalterably itself, in the sense that it is always and only what it is. Therefore there is potential for conflict between the set nature of momentary reality and the malleability of thought. This conflict comes to a head when we have learned over time to believe more in the reality of thought than in the manifest.

Stop for a moment and look at the world around you. Sense that everything you objectify is thought created. Everything is mind made and has no reality outside of what thought says it is. Now look within and see that everything you think you are—all of your ideas, images, limitations, and self-conclusions—is formed from memory, what thought has led you to believe. What would the world look like if you were quietly present without the intrusion of and belief in your memory?

Creating an abstract reality inevitably leads to resisting the reality that is occurring. That resistance is the struggle that many of us feel as stress, tension, unmet expectations, shame, guilt, disappointment, discouragement, frustration, impatience, desire, and fear. Desire, the ability to think ahead of where we are to fulfill a present need, and fear, the projection of what might happen onto the current situation, are both based solidly in symbolic language. Both are born from thought, need a narrative for their continuance, and are motivated by a deep sense of incompletion, the flaw of separation.

In Buddhism this is called the Noble Truth of Suffering[3] and comes from our learned ability to conceive our way out of danger. The brain has 1.5 million years of abstracting behind it. Why should it simply stop believing in the worlds it has created when thinking has been central to its survival from day one? In fact, the underlying and ancient fear of being naked, exposed, and completely out of control, similar to how our ancestors must have felt when they left the protective forests for the grassy plains of Africa, persists within the depths of our current psyche and keeps us reaching for thought as the final solution for our safety. Thought is the one acquired skill we refuse to retest for its effectiveness, and it has become so embedded within our consciousness that we still believe it to be central to our survival. It is no longer a progressively acquired trait but the very definition of who we are.

Abstraction has one additional consequence that I will mention here and elaborate on from time to time: it creates an echo of itself. An abstract idea mirrors back an abstract thinker. No thought, no thinker. The sense of a solid "I" comes from the solidity our brains impart to objects when we use language. You would think that a concept placed upon an experience could not create something that seems solid, since neither the word nor the experience received by the brain has any density, but it does. This is the power that a thought has; it creates something out of nothing through its ability to recognize and remember. It makes the world, and us within it, unchangingly solid because the words it uses to describe what it sees are static and fixed in memory.

This influence of thought does not stop with the creation of an imaginative world consisting of concrete objects and a central solid subject; it also envisions a complete paradigm of separation, a sort of all-encompassing and total virtual reality in the same way a computer can simulate reality. Once the world is set up as isolated objects, a set of principles comes into existence that describes the mechanics of living in that world. These rules govern the paradigm and are inescapable once we have acquiesced to living within symbolic language.

The more we believe in thought, the more we attempt to think our way out of difficulties and the more we become bound within the principles thought imposes. We usually end up blaming the objects that thought created for our troubles, but we rarely admit that thought itself may be problematic. The virtual reality created by abstract thinking is too all-consuming, too compelling and persuasive. Conditioned by our ancestors, the need to think has become genetically imbued within our cells and is inextricably tied to our survival. To this day it can be very threatening to look at the limitations of thought because our biological system still projects danger at every turn.

Early on, when abstract language was still a tool for surmounting the hazards of the environment and we were not completely identified with our thinking, the repercussion of a fixed, thought-based world could be averted, but once thoughts formed the basis of our identity, we had to yield to the paradigm that thought imposed. Now, many generations later, a few of us that feel the limitations of thought can begin to ask questions that our ancestors were unwilling to pose. Let us begin by looking at the world of form as created by language and the formless that is language free. In the beginning of our spiritual journey, form and the formless need to be differentiated until they are thoroughly recognized and understood, and only then can we allow them to return to their natural state of union.

There are a few principles of language that prohibit seeing the world in any other way than as formed objects. Let us explore these principles so they no longer restrain our perceptions. Perhaps with this renewed interest in investigating the limitations of language, we can see if anything exists that is thought free.

FORM AND THE FORMLESS

There is a familiar optical illusion that when viewed in one way is an old woman and when viewed in another becomes a young girl. What we see in the picture is dependent upon how we focus, and the perception of one excludes the perception of the other. Both perceptions are totally and completely available within the whole, but within each perception the field yields only the subject matter that is aligned with the way the brain is

looking in that moment. A principle of language then comes into play that limits what the brain is able to see. When we see a young woman, language prohibits another perspective. This principle, simply stated, is that when an object is determined to be something (in this case a young woman), it cannot simultaneously be something else (a young woman cannot also be an old woman), which excludes any other possibility from being seen. Much like the view stated earlier from quantum mechanics, reality free of language does not create a single object but leaves the picture unformed, rich with an infinite range of possibilities, and not limited to any choice. According to Dr. Amit Goswami, a theoretical quantum physicist, "In quantum physics objects are not determined things. Objects are possibilities."[4]

The worlds of form (objects) and the formless (awareness[5]) are partially analogous to this illusion. Words create independent objects that are no longer tied to any sense of unity by literally placing them outside the whole. The sense of being a person is a remnant of abstract language and limits what we are to only what can be described by words. When we look at the world through the perceptions of a person, we see the world of objects, and that is all we will see. The person of form can only see objects of form because the eyes are trained to look at shape and color for the objective reality. It is not that the formless is unavailable but that our brains are wired to see only from the form perspective.

Most of us have spent our lives living within the field of form, and it garners our attention because there is a great deal that we still want from objects. Not only do objects give us a sense of purpose and meaning, but also defining the objects we see enables our sense of self-definition. The clearer we define the objects of our perceptions, the clearer we are defined as a person seeing those objects. Objects reflect back their history and importance in our life and reconfirm our place in an object-filled world, and this internal monitoring keeps us within the formed and objective view of reality.

When our perceptions are fixed within form, we see only half of the optical illusion. Waiting in the wings is formless awareness, which is not an object. It may sound obvious that we can only navigate in this world when we objectify what we see, but what is astonishing is how invested we are in the objects and how little we notice the seeing. We usually take the seeing for granted, thinking that is just what eyes do, but formless awareness does not come from the eyes or the brain or the person and preexists all forms.

> An easy way to differentiate form and formless awareness is that form is what you see, the objects of sight; formless awareness is what sees the objects, the seeing itself. To get a sense of this, try asking, "What is seeing in this moment?" (not, What is being seen?). With this question, there may arise a felt sense of awareness that is the seeing. The sense of a person forms around the seeing as a specific object within the seeing, but awareness is not dependent upon the person for seeing.

Formless awareness is as close as the seeing that is occurring now and therefore can never be far away. All states of mind and their accompanying story are what seem to obstruct formless awareness, but formless awareness is always present, flooding the moment. Once our attention has been confiscated by the words of our personal narrative, we no longer care about awareness; we become concerned only for the safety of our passage through form (remember that our evolutionary mandate is security, and that means fulfilling our desires and avoiding our fears). If we would just stop for a moment, softening our minds so that objects were no longer our central focus, we would sense the formless psychic space that holds all objects. We would know that we are surrounded by, integrated within, completely enveloped by, and literally bathed in the formless at all times.

Formless awareness is the sacred because it is whole and complete, undifferentiated and not separated. The best a person (form) can do to touch the sacred is to use an intermediary that hints that the sacred is near. The Christian cross is an example because it suggests the presence of God even though as an object it excludes that very presence. We may attempt to evoke a connection with the sacred through various rites and rituals, although these activities all remain within a formed structure. All of this structure and activity can be helpful at a certain stage of our understanding, but at some point it begins to limit us by keeping us dependent upon the objects of sight and not upon the seeing itself.

We feel so cut off and isolated as individuals from the formless that we need holy men and women and religious texts and traditions to convince us there is something beyond our ordinary perceptions. We then end up believing in and defending the symbol of the sacred rather than accessing the formless that is ever present. As Christ said, "Heaven is spread out upon the earth, and people do not see it!"[6] Our reliance on these intermediaries solidifies our place within an objective reality and assures the continuation of our dependency on all forms.

There is a law in science that fits nicely into this discussion, and that is the first law of thermodynamics. This law is often called the law of conservation of energy, and it states that within any closed system, energy can neither be created nor destroyed. Therefore the sum of all the energies in the system is a constant.[7] For much of our human history, our species has invested in seeing and knowing the world of form, first for its survival and security and later to maintain the virtual reality that language creates. But over time the flaw of separation, the pain of isolation from the world, begins to wear thin, and no matter how meaningful we try to make our lives among objects, a struggle remains that cannot be resolved. We begin to realize that this world does not offer what it once seemed to promise, and that realization begins a slow divestment from our pursuit of and dependency on objects. Since the energy of any closed system is preserved, where does the energy we were using for worldly gratification go? There are only two places it can go, either to the young girl (form) or to the old woman (the formless). So it goes to the formless; it goes to the sacred.

The energy now diverted from the world of form goes effortlessly to formless awareness. Said in another way, the energy goes out of thinking of the self as an object and into the infinite expanse that has no boundaries. The self is built from conceptual boundaries, but in the absence of language, the boundaries break down and flood the infinite. The sense of self so long thought to be real and solid is seen as a residue of blocked energy. This is an important spiritual point because the emphasis within our spiritual journey cannot focus on extracting ourselves from form to get to the formless. Form does not have the power to dissolve itself. Form energy just goes back into form by re-creating other forms from the unused energy. The dissolution of form is handled nicely on its own when we move beyond conceptual boundaries. The energy is converted from form to the formless through wordless stillness. Our spiritual work is to understand the limitations of language and allow the natural conversion of energy to access the formless through quietude.

TIME, DISTANCE, AND SEPARATION

I was meeting with a lifelong friend whom I had not seen in several years, and we had arranged to renew our friendship over a three-mile walk before both of us departed to different areas of the country. Because we had not seen each other for a long time and the time together was so short, our walk was a little pressured as we attempted to quickly get caught up with each other's lives. My friend speaks very rapidly under normal circumstances, but that day her conversation was even more pressed. I conversed with her as best I could, responded with my own stories, and generally felt the quickened conversation was compatible and lively. We talked and laughed back and forth for about an hour, when our walk came to an end. She then looked at me and summarized what she had been saying, upon which I instantly realized I had misunderstood her entire conversation, thinking she had been speaking about one subject when she had actually been speaking about another. I, embarrassed, admitted my mistake as she, looking rather shocked, realized she had misconstrued my entire conversation as well. For more than an hour we had both missed the common thread of the dialogue, but what was even more astounding was that it had not mattered. Empathetically and affectionately, it was as if we had been speaking straight to each other's heart in two different languages. We laughed and laughed, shook our heads in amazement, hugged each other, and went our separate ways with our relationship fully intact.

The walk with my friend turned out to be the perfect meeting because the bonding we both felt had nothing to do with the missed conversation. We had initially attempted to use language as the means to reconnect, but ultimately the words did not matter. It was the love of the friendship that was the essence of the walk, and the shared affection found its way to our hearts despite the words. It would have been just as beneficial to walk together in silence. We frequently fill with words the quiet spaces that naturally occur during a relationship. Those words not only dissipate social anxiety but also establish our present position. The words say, in effect, "I am here, it is me you are relating to." The words often substitute for the affection of the heart. My friend and I were attempting to consummate our caring through our speech, but in the end the silence said it all.

Within the paradigm created by thought, words isolate each object from another and create an imposed distance between objects. The distance between objects is perceived as real, and when distance is established, time is needed to travel that distance. Once consciousness becomes identified with a thought, the sense of self becomes dependent upon the time and distance to navigate through the world. When I want something, I must first isolate the wanted object from other forms and accomplish that by thinking about the object. Now I must travel the distance to procure that object, and that journey takes time. Time and distance came from the world-view created within the thought and are fixed notions that logically follow the abstract reasoning of thought.

Thoughts also keep the sense of me separate from the sense of you, which is similar to the way conversing during a relationship establishes our individual positions. To maintain our individual place in life, we have to keep speaking to ourselves in the form of thought, and as already mentioned, time and distance then arise within the thinking. We think ourselves into place, and our thinking has become the binding narrative of our lives that connects us to all other objects. Our thoughts are so continuous they follow us into the dream states at night. Thoughts are our attempt to establish companionship in an otherwise empty universe. Like hearing the echo bounce off canyon walls, we keep self-speaking to assure ourselves that we exist and others exist with us.

Form establishes itself through time and distance, but time and distance also create the isolation that haunts our lives. Form can never release us from this separation because by definition it must be distinct from everything else to remain as form. To live in form means we will be distant and alone, governed by time. We try to use words to reconnect to other objects, but in the end the words do little to cross the great divide. To see how time, distance, separation, and form all work together to construct our current paradigm, let us look at a typical mind sequence of an average busy human being.

Mary wakes up in the morning with her head busy with the day's responsibilities. She has to shower, eat breakfast, drop her son off at day care, prepare for an important work-related meeting, and process a complaint by an employee, all before noon. She tries to plan her way out of the anxiety she is feeling by sequentially thinking of all the actions that will need to be accomplished in the limited time she has. Mary thinks about what is likely to occur and her responses to each situation. Planning and thinking into the future allows the anxiety to dissipate slightly. She feels more in control and self-empowered as she rehearses the important morning meeting. Thinking about the day seems to distance her from the anxiety she is feeling and allow her confidence to re-emerge.

When Mary thinks about what she needs to do and the time pressures on her, she is creating her own isolation. She is calling herself back into form by thinking, "It is all up to me." The image of herself as a strong and independent woman able to handle her role competently brings up the shadowed image of her opposite and fear of the unknown events. All time driven. She tries to solve the problems generated by time by planning the future, which is time feeding upon itself, creating more distance from the actual events and a stronger sense of self-formation.

Let us return for a moment to the first law of thermodynamics and the conservation of energy. The energy that Mary is using is going toward the time sequencing of past, present, and future. The present is troublesome because it holds the limits of her power. All she feels in the present is the vulnerability of the anxiety she wants to get over. The future is where she invests her energy because it represents relief from her fear by allowing her to plan her event. If she were to quiet herself so that her thoughts were not compelling her forward, the energy would leave her thoughts, but where would that energy go? The energy would go into formless awareness that *is* the present moment. This present is not the oppressive present that is wedged between the conditioned past and the feared future but the living present, the present that holds the entire content of her life. The energy would shift into a new paradigm that is no longer time and distance driven. From here she could handle each event as it arose without anxiety. This is not to suggest that planning and preparation are inappropriate, but Mary will lose her bearings in the present if she attempts to promote her image into the future. It is possible to prepare for a future event in present time but not if you worry about how well you are going to do during that event.

This living formless present is always accessible but cannot be seen when we are identified with time, when we want time to have a specific result. The formless present is not the content of the moment; the content is the form the moment is taking and the image of ourselves we want to sustain. The living present is the formless surround that holds the past and future as thoughts but not as reality. A thought is an event within the here and now, but when we identify with the thought, thinking fools us into believing that the sequence of time is real, and the new paradigm is lost.

Take a moment and see if you are able to access this living present; it has to be here and available or it is just another mental abstraction. Quiet down so that your senses become alive and you are less directed by your thoughts. Awareness discerns the sense of I becoming more vague as presence becomes acutely sensed. You cannot carry yourself along with the growing sense of presence because presence takes away the past and future, the very way you form yourself. Hear the sounds, smell the odors, and softly see the forms arising in this moment. Resist investing energy in thinking about what is sensed and hold the sensation just as it is, free of thought. Let awareness be expansive so there are no limitations. Now sense what holds all the shapes, sounds, and sensations of this moment and feel the living moment itself.

Once again, this conversion into the living present can occur only when we have seen the limits of abstract thought and the sequencing of time. There is a Buddhist story of Venerable Anuruddha going to Sariputta, one of the chief disciples of the Buddha, and discussing this point. Venerable Anuruddha has very keen concentration and speaks about some of the powers he has acquired and finishes by saying, "I have accomplished all of this and . . . yet my mind is still clinging to thinking." Sariputta skillfully directs him away from his self-enhancing thoughts, showing him the limitations of how he has been addressing his spiritual practice, and points him to the unconditioned formless.[8]

There are a myriad ways the world of conditioning can seduce us into form. Venerable Anuruddha was known as one of the more accomplished disciples of the Buddha in seeing other realms of existence, but other realms are merely substantiated through their own forms of abstract thought. We begin to see that thought gives substance to all things but does not impart essence to anything. The essence of all things is formless awareness, and nothing exists except that the formless makes it so.

When we identify with the forms created by thought, we live within an abstract virtual reality that governs and distorts the truth. We have looked at several of the assumptions that are tied to thought, including how thought limits a perspective to one possibility and the way thinking creates time and distance. There are many other laws created by thought, but one worth noting here is the appearance of birth and death. We assume the truth of birth and death only because thought limits our understanding of what we are. When we think of ourselves as isolated entities, we are governed by the time sequence of individuals (he was born on such and such a date and died seventy years later). But the formless is timeless and therefore not defined by a beginning or an ending.

As formless awareness comes to the forefront, the sense of being formed diminishes proportionately and peace deepens. Now the words of the Buddha carry a message of unmistakable truth when he says, "The sage who is at peace is not born, does not age, does not die, does not tremble, and does not yearn. For him there does not exist that on account of which he might be born. Not being born, how can he age? Not aging, how can he die?"[8] This, then, is the end of birth and death.

The principles of perception formed through abstract thought shape the worldview that we consider normal. Once we are within that worldview, its inherent logic prevents any escape. How could anyone dispute time, distance, separation, birth, and death when that is what we see and experience every day? There is no way out of this psychic container except by questioning the assumptions that hold the view in place. When we question time, distance, and separation, the view becomes transparent and we see what is actually true, not what is conventionally believed. The more fundamental question may be about how many of us are willing to question consensus reality, or have we become like institutionalized inmates that sabotage the time of their release?

BOTH AND NEITHER

The world of thought and objects and the paradigm of formless awareness when seen from each perspective seem to exclude the truth of the other. The fact that we can flip between the form and formless perspectives as we can between the views of the young and the old woman indicates that both are as real as the two pictures in the illusion, but until they are seen as two forms of the same truth, we can become trapped in either perspective. Both contain a complete and total worldview within their vantage points, and each one denies the possibility of the other—you are young or you are old, no other option. But all boundaries are conceptually applied, and life, before we abstracted it, held no boundaries whatsoever; therefore the division between form and the formless is simply an idea believed.

Once freed of this idea, the formless spreads out immeasurably and perfectly over the world of form without contradictions. But how can two very different configurations such as objects and awareness be one and the same? How can a conceptual boundary hold the union of these two in check? Again, science may point a way through this puzzle. In the book *Quantum Enigma,* the two physicists who wrote the book state, "Most of us share some commonsense intuitions. For example, is it not just common sense that one object cannot be in two far apart places at once? And, surely what happens here is not affected by what happens at the same time some place very far away. And does it not go without saying that there is a real world 'out there' whether or not we look at it? Quantum mechanics challenges each of these intuitions by having observation actually *create* the physical reality observed." The authors continue by stating that quantum mechanics "has revolutionized our world" and "not a single one of its predictions has ever been wrong."[10]

In quantum mechanics a subatomic particle is not created *until it is observed,* at which point it becomes formed. Before it is observed, it can best be described as a potential, not a discrete object, and the observation, consciousness, determines its final state. Neils Bohr, the great Nobel Prize–winning physicist, said, "When we measure something we are forcing an undetermined, undefined world to assume an experimental value. We are not 'measuring' the world, we are creating it."[11] Although this theory is usually applied to the subatomic world of the very small, according to physics professor Vlatko Vedral, "quantum mechanics is not just about teeny particles. It applies to things of all sizes: birds, plants, maybe even people."[12]

If consciousness determines the existing state of reality, then there is no absolute or final perception. It exists as a potential, not a conclusion. There is nothing "real" until consciousness determines it to be so. Returning to the optical illusion, if nothing is made from either perception (neither a young girl nor an old woman), then everything can remain within that state of potential, within a state of wonder, with endless possibilities. Again the Buddha, speaking about that unformed perception: "There is a state where form ceases to exist. It is a state without ordinary perception and without disordered perception and without the lack of perception and without any annihilation of perception. It is perception, consciousness, that is the source of all the basic obstacles."[13]

With that there can be interplay between the young woman and the old woman. Focus on life one way and the energy is converted into form, focus another way and it appears as the formless. Do not assert the truth of either, and both exist simultaneously as possibilities, yet neither exists as a fact. Within this raw, undetermined expression of life, wonder becomes the architect.

For much of our spiritual practice, there usually remains a tension between these perceptions. Life, we say, is either form, in which case we need to defend ourselves from other forms, or formless,

Anekantavada

where we can relax knowing everything is mind created. We usually think in either/or terms, so one has to be right and the other wrong. But this is still division created by thought. We begin to notice in moments of utter stillness that consciousness expands beyond any certainty, and there remains a simple "isness" to life that is not now, nor ever could be, divided. The coming and going of self and emptiness, of form and the formless, are all part of the dance of the wonder of being. Take a side and we are lost in the aging woman or the frivolities of a youthful girl, neither of which is the complete story.

Usually spiritual practice is defined by the moments you are aware, mindful, and awake, and the moments in which you are totally engrossed in and reacting to objects are the worldly times. You usually pit these times against each other, trying to decrease the worldly moments while you increase the spiritual moments. Based on the previous paragraphs, what are the limitations of practicing like this? Is there a way to hold both the spiritual and the worldly so they are not antagonistic but actually feed each other? What would be the benefits of this total embrace of form and the formless?

Now let us look at how the mind arranges itself to convince us of separation. How does the mind configure itself internally so that we believe we stand outside the world looking from a distance at it? If we can actually experience how and when this is occurring, then the fallacy can be investigated and corrected.

3

The Divided Mind

If you don't know where you are going, you will wind up
somewhere else.

—YOGI BERRA

The simulated reality created by abstract thought is a closed
system very similar to the way a dream is a closed system.
Everything that happens, even external sounds, is incorporated into
the story of the dream. Once a thought is believed, the simulated
reality closes down and becomes hermetically sealed, completely
isolated from other systems that are not conceptually based and
without an exit from abstract ideas. There is no logic, reason, or
strategy that can open this paradigm beyond itself, because all forms
of willful effort come from within the system. In fact, all attempts to
find an escape route simply strengthen the hold this reality has on us,
in precisely the same way all attempts to escape a dream reinforce the
truth of the narrative of the dream to the dreamer.

For instance, if we are dreaming and are fleeing a charging lion,
the emotion of fear and the urgency to escape the lion's attack actually reinforce the identification with both the narrative of the dream
and the dreamer. So, too, when we believe a thought, we are identified with what the thought says. The accompanying emotions

Dreamer & the Dream

arising from that belief affirm the truth of the narrative and prohibit any exit from the prevailing paradigm as long as the thought is held to be true, and there is no way logically or strategically to escape the bonds of thinking by using other thoughts to pry us away.

We can get a sense of why this is so if we return one more time to the first law of thermodynamics. The energy contained within a vanishing thought does not die with the thought but moves on to the next thought and continues to feed the laws governing this closed system. The energy never leaves the system, and thoughts literally feed upon themselves. In addition, thought creates the idea of time, time defines space and distance, and all three reinforce the sense of separation that ultimately strengthens the belief in a separate object called "I." The energy that is trying to escape the system actually feeds back into the system and affirms the sense of the controlling "I" who is attempting to think his or her way out of the paradigm.

When has time or thought ever put an end to itself? Thought does not stop with the ending of a particular thought; it thinks on into the next thought. There is always something else to think about, and there is rarely a moment when thought is not relevant or time is not sequential. As long as thought is occurring, there is the idea of time going forward. When the thought of time-future becomes the present time, we don't suddenly stop planning or worrying; we simply move on to the next area of concern, which is either in front of (future) or behind (past) us. We end up with a never-ending succession of thoughts defining the simulated reality and with the solutions to problems always contained within further thinking.

See if thought ever puts an end to itself. Take a simple interpersonal encounter as an example and notice whether thought comes to an end after parting or whether it continues to build upon what just occurred in the exchange. Notice that the past (what just happened) and the future (what I will say or do in our next meeting) are part of what is brought into the narrative that centers on the theme of self and other. That particular story line will end, but another will replace it, with the sense of self central to the new theme as well. Notice that the more you narrate a story line, the further you stray from the truth of what occurred.

Dissipated energy from thought circles back into the system as an elaboration of the story we tell ourselves. Once something becomes known and thought about sufficiently, the energy recycles back into the process by wanting to know more. There is never a time when our knowing seems complete, and the need to know more projects a future through which this can happen. Now time and thought become mutually supporting. This cyclical reemergence of the endless rebirthing of reality is what must have led the Buddha to say, "Inconceivable is the beginning of this samsara; not to be discovered is any first beginning of beings, who, blinded by ignorance and ensnared by craving, are hurrying and hastening [and thinking themselves] through these rounds of rebirths."[1]

This uncontrollable and never-ending thinking is being studied by scientists who are demonstrating that the brain "runs largely on autopilot and sustains a sense of unity amid a cacophony of competing voices [thoughts]. The neurological network in the left hemisphere is providing a running narration. The left hemisphere takes what information it has and delivers a coherent tale to conscious awareness. It happens continually in daily life, and most everyone has caught himself or herself in the act—overhearing a fragment of gossip, for instance, and filling in the blanks with assumptions. The interpreter creates the illusion of a meaningful script, as well as a coherent self. Working on the fly, it furiously reconstructs not only what happened but why, inserting motives here, intentions there—based on limited, sometimes flawed information."[2]

Science is corroborating our wisdom, and encourages us further to question conventional reality. When we know our perceptions of separation are not supported by either wisdom or science, we are left wondering why we believe so strongly in thought and time at the expense of a greater unity. The first step in untangling our confusion over reality is to see directly the derivation of self and other as a single mental experience.

A few definitions are needed at this point. The brain, as I am defining it, is a biological organ with billions of neurological pathways mechanically carrying bits of information for processing. That differs from the mind, which is the coordinating center of sensation and intellectual and nervous activity. It receives all the data from the brain and sets a view, a corresponding story, and a course of action through thought. "A core aspect of the mind can be defined as an embodied and relational process that regulates the flow of energy and information. One thing to note is that this definition means we must separate 'mind' from 'awareness.'"[3] Awareness is what sees the entire subjective and objective process but is itself not a part of that activity.

The Divided Mind and Authentic Spiritual Practice

Why is thinking so out of control? Why does the mind feed incessantly on thought even when the experience does not call for further elaboration? The root cause of the insatiability of thought has to do with how the mind thinks it is organized. The mind behaves as if it were divided between the sense data coming into the brain and the person receiving the impressions somewhere outside the brain. The person thinks about the experience at hand and then acts in accordance with his or her thoughts and emotions. But the person the mind believes is behind the scenes controlling the thoughts and actions is actually arising within the mind itself.

It is as if the main character within a movie believed she was the director of the film. She thinks she has control over the content of the movie, when she is actually formed by the same script and composed of the same material as everything else in the movie. The person is a product of the mind, not the other way around, and the incessant mind chatter has to be maintained for the person to believe he or she is outside looking in. We know ourselves only by making mental noise, and if the mind gets quiet, this false dichotomy of "me" separate from "my" mental experience cannot be maintained.

The concept of "I" is another thought coming from the mind, but it is a weighted thought, one that carries memory impressions dating back to our birth. When those memories are received by the mind, the next thought concludes that since "I" existed back then, "I" must exist now. The egoic identity successfully argues that since all of those thoughts are coming from somewhere, they must be coming from me, and then assumes a thinking subject. But when we actually look inwardly with awareness to see this "I," we see only thought, emotion, and memory. There is no entity apart from these thoughts.

Let us experientially look at this sense of separation by looking up from this book and taking in the surrounding moment. Let your mind be soft and pliable. Without trying to identify anything specifically, get a felt sense of the moment. Allow everything to be included and at rest. Notice whether the mind is fracturing or arguing with the content of the moment. Release the need to resist any aspect of the present. Feel the felt sense of wholeness return when the mind becomes quiet. Incline your attention back into your mind and look without adding any thought about what is observable. If there is no resistance, you will not find the person who is looking, but you may be able to sense the space that surrounds all form. From here you can discern how the mind divides the space with thinking and assumes a placeholder within that noise and how quickly the quiet is lost once that placeholder called "me" arises.

Michael Gazzaniga, a noted psychology professor who has done extensive brain research at the University of California, Santa Barbara, when asked about what the sense of self is, put it this way, "There is no you, there is no free will or someone sitting up there in your head making the decisions. The science does not support that fact. Now we just have to get over that way of thinking."[4] Getting over that way of thinking is easier said than done. As mentioned in the previous chapter, this organizing principle occurred more than a million years ago as a response to the physical vulnerability of our ancestors and is now well rooted in our genetic code.

If you would like to see the remnant of this ancestral division that separates the thought from yourself, stop for a moment and ask yourself whether you are a thought within the brain or whether you are outside of the brain having a thought. In the latter case the thought is happening to you; in the former, the sense of yourself arises from the thought itself. Now expand your attention so that it covers both the felt sense of yourself and the "I" thoughts arising. Once you are quiet enough to include both, you will see the sense of self attempt to relocate to a new place outside the thoughts. Continue to become quieter until you realize that any location the sense of self establishes is actually a subtle identification with the thoughts arising within the mind.

Most of us would say we have a brain, and we are more than just a thought about ourselves. Somehow we think we are more than the simple functioning of the brain but still think of ourselves as the person having ideas, drawing conclusions, making decisions, planning, organizing, and emoting—the precise functions of the brain. We never tire of finding a new location where we can be the person thinking, but we cannot find that person separated from the thoughts that he or she is thinking.

During our evolution, as the "I" began to differentiate out more and more, the entity started to compare itself with other organisms that were also thinking thoughts of separation. Competition and evaluation arose, which further strengthened the image of self. A threshold was reached when the idea of "me" became the socially acceptable foundation on which society was built and everyone conceded the truth of "me" and lost the unity that was present when the thought and the thinker were together as a common function of the mind. When that threshold was crossed, our species lost its bearings, and our perceptions became entrapped within an imagined reality of separation, where all subjects were alienated from all objects. Thoughts from the subject, "I," then became primarily important in determining reality.

This is an essential point that is worth repeating to fully understand. For this discussion let us say there are two parts of the brain: the first part is composed of the data that comes into the brain that is organized into a coherent worldview, and the second part thinks about and reacts to the data, forming the sense of I within that reactive process. The thoughts of the brain and the sense of I are one and the same thing. An idea took itself for something other than an idea—it took itself to be "me." An idea is obviously a part of the working of the brain and includes thoughts, memories, emotions, and attitudes, which are all mental functions of the brain. Over time these mental functions assumed themselves to be a person, and once that occurred, the person set him- or herself up to be the overseer and owner of the brain. The person who was just created out of thought now became the person *outside of the brain* having the thought. The person grew in stature as memory retained more and more ideas about "me" over time, and the weight of this remembering began to reinforce the thoughts of separation and isolation from other objects (I have my history and the objects have their history, therefore we must be separate), and that gave rise to time, distance, and separation.

When the sense of self arises and separates from the data coming in, a time gap is imposed between the thinker and what is perceived. This gap allows us to pull back and consider the reality and reflect upon the details of the situation. What is actually occurring in the brain at that moment is a perception and a thought about the perception. The two have different roles that are frequently contentious with each other. The tension arises between the perceived reality and the thinker, who is considering other options: "Is this moment safe? Is it pleasurable enough to relax? What is missing? What is my role here? What are others expecting from me?" On and on it goes, with each thought creating an artificial distance between the thinker and the reality perceived. This imposed distance is the reason we believe that "we" are outside of "life," looking in, as if life were happening to us.

All authentic spiritual practices, meaning practices that move from form to the formless, simply attempt to close this time/distance gap by showing that the thought does not come from a person but rather from a conditioned reaction to the perception. But here is where our spiritual journey can easily go awry. We must be very cautious at this juncture or the view we have of the spiritual journey may inadvertently complicate the solution we apply to resolve this perception/thinker separation. How we approach this question of division will define everything we do, and that approach will be characterized by how well we understand the differentiation that occurs within the brain between thought and the thinker. If we believe there is a thinker thinking the thoughts, our efforts will look away from the thinker, sustaining its reality, as we work on the troubling thoughts and emotions that arise. Remember that once we make the thinker "real" in any sense, we will be working within the closed simulated reality of separation that has no exit. A paradigm closed unto itself.

Many spiritual systems do just that. If the tradition uses strategies derived from the sense of self (thinker), the energy applied to close the gap will be recycled back into thought, and a stronger sense of self will result (remember the first law of thermodynamics). Practices that do not question the sense of self maintain this divisive energy in very subtle and clever ways, because from the perspective of the thinker, these strategies are a sincere attempt to move the process forward. To the sense of self it feels as if real progress were being made. Unfortunately, the sense of self is part of the system the thinker is attempting to extricate himself from, and therefore he cannot grasp the fact that he is also moving along with the thought, building upon himself as the system moves, and thereby limiting the definition of his success to what he thinks is successful. His definition of success has to do with how well he is progressing "in time." As he practices, he might see his thoughts mellowing and experience enhanced mental qualities, both giving him the perception of closing the gap by advancing forward in time. Even his sense of self may feel more subdued as the practices continue, but the system as a whole will still be dependent upon thought, time, distance, and separation for the conclusions of the journey.

As an example of how the beginning and the perceived ending of our journey can be enclosed within the same paradigm, I use my practice as an illustration. Though this example may be obvious, there are many more-subtle ways we get lost in the same paradigm without any clear resolution. I suggest that the reader review his or her practice thoroughly to see whether he or she may be caught within the consensus paradigm.

Early on I was motivated to overcome my self-dislike and created a strategy for bypassing myself altogether on my way to enlightenment. If I could just put myself on the back burner, maybe I would not have to deal with myself at all and could move straight to the goal. I was very stubborn but also sincere. I felt real progress was being made when I accessed quieter states of mind. Here were states that did not represent the person I thought I was. I found my practice attempting to build upon these states whenever possible, but unbeknownst to me, I was feeding my attachment to these states while thinking I was moving toward my goal. I had read in Buddhist literature about how these states were factors of enlightenment, and all I needed was more time to cultivate them and complete the journey. Even my definition of enlightenment, to live free of myself, was being defined by the aversion I had of being the person I thought I was. The more I tried to leave myself behind, the more I would appear through judgments and reactivity, and it took a long time to understand my way out of this fixed perspective of freedom.

So what is the solution when there is no exit? In Dante's *Divine*

Comedy, above the gates of hell is written, "All hope abandon ye who enter here."[5] Most of us would read that inscription with despair and give up, but giving up is not giving up when applied to the gap between the thought and the thinker. Giving up in this sense is surrendering the thought of escape. When a thought is completely surrendered, it is no longer tied to the narrative of self and cannot be recycled into more thought. The thought of escape prior to surrendering feeds the division within the brain and maintains the perception of a thinker outside the thinking mind. Once the thought is surrendered, the sense of self is left without an object and the "I" disappears, closing the gap. When separation ends, so does the problem, and the desire to escape ceases. When there is nowhere to go, time and distance also come to an end and the abstract reality transforms itself into the formless awareness.

The Buddha talked about this collapsing of sequences as dependent arising, or the conditions necessary for something to arise or cease. "When this is, that is. From the arising of this comes the arising of that. When this is not, that is not. From the cessation of this comes the cessation of that."[6] As one condition puts an end to another, what remains is the unconditioned, that which has no conditions for its formation. Returning to the thought and the thinker, as the thought is surrendered, the word comes to an end but not the energy contained in the thought. The energy within the thought now becomes available as formless awareness. Formless awareness is what is left after conditions are removed and the division ends. Formless awareness knows no boundaries, no gaps, no differentiation between thought and the thinker. Formless awareness is seeing the totality and is not formed from conditions. The whole leaves nothing out, and so the thought and thinker become undifferentiated in stillness.

We have now seen that the realities of form and formlessness as mentioned in the previous chapter manifest according to whether the mind is seeing in totality and is therefore undivided and unified, or whether the thinker (sense of self) is seeing, in which case the mind is fractured and divided. The end of the thinker is the opening of the formless. As long as the thinker "thinks" of him- or herself as formed, life will form around the thinker as objects, and he or she will be unable to access the sacred. If the distance between the thought and the thinker is surrendered, the mind reunites, objects lose their individuation, and formless awareness reappears.

Authentic spiritual practices attempt to quiet the mind sufficiently to provide glimpses of the unified mind, and at the same time, these practices encourage a deeper understanding of form so that there is complete ease within all formations. For a person to walk this balance, the practices taught need to be aligned with the truth of formless awareness and yet have no resistance to the arising of form. By definition, we "practice" to establish that balance even when that reality is not fully realized by us. We learn to see all experiences arising from stillness and arrest the impulse to differentiate any single aspect of mind, such as the thought or the thinker, as special or unique. When the thinker of the thought and the object of thought are not isolated from each other, a pure awareness that is not being initiated by the meditator envelops the mind. This pure awareness has nobody watching even though everything is being seen. It is from this point forward that all transcendent realizations arise.

Allow awareness to arise and surround whatever the mind contains. Do not try to change or rearrange anything. Include thoughts and the sense of yourself within what is seen. Wherever you locate, quietly surround that place with awareness so there is nothing outside the formless. Is this all-encompassing awareness coming from you or is it preexisting? How do you know? Is it more accessible when you think about what is occurring or when you are completely quiet?

Buddhist Practices

Addressing the Divided Mind

It is important to ask how Buddhism addresses the divided mind given the fact that both science and our direct seeing (wisdom) have substantiated the truth that the mind is innately unified. Buddhism questions the subject, the object, and the assumptions asserted by conventional reality to eliminate any divisions within the mind. To understand this, let us look at the following diagram.

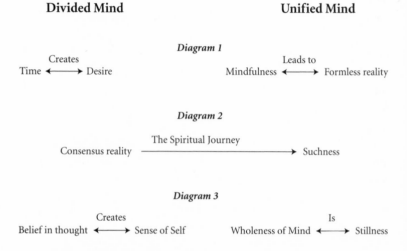

Divided Mind   **Unified Mind**

Diagram 1

Creates   Leads to
Time ⟷ Desire   Mindfulness ⟷ Formless reality

Diagram 2

The Spiritual Journey
Consensus reality ⟶ Suchness

Diagram 3

Creates   Is
Belief in thought ⟷ Sense of Self   Wholeness of Mind ⟷ Stillness

As we traverse diagram 2, consensus reality to suchness, the practice moves from a thought-based reality highlighted by a division between subjects and objects to *suchness,* which is the Buddhist terminology for the true nature of reality. The Buddha is sometimes referred to as the Tathagata, which means "the One who has arrived at suchness."[7] We might think of suchness as reality free of the belief in thought. That means that when thought does arise, it is not associated with a person who is thinking or an object that is being thought about. If we now look at diagram 3, from the belief in thought to stillness, we see that the sense of self forms around thought, as we have already discussed. This diagram also indicates that through spiritual practice we move toward wholeness of mind, and the quieter we become, the more whole and unified is the experience of mind. Conversely, the more we believe in thought, the noisier and more divided the mind becomes and, ultimately, the more isolated we feel from everything around us.

And finally diagram 1, from time to formless reality, demonstrates the way desire needs time to satisfy its wants. Desire creates the idea of time so we can secure a future more fulfilling than the present. When a desire arises, we look ahead of ourselves for the promise of contentment. Satisfaction from desire comes by obtaining the desired object, and with our eyes focused exclusively on the forms of the world, formless reality is bypassed completely as irrelevant.

Buddhism uses the practice of mindfulness to question consensus reality by showing us the limitation of thought and begins to reveal the face of reality free of thought. The more mindful we become, the less the forms of the world entice us and the quieter we are. The quieter we become, the less thought intrudes within our actions and the less divided we feel. As awareness increases, we find ourselves more present and less dependent on time and the images time creates. With fewer images, the formless reality begins to reveal itself.

Pick one of the diagrams above to explore in your practice. If working with diagram 1, time and formless reality, notice that the stronger the desire, the more lost you become in the images of the future and how little mindfulness (awareness) there is of the pattern. If you investigate diagram 2, consensus reality and suchness, you will see that the mental noise of consensus reality keeps you from the stillness of suchness. Diagram 3, the continuum from belief in thought to stillness, will demonstrate how predominant the sense of yourself becomes when lost in thought and how unified you feel when thought is quieted.

Much more will be discussed in chapter 6 about these continua, but Buddhist practices attempt to move us from the left to the right sides of these diagrams. The practices show us insightfully that the views, assumptions, and intentions built by the sense of self are based upon a consensus reality, not the "suchness" of the way things actually are. One of the first insights that many practitioners of Buddhism have is the insubstantiality of all experiences. When the experiences of reality were hidden under the ideas we had about them, reality seemed solid and enduring, but once the practice begins to remove the layers of thought covering reality, reality is seen as unstable and unreliable.

When we see that objects are not as dependable as we once believed, our desires for them begin to wane. As objects hold less of an attraction, our thoughts no longer stray into the future, where we believe our desires can be satisfied, and we begin to shift away from endlessly thinking about future possibilities toward stabilizing our consciousness here and now. Mindfulness becomes the tool of choice that both limits needless thinking and connects us firmly to the ground of our experience so that experience can be explored and understood. As this process unfolds, mindfulness discerns that thought is without real substance or validity, and the mind gets quieter on its own. With less thought and more stillness comes the flowering of formless awareness.

We begin to see that awareness arises in the absence of identification with thought and is not an experience that needs cultivation. In fact, we see that awareness is not an experience at all but the ground from which all experiences arise. This is an important distinction because it clarifies the role of effort in practice. Wise effort is the understanding that what is intrinsically here cannot be willfully induced. The sense of self arises with willful effort, and therefore wise effort is the release of all tension associated with will. The sense of self, with its need for volitional control, is restricted to the left side of the continuum and cannot itself journey to the formless right side. As we mature in our practice, we see that our role is one of release rather than resistance, allowance rather than avoidance.

We have already learned that the unified mind becomes divided when the sense of self assumes authority over the whole of the mind and pretends to be outside looking in at the mind. Under its own influence and control, the self attempts to spiritually maneuver its way toward the formless. The self does not realize that its formation arises out of noise and cannot enter the world of quietude. As the diagram convincingly shows, this is not possible and all willful effort must end if the formless is to be discovered. Effort from the sense of self can only move consciousness further to the left side of the diagram because effort carries the noise of thought within it (where I am going and what it will be like when I get there). As the Buddha stated, "Every form of suffering [division] grows out of effort. But when all effort has been abandoned, there is freedom of the effortless [formless]."[8]

Even mindfulness needs to be freed from the sense of someone's doing it in order to work properly and move consciousness to the formless right side of the continuum. If mindfulness is strongly controlled by the sense of self, it will subvert the usefulness of the method and keep it contained on the left side. Mindfulness usually begins as a self-controlled technique that effectively tempers difficult states of mind and cultivates skillful states. As useful as that may be at a certain time during one's practice, we need to be aware that ultimately any self-driven strategies will restrict consciousness to the divided mind.

The words we use with the techniques are often an indication of whether the energy is being derived from the sense of self. For example, words regarding time or distance come from the consensus paradigm. Notice that the word *cultivation* implies continuous evolution, never completion or stopping, and therefore uses time to move forward. The appearance of time-based words that are hooked to strategies promising results indicate left-sided (the left side of the continuum) dominance. Words like *cultivation, effort, overcoming, becoming, advancing, expanding, increasing,* and the like are clear indications that the sense of self is at the helm. Sometimes these words are used to indicate a period of time of cultivation before a sudden and complete arresting of movement (enlightenment), but if we consider the unified mind, we see that the divided mind can only be unified when those very words, and the accompanying views, are abandoned. The divided mind cannot unify itself; it simply surrenders the words that appear to divide it.

What time-based words guide your practice? How much reality do you give to them? For example, when you think in terms of cultivation (a time-based word), you cannot help but also invite the polarities of more or less, past and future, increasing or decreasing. Our practice then becomes oriented to time, and our efforts attempt to overcome the perceived limitations of the present in order to cultivate more in the future. But this is all divided-mind dharma. The words will end their control over our practice only when we understand that they offer no clear resolution.

Mindfulness in the beginning seems to be directed by the sense of self, and both are often driven by words like those above. We say, "I want to be more mindful," and we set out to "cultivate mindfulness" because we feel we do not have enough of it. The key here is that the sense of self never feels that it has enough of anything, and that is what needs to be learned. Though cultivation is an important phase of practice, it must be eventually passed through or these terms can eventually corrupt our practice into thinking in terms of time and self-improvement. The only way to keep the practice unspoiled is by using mindfulness to thoroughly uncover the nature of self in order not to follow its mandate. We are called upon to use mindfulness to investigate what the sense of self is, what it runs on, and how it arises rather than act from the conditioned belief that we are insufficient or need something we believe we do not have.

In Buddhism we explore the nature of mind that ultimately opens beyond the belief in self. Belief in the self inhibits awareness from seeing what lies outside the control of self. Through careful observation (mindfulness), we see that all thoughts, emotions, and sensations that arise are not self. We know they are not self because they can be seen as dependently arising from conditions. "When, Bahiya, there is for you in the seen only the seen, in the thinking only the thoughts . . . then, Bahiya, there is no 'you' in connection with that."[9] And through this direct seeing, mindfulness opens beyond itself to awareness.

In the course of practice, we also notice that objects are born from memory and are imprisoned within the context of our past. Something is what it is because we remember it to be such. Infused within this memory is our conditioned liking or not liking of the object, which prepares us to be attracted to or averse to the object when it does appear. Trained meditators become aware of this attraction or aversion and prevent the proliferation of their narrative into a negative or positive theme when the subject does arise. The quieter we become as each experience arises, the more the experience returns to the empty state of its origin.

As resistance decreases, the nature of objects (and the subject) becomes known. It was resistance, the fear, avoidance, or wanting something from it that kept an object from the formless, and it is to the formless that all objects return when not invested with our preferences. It is a little like trying to see the screen of a movie as the movie runs. In this analogy the movie is the forms and stories of our lives and the screen is the formless awareness that is the ground of all experiences. Our investment is in the movie, to understand and empathize with the story and drama, but when we focus on the movie alone, we miss the backdrop of the screen. The screen is unimportant because it says nothing about the story unfolding from the movie. The screen is present the entire time, but it's the forms on the screen that hold our interest. So, too, when the objects of the world become less persuasive and when the subject becomes more porous and insubstantial, the formless background begins to hold our interest. As we begin to notice the backdrop that holds the form, the divided mind opens to the sacred unified mind. The patterns and images on the movie screen are never separated from the screen; in fact, they are of the same composition. Much like the movie, the foreground form and the background formlessness are understood as a single essence. As the Buddha said, "Merging with the deathless are all things. Terminating in Nirvana are all things."[10]

We see our way through all distinctions. There is absolutely nothing else except "seeing" that we can bring to our spiritual journey that does not eventually shackle us the divided mind. We have to bring unified-mind strategies to divided-mind dilemmas in order to open the mind beyond division. Seeing is the only strategy that does nothing but see. It adds no evaluation or self-control; it only sees and discerns, and that is all that is necessary for the resolution of the divided mind.

When experiences arise within a divided mind, judgment results. When experiences are perceived within a unified mind, there is just seeing without judgment. Get a sense of the two forms of perception throughout the day. Notice that the unified mind is without a commentator and free of a story, while the divided mind has a strong narrative full of opinions. Is it possible to move from a divided to a unified perception? What must happen for that to occur?

To set up enlightenment as a distance from where we are or as the time needed for preparation is to look through the old paradigm at the new. It is to place us back within the diagram of time and desire. There is no distance or time from the present, and to conceive of awakening as such puts us back to sleep. We cannot awaken from sleep without realizing we are asleep, and that is accomplished by understanding how time and distance deprive us of natural wakefulness. We have to probe even deeper into the mysteries of the mind to discover our patterns of sleep and from there garner the courage to awaken. It takes extraordinary courage to admit there is no delay to wonder and that there is no separation from the mystery we seek and the one who is seeking it.

4

Governing Laws of the Formless Paradigm

Broken and broken, the moon upon the sea mends easily.

—CHOSU

In the previous chapter we summarized our everyday perceptions by seeing how the mind has learned to falsely divide itself into the thinker and the thought. It projects this schism onto the sense data that is coming into the mind as a subject, me, seeing objects out there separate from me. We then act from this untested premise despite the difficulties that arise from that belief. After some time this projected realism wears on us, and we recognize that fulfillment can never be fully realized within the divided mind. We thereby begin to retract our investment in objects, and as they become less enticing, the energy that was used toward their pursuit shifts out of form into the formless, and the sacred is realized.

The thinker and the experience seem to have a space of time between them as the thinker, "I," ponders the images of reality the mind is revealing through the senses. This gap makes us feel as if the "I" were in control, making decisions and exerting the necessary effort to correct whatever problems arise. All of this is an illusion, of course, since the "I" and the images from the senses are all arising as mental activity within the mind, and there is nothing independent of this mental activity and no time gap between them. More thoughts occur after the image is seen, but the image and the sense of self arise simultaneously. As sobering as this may seem at first, it is directly observable, and therefore the perception can be corrected and, most significantly, separation ended.

Authentic spiritual practices are systems that directly address the subject/object separation and question the false assumptions of the divided mind. As we saw in the previous chapter, Buddhism is meant to do just that. These false assumptions include the sense of time, distance, and our egoic image and identity, which result in struggle, isolation, separation, fascination with objects and the pursuit of pleasure. Authentic practices encourage the understanding of the entire range of self-centered activity, from reactivity to willful effort, and work to extract the sense of self from all that arises, including all states of mind. Each self-invested state of mind obscures the formless because the energy from the attached view recycles back into the formation of self. When energy is released through understanding the sense of self, rather than supporting its formation, the energy moves into the formless.

Essentially, spiritual practice dismantles the entire paradigm of self, the complete virtual reality constructed from thought. This is where most of us fear to tread. It is one thing to play spiritual hide-and-seek with the egoic identity, looking and seeing how it forms and observing its composition and dependency on thought. This feels as if everything were being seen but only from the safety of the seer and within the established world order. It is another thing to dismantle the misconstrued life on which the self is built. When we do that, we deconstruct our worldview: what we have taken life to be and our entire life set of assumptions. Like a house of cards, the sense of self comes tumbling down, pulling with it the entire paradigm of self. Though we may be hesitant to go in that direction, that is precisely where awareness must inevitably flow.

Many of us assume that taking ourselves apart will be a spiritual adventure. It is fascinating to discover what we are and the causes and conditions in which we arise—but we expect something to catch us at the end. We might be willing to deconstruct ourselves if everything else in our world remained intact, or we might be willing to dismantle everything else as long as we remained intact, but disassembling both can seem pointless and scary. What is left of our world, what is left of "me"? If it were not for the compelling force of the heart, few of us would venture into this arena, but the heart holds not only the urge to move beyond the perception of separation but also the safety of its own love. And that is why we move: for the resolution of the heart and the fulfillment and embodiment of love.

Look around for a moment and become aware of the reality the mind has created; everything you know or have known, all of your plans, expectations, and directions. Imagine you are an anthropologist entering this reality for the first time in order to study its composition. What you think about life, how it is configured, what you take it to be, what you want from it, and where it is going—all of that without exception is thought created. Relaxing into the view without asserting or forcing a particular vantage point begins to reveal a non-directed life. Notice the sense of abiding that was absent when thoughts formed your life, and the sense of space and ease. Here life is lived within the playing field of wonder and innocence and is not built upon time, distance, separation, or struggle.

In both practical and spiritual ways we can make life more heart-felt when we support the holistic principles rather than operate from the misperception of dualism. The heart is always present, waiting patiently for us to tire of our narrative. Within this new paradigm of the heart is a set of governing laws that spring forth from the holistic nature of the mind and that, when utilized, help us live more harmoniously within it.

THE CROSSOVER EFFECT AND
THE LAWS OF THE MIND

During a medical procedure a few years ago, the doctor sedated me with a drug called Versed. Versed has profoundly potent amnesiac qualities, and as I was awakening from the drug, I had the most unusual experience of speaking to the doctor, who was bent over listening to me attentively, and simultaneously having no idea what I was saying. The awareness that I was speaking came before the knowledge of what I was saying, and I remember this very awkward moment when the two time frames merged and I, now fully returned, was supposed to say something but had no idea where the thread of the conversation was going. Fortunately, the doctor nodded and left the room at that very moment, and I was left wondering what we had spoken about. A few weeks later the doctor showed up for a beginning meditation class I was teaching and mentioned his appreciation of learning about the class during my medical procedure. I had no memory of that conversation at all.

This experience and others have shown me that my thinking and communicating do not always rely on a formed sense of self. This is in conflict with conventional beliefs, where communication depends upon my being the spokesperson and cannot occur in any other way. There is clearly something else going on here, which may be that two different realities are interfacing, and this crossover effect becomes evident when an event does not play within the convention of our assumed reality. What may well be occurring during these mystifying moments is the overlapping of the consensus and formless paradigms, where the rules of one are being expressed within the parameters of the other. The event is puzzling only within the laws that govern the paradigm from which we are observing.

We have all had completely mysterious events happen without any rational cause, but we dismiss their occurrences because they are not consistent with the principles of our everyday life. We call these anomalies outliers or coincidences because there is no way to define them within the context of consensus reality. Extrasensory perception, or reception of information not acquired through the five senses, is an example, as are insights, revelations, and creativity itself, but for this chapter we will limit the discussion to how the mind works as a totality within the formless paradigm but crosses over continually into conventional reality.

The laws of the mind that are outlined in the next sections are well known to many of us but cannot be explained by orthodox theories and make sense only when the mind is understood as unified. Since the mind in its essence *is* unified, these laws are the intrusion of unity into our ideas of separation. We believe that if we are separate from the mind, we should have control over the mind, and the mind continually shows us we do not. Changing our assumptions of separation would cause too much disruption, so we keep trying to fit these outliers into the consensus paradigm, which cannot be adequately done. Even mental-health professionals may utilize these laws because they see them working effectively with their patients but miss the underlying principle of the unified mind that explains why they work.

The effort we impose on the mind is the mind affecting itself.

This overriding principle of the unified mind establishes one clear reference for our spiritual journey. We are not in charge, and the more we attempt to assert control, the more we force the mind into a divided subject/object mode of perception. Since the unification of the subject and the object is the direction of our spiritual journey, we need to come to terms with this law and attune our practice to it as quickly as possible.

This may be a difficult task, since we are so conditioned to think of the spiritual journey as a movement from one state to another rather than from form to the formless. We think the present state of mind needs to be changed and a new state cultivated, but that is the way the divided mind thinks, and *that* is what needs to change. The divided mind thinks in terms of distance and bridging separation through space and time. Since it knows only form, it thinks in concrete and quantifiable terms: "I am here and I need to be there." When we go along with that thinking, we rely on form to close that gap: "I am quieter today and feel like I am making progress; I am more settled and attentive, calmer and more loving. This practice is really working." We are looking for some expression of ourselves to satisfy our thirst for completion, but any conclusion drawn by the sense of self keeps us within form and bound to our narrative.

It is very difficult to stop thinking about where we want to go and what we need to do to get there, but even when this thinking continues, at least we can question its direction. Such thoughts when believed take us deeper into the quagmire of our conditioning and lead to the assumption that time and adaptation will heal our spiritual dilemma. We can begin to correct the direction of these thoughts by asking, "What is wrong with this moment?" and then observing what we believe is wrong that time and effort will correct. We can also begin to question the strategy of seeking a better form of "me" as the ultimate remedy to ending mental division, since the belief in the idea of "me" is what creates the division in the first place.

Self-effort is a disguised expression of the same belief that something is wrong and needs correction. When something seems to be missing within the present, a corresponding emotion arises that confirms that belief, and the sense of self takes the reins of control and applies a corrective force. This applied effort comes from the "I" part of the mind in disagreement with the emotive part of the mind. "I shouldn't be feeling this way" or "Something is wrong here" and the actions we take from this conclusion further divide the whole. Effort seems to put us firmly in control, but what is actually occurring is a strong identification with the "I" formation and an antagonism with the emotion. When one thought is strongly opposed to another, a battle of tension ensues and the emotion is repressed or acted out. If the association between the emotion and the thought of "I" is strongly negative, the next conclusion after "I hate the emotion" will be "I hate myself."

To correct this errant tendency to effort our way toward wholeness, we need to remember that ultimately there is nothing wrong with the mind or the "I" within the mind. States of mind do not say something about "me," and nothing the mind emits implicates me.

This is so because there is no "me" outside these thoughts. There is only a momentum of past conditioning, nothing else. We are so used to reacting to and identifying with the conditioned story that accompanies the state that we are convinced the state of mind expresses what we truly are. States of mind are conveying the mind's conditioning, how it behaved in the past when certain conditions arose, and are not imparting some fundamental truth about our true nature. Once we realize we are a set of mental constructs and the conclusions we are reaching are composed of the narratives we have believed, we can step out of this confusion.

What is wrong with you that needs to be corrected? You may think there is something wrong, and emotions seem to validate that assumption, but when you look at the emotion you will see that it is just a feeling about the thoughts you are thinking. The emotion is not actually connected to any truth other than the belief you give your thoughts. Those emotions become a conditioned part of the image of yourself. Experience the emotion free of thoughts by not letting the story of the emotion play through the actual feeling. Let the emotion be just what it is. Now ask yourself again what is wrong with you and do not let your answer be determined by an emotion or a thought.

A corollary to this law is that "I" cannot end my suffering because the "I" is creating the division that *is* the suffering. We cannot create wholeness from division. All we can do is understand why we suffer and surrender all of our reactivity. Awareness, which is whole and cannot be divided, puts an end to suffering. All of this reaffirms the statement made earlier that we are not in charge, but if we are not in charge, what is? If we attempt to answer this while we are still strongly identified with form, we will conclude an answer in form, and we will make a god or a higher power the responsible party who is ultimately in control. But as awareness quietly evolves out of form into the formless, it is obvious that formless awareness is in control, and that is shapeless and silent.

Awareness is not a form and therefore not a person, place, or experience, but it is the essence of all things. Since everything is composed of awareness, there is no need to externalize a creative force as God. As the physicist Stephen Hawking states it, "Spontaneous creation is the reason there is something rather than nothing, why the universe exists, why we exist. It is not necessary to invoke God to light the blue touch paper and set the universe going."[1] When the formless is realized, we no longer need God. God is seen as a holdover from the consensus paradigm, and belief in God keeps us bound to form.

The more we avoid an experience, the more we ensure its return.

I remember when I first saw an Asian centipede while I was in Thailand. I had an unusual bodily reaction that forewarned me about our relationship. I had such aversion I tried every way to limit our contact, placing oil-soaked rags around the base of the wooden pilings that held my small cabin aloft and searching the cabin thoroughly at night before retiring to bed, both recommended by the elder monks who knew the dangers of the centipede's bite. Still the centipedes found their way into my shelter on several occasions. Once I awoke in the middle of the night to see a centipede hanging down from a shelf about a foot above my head, eating a scorpion. Another time I heard the sounds of a rustling centipede in my hut and spent all night trying to dislodge it, only to have it leap forward and bite my hand as the morning sun arose. Many Westerners came and left the monastery during the years I was there, but no one that I knew had even a minor problem with the centipedes.

As I look back on those episodes with the centipedes, I am convinced my aversion brought the centipedes to me. It was an outward manifestation of an inward principle I had understood for years: the more an experience is pushed away, the more it returns to haunt us. This may not sound reasonable, since the inward world of thought and emotions seems so disconnected from the outward movement of centipedes, but once the mind is unified, we sense that everything has always been integrated under the same laws. The mind created the outward perception of division when it assumed the self was separate from what it observed, but once these two are brought into alignment, the division between inside and outside vanishes and the governing laws of the mind become universally applicable.

This law can easily be understood when we apply it to the mind alone. Suppose I were to suggest a single word, such as *apple,* and state that you can think about anything you wish except that word. I am sure if you then recorded your thoughts you would find the word *apple* arising repeatedly. A repulsive word, idea, emotion, attitude, or action has a strong identifying link back to the thought of "me" and requires an equal force from me to keep it repressed. We identify with an experience as much through fear as we do through attachment, and turning away from an experience holds us to that experience with the same tenacity as grasping the experience does. With enough mental willpower, we can suppress an aversion experience, but we cannot eliminate it from our consciousness and it will return. Reactive outbursts are an example of a denied or repressed pattern springing back into consciousness under the right circumstances.

The broader impact of this law is when we try to separate what we like from what we avoid and thereby create an unconscious boundary of mental tension that forces further division. Now the repressed idea is no longer a single word but an entire category, like all unpleasant experiences. Since the mind is not under our control, we cannot decide what will be included and what will be omitted. All the self can do is simply turn away and pretend the unwanted fact does not exist. It often does this by thinking about the opposite, pleasant experience. But we cannot get rid of the unpleasant fact by turning our mind away; we can only deny the fact of its existence, and that leads to the creation of a mental shadow.

As an example, let us say you have a strong investment in your image as someone who is kind and considerate and will go out of your way to help a person in need. Now let us say a neighbor has repeatedly asked for assistance, and, wanting to be helpful, you have accommodated her requests over a number of months. Recently when the phone rings you notice a slight tinge of reaction related to the probability of another request. There is a growing resentment that you refuse to acknowledge because it does not fit your self-image. At some point the neighbor calls and, before she can say anything, you explode, telling her how selfish she is in her repeated demands. This time she was calling to share her summer tomatoes, but the damage is done. Your shadow erupted upon the scene because it was never accepted within the totality of your consciousness even though it was there all along. What is not included controls us. Christ said it in this way, "If you bring forth what is within you, what you bring forth will save you. If you do not bring forth what is within you, what you do not bring forth will destroy you."[2] The tension of resistance is due to our strong identification with our state of mind. We resist undesirable qualities because we believe they represent who we are and through this identification we can be assured we will become those very qualities.

A self-image is always composed of what we accept about ourselves pitted against what we do not. The only way the mind can regain its wholeness is to drop all images and allow the polarities to coexist. To release the image is to relinquish the idea of who we are, since the sense of self is composed only of our personal narrative as it relates to our memory. In fact, all images have to be abandoned, because each contains a mental script of what something is, and by inference, what something is not, and that subtle form of distinguishing divides the world into individual objects. This again brings us back to the central fact that division is created through mental investment, and that investment has to be released in order to see reality clearly.

Write down a list of traits that fit your self-image, starting with the most important and adding in decreasing order. Now, across from that list, write down the opposite of the trait (for example, honesty . . . dishonesty). You can now see the shadow of your identity. The opposite qualities at the top of the list will be the ones you struggle with and fear the occurrence of the most. These will be the qualities that will create the most inward tension when they arise. Since all qualities of mind exist within everyone's consciousness, both sides of the polarities will arise. The more you fear a state of mind, the more ferociously it will erupt into consciousness through your reactions. Try allowing the two opposing qualities to meet in your mind without tension. For example, if you see yourself as a kind person, allow unkindness to coexist when it is present. Offset the fear of having unkindness arise with the willingness to learn about it when it does arise. What does unkindness feel like in the body and mind, how does it express itself in thought and action? Do not judge it; just see it. Opening to both sides of the polarity will diminish and finally end the tension that creates mental division.

One of the consequences of realizing the law that states the more we attempt to avoid an experience, the more it controls us, is that we perceive the mind has no natural boundaries. All boundaries are conceptually conceived by abstract thoughts attempting to categorize and separate one experience from another. This includes distinguishing the inside from the outside, the body from the mind, one object from another, and "I" from the rest of experience. When something is without boundaries, it is by definition limitless and inclusive. When the mental boundaries are eliminated, the mind has no edges, no partitions, and cannot be measured. This law throws the universe wide open and exposes the whole heart-mind to oneness.

When we see people in our culture acting at the expense of a greater good, we may wonder why so many miss the pain inherent in a divided mind. Our culture does not encourage an examination of the cause of our dissatisfaction because our economic engine is built upon the pursuit of pleasure and the avoidance of pain, which is the cause. In this sense, separation is consistent with our cultural values. It is important to note that reality does not contain pleasure or pain; the mind imparts those qualities through its conditioning. When the image of the object is identified, it adds a pleasant or unpleasant tone, and we chase after or avoid that feeling as if it were intrinsic to the object itself. It then pursues the object it has assigned as pleasurable and avoids the opposite, forcing another polarity within consciousness.

We cannot force the mind to heal or compel it to bring forth what is hidden.

We have all had the experience of being unable to remember something that lies just below conscious awareness as if it were "on the tip of our tongue." Trying to force the forgotten thought forward does not help, but what often does is to back away entirely from all tension around remembering, and out of nowhere the thought usually emerges on its own. Forcing our authority on the mind only represses the experience further by increasing the tension between the sense of self and the emerging idea. As we learn to work within the governing laws of the mind, we sense how closely healing and forgiveness are related.

Many of us remain unhealed to our past because we do not understand how to forgive. Forgiveness is bestowed through the unified mind, not through our efforts to release the burden of a memory. The part that feels ashamed or outraged is unified with the memory of the incident by exposing and releasing all contrition or reaction over time. We simply allow the memory and our reactions to coexist without disruption until the tension between the two can no longer be sustained.

The mind will repeatedly attempt to come up with other possible actions that should have been taken. Thoughts like "I should have handled this differently" or "I will always remember the effect my anger had on him" may feel as if we were offering the necessary penance to move on, but healing does not come from self-deprecation or from perpetuating animosity. When we are attempting to forgive a harm caused by another, we have to allow the person to be more than the sum of his or her behavior. That understanding takes a thorough exploration of what a person is and involves seeing the behavior as the residue of the conditioning around which the image of the person was built.

When the unified mind is understood, these thoughts are seen as divisive and limiting. Instead, when the memory surfaces, it is left to express itself however it will. The subject, "I," must be careful not to further condemn him- or herself or the memory. Like a child who is made to sit in the corner, the memory is allowed to stew within its existing emotions, while the actual facts of the incident are left undisturbed. This is an important point, because we often attempt to rearrange the memory to suit our justification of why we acted the way we did or to further condemn the person who harmed us.

This may be a lot to ask when the memory has a heightened charge, but remember that we are talking about what it takes to be completely healed, and that may require repeated exposure to the divisive memory. Each time the memory is observed without disruption it loses a little of its reaction—on its own—until it eventually simmers into a nonissue. The memory will often carry layers of emotions such as fear, guilt, and, shame, but if these are left as part of the residue of the memory and not identified with as our current condition, then the emotions will soften with the memory. As the emotions moderate, so do the accompanying thoughts, and the rift begins to heal. Though the memory may bring up residual feelings from time to time, what remains can become manageable and unobtrusive.

With the exception of trauma,[3] there is a natural timing for reengaging the memory and returning it to quiet. Wisdom develops through a simple and peaceful vigilance, and it is this clear awareness that heals the rift. Bare and simple awareness is enough because it is formless, adding nothing to either side of the issue. Learning is a byproduct of this attention, and over time we see why we did what we did, and, given our disposition in that moment, we understand that we could not have acted in any other way. We know we are a completely different person now from when the incident took place, and it dawns on us that there is nothing to forgive between unrelated images of ourselves. This entire process will be discussed in much more detail in a later chapter, but for now the important point is that the optimum environment for healing is noninterference.

The mind heals when left alone. There is a corresponding process in biology called homeostasis that supports this law. Homeostasis is the self-regulating biologic processes that maintain a constant state of balance under various conditions of stress.[4] In other words, a system (the mind) will come back to balance (healing) on its own when freed from internal or external stressors (division and separation). We can get a sense of how homeostasis works within the mind when we remember that the unhealed mind is the divided mind. Any unresolved tension between the observer and the perceptual image creates disharmony, and the balance is lost. We normally force the mind away from balance by weighing in with our opinions, which compromises its mental resilience. The divided mind believes it is our contrition that accomplishes the healing, but the effect of self-deprecation actually prevents the mind from unifying.

The next time you feel guilty or remorseful, stop the self-critical thoughts and just hold the memory of what you did in your consciousness without altering the experience. Feel the pain of not being perfect and hold that pain with the memory. Do not add any more to the story than what is arising within that memory. Be patient with the memory and the pain, but do not encourage any further guilt by adding more commentary. Just let the experience and your inadequacy be what it was. When it fades away naturally, let it go. If it reappears, be willing to stay with it as long as it lasts. Over time it will lose its power.

Learning what healing is and how to access it is perhaps the only realization needed for the fulfillment of a spiritual journey. Healing is learning how to do nothing and abide in formless awareness. It is stepping out of form and into formlessness. Doing nothing usually requires doing something before we can do nothing. Doing nothing often entails learning what doing is and is not, from the perspective of both form and formlessness. Stated simply, there is often a lot of learning necessary to do nothing. For most people it is not just a matter of trying not to argue or resist. Surrender is what is necessary, and that subject will be the topic of the next chapter.

A corollary to this law stating that we cannot force the mind to heal is that we cannot meet the mind with the same energy it is emitting. For example, we may find that we have a strong need to control situations and have felt anxious when we are out of control. A sincere intention may arise to move beyond this pattern, but the wrong solution is to try to force ourselves not to be controlling. Trying to assert power over control reinforces the same pattern and ends up reinvigorating the self who is in control. The only option available is to understand our way out of control—see it, learn from it, and let it be. When we are attempting to understand a problem, we are not trying to control that problem or there would be no learning about the nature of the problem. Likewise, if we are trying to learn about our anger but become irritated with our progress, that irritation reignites the flame of anger and reconditions it back into the brain. We may believe that our reaction is justified, but it would be justified only if the sense of self were outside the anger and therefore able to influence it. We have learned that the anger and the "I" who feels the anger are both mental phenomena.

To fully align our spiritual journey, we have to include the entire disposition of self. The only authentic strategies we can work within are clear observation and simple understanding. Any other actions on our part are strategies from the consensus paradigm and the divided mind, which will return perception to its subject/object default setting. Perhaps the hardest lesson for the sense of self to learn is that seeing is enough. Pure seeing eliminates our influence, and the sense of self feels helpless. We cannot leave any part of ourselves out of the observation or that part will inevitably regain its power and control. We find ourselves living the Christian phrase, "Be whole as your Father in Heaven is whole."[5]

We cannot strategize our way to freedom.

The mind is extraordinarily cunning and loves any journey where it can define its own progress and establish its own direction toward a goal. But if the real journey is the unification of the subject and object, the two halves of the divided mind, then the divided mind has no clear way of progressing toward that goal. The mind has no way even to conceptualize a framework about where it is headed, since it can reason only from its current perception of the problem. Any and all mental maps will be clearly irrelevant to moving our spiritual journey forward, since all maps will arise from one side or the other of the very division we are seeking to cross. The great twentieth-century spiritual teacher Jiddu Krishnamurti stated it this way: "I maintain that Truth is a pathless land, and you cannot approach it by any path whatsoever, by any religion, by any sect. That is my point of view, and I adhere to that absolutely and unconditionally. Truth, being limitless, unconditioned, unapproachable by any path whatsoever, cannot be organized [by the mind]."[6]

An authentic spiritual journey must eventually lead to a total stopping and arresting of all movement forward, where we have no power to advance and no clear direction to proceed toward an end result. We have already hit this "wall" several times in this book, and we will do so again, but where does this wall leave us? What are we to make of our total personal failure to resolve spiritual issues?

Again I find an equivalence of this same predicament in science. In quantum mechanics, the Heisenberg uncertainty principle states there is a fundamental limit on the accuracy with which certain pairs of physical properties of a particle, such as position and momentum, can be simultaneously known.[7] The physics professor Richard Wolfson explains the implications of this law by stating, "At a certain point we become a factor in the very experiment we are performing. No longer are we an objective disconnected observer. We become part of what we are observing. We become part of the world we are trying to interact with. We cannot observe the universe without affecting it. You cannot say something has a position or a velocity if you cannot measure them, and nothing can be measured absolutely."[8]

Clearly science has seen that the observer is not independent of the observation, and it is at this identical point where our spiritual journey abruptly stops. When this is fully realized by directly observing the limitations of all forms of self-control, then the consensus paradigm ceases to work and the formless paradigm is entered. Stated in the metaphor of this chapter, the divided mind discontinues its divided ways and subject and object reunite within the unified mind.

> Have you seen the limits of using yourself to advance spiritually? If so, what is left for "you" to do? You cannot thoroughly understand this dilemma until you realize what you are and what remains after you have taken yourself out of the picture. What remains will then carry you forward. Allow your energies and intention to move toward that discovery.

This makes sense, does it not, because as long as the sense of self believes it holds the power over the object, it will maintain its independence from the object. There is no way to persuade us out of this conclusion, but there is the realization of its untruth. Since neither side of the divided mind possesses awareness, then unencumbered free awareness can see what is actually occurring on both sides. What it sees is free of any influence by either side, and so it sees the truth. This information does not come from discursive thinking, which is a by-product of the divided mind; it comes through the unified mind/ heart/body. Realization is this direct infusion of discernment into the totality of the unified mind that includes the body and the heart.

A unified mind does not deny either side of the division but holds whatever is arising within the synthesis of formless awareness, but there is an additional point that needs to be expressed. There is perfection that holds all of it together and embraces unity and conflict, division and nondivision. It holds both the perception of self as the center of life and the perception of self that is empty.

A unified mind offsets our tendency to believe in the arguments of our divided mind, but the divided mind is also a manifestation of the perfection of all things possible. The coordinating and organizing quality of the mind that successfully allows us to navigate through the world does not cease. The form of our bodies and minds continues forth with none of it discounted or ignored. Our ignorance and our wisdom are both subsets of this greater perfection. The whole of it, all without exception, is what we awaken into without contest and resistance.

We have now explored a few of the laws that arise from a unified mind, but what we have not examined is the mechanism through which this unification occurs. How does the divided mind transcend itself? We have noted that this passage cannot be accomplished through self-empowered will, so how is unification possible when we have no power to change division? What is the passageway between the consensus and formless paradigms?

The consensus paradigm works through the mechanism and slow process of adaptation. It alters its narrative to accommodate the changes it needs to make. It literally talks itself out of one fixation and into another, but words do not assist in entering the formless paradigm. Surrender is the ending of the narrative and the gateway for accessing the formless.

5

Comparing Strategies

Adaptation and Surrender

We must be willing to let go of the life we planned so as to have the life that is waiting for us.

—JOSEPH CAMPBELL

E ver since the origin of life on this planet some 3.7 billion years ago,[1] all of life has been in a constant state of evolution. When that single-celled organism arose from the primordial soup, it started to adapt, change, alter, and move, and that one-celled organism eventually evolved into all life forms that we now see on this planet.[2]

If we just focus on our species for a moment, the range of modification and adjustment that we have gone through is astonishing. Some of us have adapted to the rigid icy conditions of the Arctic, while others live in the drought-laden and arid wastelands of the Kalahari Desert. Humans have covered the face of the earth because of our genetic predisposition to adjust to almost any set of circumstances and to move when that environment can no longer support life.

No matter what conditions we live within, what is equally amazing is that our minds will eventually settle within that setting and call it home. Once we call a place home, we have strongly identified with the surroundings and resist further migration. At that point many of us are willing to defend and protect our home regardless of where it might be located.

> Notice the tension between home and adaptation. Home is where you want to be; adaptation is what you have to go through to get there. Once you find your home, you no longer want to adapt. Home is where you have stopped changing and now belong. The feeling of being at home touches a deep yearning to belong. The need to belong may be more primal than your evolutionary disposition to adapt. Notice when you refuse to leave a comfortable situation and object to further adaptation. Is this expression of belonging ultimately satisfying? Is it the place that is the problem or the emotion that is paired with the place? Is it possible for you to feel at home regardless of where you are located?

The conflicting forces of home and adaptation, comfort and migration, play forth through our internal lives as well. We have each grown up within a certain psychological configuration that consists of our self-image, attitudes, convictions, assumptions, opinions, and views, and these are how we know ourselves, our cultural heritage, and what we have learned to call our internal home. We are comfortable there, and though it may not always be comfortable to be there, we will nevertheless argue, resist, and fight to defend this home just as we would our physical environment. We often have to be forced to modify our internal comfort level, and that usually results only after a level of suffering that we can no longer bear. Then and only then will we consider adapting and changing our internal world.

Just as human beings have learned to live within extremely diverse physical conditions, so too have we learned to live within dissimilar internal environments. One person may appear calm, serene, and equanimous while another person's inward life may be tumultuous, full of drama, volatile emotions, and intense reactivity. Each of us has found an adaptive comfort within our state of mind that we now call home. We do not like to change because it means we will have to readapt to a new array of mental conditions with which we are unfamiliar and that will take us out of our comfort level.

Changing our internal world occurs more frequently than we might expect. Any time we meet the variances of life with a consistent response, we will feel the pressure to modify our conditioned response. The changing nature of life requires an adaptive response, and one of the easier ways to do that is simply to change our attitude to fit the occasion. Once I was standing in a long line with my twelve-year-old niece, grumbling as I often do about the long wait. She looked up and said, "Just change your attitude, Uncle Rod." And so I did.

But here is an important dharma point. Not long ago I overheard one dharma student saying to another, "Just change your attitude and all will be well." We sometimes link "being with things as they are" with simply adjusting our mind-set about the way things are. Given our evolutionary tendency to adapt and modify, it is not surprising that we fall back on adaptation for our dharma response as well. The question is whether the Buddha teaching can be distilled down to a simple change of attitude as the path to end suffering.

There are many times during the day when a mood colors an action. "I just can't meditate," we might say after a problematic morning. Seeing through these moods and the accompanying attitude is important if we are to proceed through difficult times, and we do learn that we can accomplish what we need to do despite the emotions we may be experiencing. However, spiritual practice is much more than keeping a positive attitude. Having a positive attitude can be very helpful in sustaining our spiritual journey over time, but thinking of the spiritual journey as changing our emotional response relegates the practice to behavior modification and is similar to saying that dharma practice is seeing the glass half full rather than half empty. Spiritual practice is more than mastering the power of positive thinking.

Most of us discover relatively soon in practice that we can bolster our attitude by discounting some of the illegitimate thoughts and accompanying emotions that sustain it and by encouraging more uplifting thoughts. We walk a very fine line between the spiritual directive of noninterference and our discomfort with our arising attitude. All of us would like our minds to be easier and more cooperative, but we may not know how to do that without rejecting the mood we are in and deliberately thinking in a more positive direction.

What does noninterference look like when we are facing a deluge of difficult emotions that we know we have the power to transform by nudging our thoughts in a different direction? At this point we have to rely on the discerning wisdom of awareness. When wisdom meets an obstruction, it surrenders all resistance to it; when our reactions meet an obstacle, we strategize on how to overcome the difficulty. Wisdom lives all states of mind but believes in none; reactivity identifies with each state of mind and lives out each one. Wisdom does not resist or attempt to change anything, but reactivity wants to change anything that is difficult to accommodate.

A common meditation instruction is to see all states as visitors passing through the mind and allow each guest a safe passage free of judgment and condemnation. The reason we leave each state of mind alone is that we cannot realize the true nature of mind if we are busy changing its composition. By allowing mental states to be as they are, we realize we have nothing to fear from what they are. We alter an emotional state or attitude when we do not trust it, when we give it more substance and truth than it warrants. We cannot touch the Buddha's teaching on emptiness if we are busy tweaking what we see, so we drop our resistance and simply be quiet with the experience. The quieter we become, the less we infuse the story of our life within that experience. It is the narrative we fear because the narrative binds the experience to our personal point of view. "It is all about me!" we think, when actually the narrative is empty words pointing to no one.

There is a place for uplifting our emotions and discouraging difficult thoughts, but we must be aware that ultimately it is through noninterference that the deepest teaching is accessed. Noninterference is simply letting something be what it is without believing in the story that supports it. With the absence of the story, we awaken to the natural alignment of all things; we awaken to their interconnected reality. That is how awareness sees reality when the filters of the ego are removed. The reality of interconnection floats to the surface like a submarine emerging out of the depths of the sea, and we recognize it as true because it is not being formed by our story.

ADAPTING THE NARRATIVE

An adaptive response in terms of the divided mind is the narrative rebuttal that the reactive part of the mind is having with the incoming sense data. The data are lining up so that our comfort level will have to be altered, and in response we have a tantrum. We are being forced to leave the comforts of our home, and we resist the data proportional to the change needed. Slowly we alter our arguments, change our narrative, and accommodate the new world order, but all of this takes time and tension.

Adaptation is an evolutionary response, which means that it is time driven and can be extraordinarily slow. We attempt to bring our adaptive responses to the fleeting moments of life, but the moment has often moved on by the time we respond. When we actually get around to modifying our responses, the circumstances that led us to consider change may have long since departed. When a moment arises where an immediate response is needed, we stop and ponder the risks of adjusting to this new situation. "Should I go along with it? Why not hold out for a better occasion? If I do, what will people think of me? Okay, I will join in. . . ." Meanwhile the configuration has changed and the engagement, if attempted, is slightly out of sequence.

Notice how often your actions of body, speech, and mind are just a little untimely, slightly out of the flow of the moment. What inhibits a more spontaneous response, and how would you access that spontaneity? Play with responding within the moment rather than from the moment.

Often we are forced to adapt to a life-altering event such as when we lose a job, someone has died, we move to another area, or we become compromised mentally or physically. Here our comfort level, what we counted on life to provide, is being directly assaulted by circumstances beyond our control. We struggle to adjust to this new reality but feel helpless. We have no response, no way to counter the forces that seem aligned against us, no answers, tools, remedies, or maps for this new terrain. Adaptation is all we know, and it does not offer another option except to grieve our loss.

Adaptation to these traumatic events requires a grieving response that leaves us lingering within our old comforting memories. We cannot move immediately into the newly altered life because the adaptive response does not activate that quickly. The adaptive response has stages where we first have to let go of what we had and then grapple to readjust. This pulls us through a matrix of struggle and suffering.

The first stage is denying the truth that we have to change, that life is coming at us in a hostile way. We try to temper its effect by turning away like Scarlett O'Hara in the movie Gone with the Wind. With the world tumbling around her, Scarlett says, "I can't think about that now. If I do I'll go crazy. I'll think about that tomorrow." We try to lessen the impact of reality by thinking about another story that gives us a little delay. The world becomes very tightly closed within denial, and we mentally shut down. The adaptive response is not flexible or swift enough to offer another strategy.

Denial is the mind's defense against the thought of having to change.[3] We are the only species that I know of that can pretend something does not exist when it does, and we do so with a sleight of mind that would amaze most magicians. We make the truth run a maze of defenses that alters it significantly, so when the truth does reemerge, it looks more approachable. We keep challenging the truth until we hear the one voice that coincides with our confusion. "What does that doctor know about lung cancer anyway? I read online about a doctor in Papua New Guinea who doesn't believe in lung cancer."

Denial is the willingness to live unconsciously and assume a make-believe world that fits our comfort level. The current resistance to climate change is a case in point. We all sense the radical change of lifestyle that would be needed to concede this truth, and so it is better left denied. But the completion of the journey from struggle to the end of struggle requires allowing the undefended fact to enter consciousness, the fact that gets through without alteration. We are beginning to see that by altering the facts, reliance on the adaptive response delays the true transformation necessary to end struggle.

> Admit when you deny a fact that needs your attention. Perhaps it is the truth about a relationship, your job, or an action that is needed. As painful as the truth is, living within denial is even more painful. Notice the toll it takes mentally and physically to pretend the truth does not exist.

The second stage of the adaptive response is the betrayal we feel about the fact. We feel powerless and vulnerable, but at least we are beginning to allow the fact in and have started to adapt. It is our narrative that adapts. We change our story when the pain of denial is disproportional to the severity of the fact. The shut-down mind of denial simply looks in the opposite direction, but even here there is some seepage of truth; if not, denial would never evolve into anger. Anger is the first faint admission that the fact is true, though the divided mind continues its protesting argument.

Anger is a begrudging realization of the truth, but it also holds a component of caring. Something precious is about to be taken from us, and there is nothing we can do except be angry. There is also a trace of fear in anger. We are afraid of where this change is going to force us to go. It can be helpful when we feel anger to sense the caring and the fear, and we will usually act less divisively when we consider these two conflicting emotions within anger.

The next time you are annoyed, frustrated, or angry, notice that there may be two other components to the emotion: caring and fear, which frequently go unnoticed. You may be afraid that something you care about is going to be lost. If you drop the rhetoric of the anger, you may be able to feel both an appreciation for what you are about to lose and the fear of it being taken away. This is the grief response, and to know that anger arises from grief can allow you to relate to it in a very different way.

The third stage of modifying our behavior to a threatened event is compromise. As each phase of adaptation occurs, notice that more light and truth are filtering through our minds. When we are willing to compromise, a relationship between us and the future event is established. We are meeting the fact, if not head on, at least tangentially. A dialogue ensues that is attempting to alter the inevitability of the time line or destination with a plea-bargaining agreement. This is a fairness issue, and we want reality to concede the point that we do not deserve this, but if we have to go through it, we are willing to compromise. Give me a few more days to finish my work; take one of my lungs but spare my life; I will concede that the climate is changing, but it is due to the random patterns of weather, not to human-induced causes. We are at a roulette table and bidding all of our chips in a desperate attempt to gain a little time and leverage.

Unfortunately, fairness is not an attribute of reality. It is a mental trait that we apply to reality to make it orderly and predictable, but it is not a facet of reality itself. How could it be, when children sometimes die before their parents? The knowledge and acceptance that reality does not impart fairness is crucial to our long-term consent to be with things as they are (the end of suffering). We have to know the expectations we are bringing to reality as opposed to what reality actually offers and concede that point quickly or our minds will remain divided and resistant. Reality can never offer fairness. It can only offer the undefended fact of what is occurring.

The fourth stage is despair. We have placed our bets, lost the gamble, and are out of the game. Our narrative now turns downward and inward. Though difficult, reality is now being starkly faced, and it is taking its emotional toll. Where do we turn when there is nowhere to turn? What happens to us when everything is gone, including hope?

Simultaneous to any loss is the arising of a new possibility. Loss does not actually leave us with nothing; it leaves us exposed. This, then, is the hidden potential within every change: it brings to light what cannot die or be taken away. If we did not fill this space with grief, we would see its vivid color and infinite expanse. We would switch into the formless paradigm of the heart. But for most of us, the loss is too disorienting not to grieve, and the emotion comes to the forefront as this new possibility falls away from view.

Adapting to change moves through one narrative expression after another. Each phase has a compelling story that captures our total attention and focuses our survival energy so that the next phase can be revealed. We have to live each phase until it moves us through to the next, but when there is nothing left to move through, it drops us off in silence. Silence then is the fifth stage of true acceptance that few people reach.

Acceptance is the quieting of the narrative, the stillness within the story. One chapter has ended and the next has yet to begin. There is nothing left to add, and all the routes out of the problem have ended, so the conversation ends. Most people do not take advantage of this ending. There is usually only a pause of quiet before a new chapter of resignation springs to life. Depression is intertwined with resignation and is not full acceptance. We feel downtrodden and hopeless, but there is still life within resignation. It is not as gray as the stage of despair and can actually contain some joy as we see new possibilities on the horizon.

Usually after some duration, we learn to tolerate, if not accept, our new reality. This new world has displaced our previous home, and what we once feared has become our newly adapted reality. With time it will become our comfort level, which will inevitably be challenged by circumstances leading to further adaptation, but for now we can call it home.

The next time a significant change occurs, see if you can access the stillness that arises preceding the grief response. When something is no longer present, there is a hole into which it falls, a hole of stillness. Do not move too quickly to cover this stillness with thoughts about the loss. Notice the stillness within the accompanying emotions of chaos and desperation as you attempt to discover your way through this cycle of change. Can this stillness ever be lost, or is it a companion to every stage of grief?

The main point here is that the adaptive response holds a variety of emotions and mental patterns that are not conducive to living free of suffering. To steer away from these spiraling and often self-defeating phases that are central to adaptation, we must find another way of adjusting to the reality of loss that is not evolutionarily based. Life is not a slowly moving vehicle that we can jump off and on at will—first denying and then allowing reality depending on how we might feel. We are in and of it, like it or not, and being of it requires a different mechanism to flow within change rather than the adaptive formulas we have applied since time immemorial.

SURRENDER

Much of our early spiritual practice uses the same evolutionary tendency to adapt under pressure. Within the simple moment-to-moment adjustment we make internally, we can find our evolutionary history of migration, adaptation, and comfort seeking. Once we change, we quickly attempt to find and sustain a new comfort level, which we fight to protect until we are forced to change again. Our growth seems to move in fits and starts, with repeated bursts of activity followed by prolonged periods of delay. We will move forward when we are forced, but we are most interested in finding and maintaining a new home with a comfortable range of ease.

As we assume a more defined cognitive map within our spiritual journey, such as suffering and the end of suffering, our willingness to respond more quickly and evenly to the tensions of life increases. An almost continual feedback loop is established between the arising of a difficult experience and the adjustment needed to release the inward contraction around that incident. We get quite accomplished at limiting the effects of suffering on our life through our adaptive response.

Though the time exposure to suffering is now limited, there is still a time lag between the arising of the difficult experience and the ending of our internal contraction. That time lag is created by the intrusion of the narrative with which we attempt to talk our way out of suffering. It may sound something like this: "Here comes Sally. Oh my, what am I to do? She is so sour and bitter, she brings me down." Now the spiritual narrative kicks in with: "Okay, just relax and release the tension. No one can bring you down if you don't buy into her programming. She won't stay that long, and if you stay soft and allowing, this experience will pass on because all things are impermanent." And finally, after Sally leaves: "See, that wasn't so bad. I caught the problem a little late, but my mindfulness finally kicked in and I settled down. My practice is working pretty well."

There are mental and physical adjustments occurring throughout this narrative as we prepare for the inevitable interaction, first through a heightened arousal and then with a calming response. The point here is that if we live within our narrative, we will first have to suffer in order to initiate our spiritual response to end suffering. Even then we did not end suffering immediately or thoroughly. We talked our way down to a lower level of suffering, but there was still a residual tension that remained throughout the conversation with Sally. When we use our narrative to end suffering, we actually apply an adaptive response that modifies the suffering but rarely ends it.

This is the limitation of internally speaking our way through the suffering process; it is an adjustment, a modification, and time driven. Adaptation is about the only strategy we have to end suffering when we carry along a sense of self throughout the process. The self is an image that is constantly adapting its narrative to fit the outcome it wants and knows no other resource but to continue to think its way through the event. When the self tries to end suffering, it does so by altering the narrative, talking us down from a highly emotional state to a spiritually normal state of mind. Toning down the volatility makes life easier and more accommodating, and for many of us that may seem like the ultimate answer to ending suffering, but there is more to the spiritual journey than this self-modifying behavior.

Through narrative adaptation jailed prisoners can conclude that they are better off in prison than outside and become institutionalized. We can story our way anywhere, and eventually the ending of the story becomes our comfort level. Our spiritual narrative can evolve to include laws, such as impermanence, that we think are spiritually important ways to live, so we start including them in our story. "Just wait, this too shall pass," we might say to offset the anxiety we are currently feeling. We can get so effective with our spiritual vocabulary that we think, by speaking the laws of reality we are actually applying them, but including a truth within our commentary does nothing but talk us down. Truth that fits nicely within our story line is a philosophical truth, not a realized truth, and philosophy does not end suffering.

> What spiritual narratives do you use to ease your way through difficult events? For instance, do you talk yourself out of a difficult situation by referencing impermanence or selflessness? Perhaps you say to yourself "This too shall pass" or "It doesn't matter; it is all empty." Do you get a sense of why you employ such a phrase? Has this truth been fully integrated, and if so, why would you need a phrase to reassure you of something you have realized?

Talking ourselves out of suffering has been the play of subtlety, the counterinfluence of self, which we will discuss in chapter 8. Adaptation is self-driven and encourages a stronger sense of self by strengthening both the story and the storyteller. We have now seen the limitation of adapting our way toward spiritual awakening as our main strategy and understand that it can take us only so far before it loops us back in the wrong direction. What, then, moves us to and through the paradigm shift? What mechanism, if not adaptation, allows actions to be perfectly tuned within the moment, does not carry a sense of self along with it, and is not driven by a story or a storyteller?

Now we are ready for surrender, but let us first define the term. Surrender is not surrendering to someone or something. It is totally releasing the narrative that has been moving us forward. Surrender is not a modification of our actions or a resettlement of our comfort. It is an ending without discourse or lag time and therefore seamless and continuous within the moment. It is based in wisdom and not self-driven.

Not too long ago I was taking some trash outside to the waste bin and had another activity to do while outdoors. After depositing the trash, I had a senior moment and forgot what I was going to do next. Not even a remnant of memory remained about what I was about to do. All I could do was turn around and go back inside. That is the way surrender feels, though free of the aging process that defined this incident. The point is that surrender leaves no trace. It is a complete letting go, not a trying to let it go, which is an adaptive response. There is no internal response offered between the changing event, the surrendering, and the next event, and therefore no grief response follows the change. No modifications are necessary because there is never a movement away, never the slightest protest to the newly arising event.

What we are really surrendering is the time gap between the moment and our reflections upon the moment. This gap is where the narrative resides that contains the sense of self and the story of what is being done. Surrender closes this gap and therefore eliminates separation. What we are surrendering is our separation, and we surrender into silence. Many of us ask how to surrender, and this is an important point: the "how to" is asking for an adaptive response so we can learn to surrender. That would reinsert the gap of time and continue the narrative necessary for surrender to happen, and that would not be surrender.

What if we asked a different question other than "how to," a question that does not encourage a further dialogue but, rather, attempts to close the gap of the narrative? A question such as, What is happening during surrender? A "what" question that takes us directly into the experience of surrender without any intervening gap of time. Such a question may help us understand the difference between surrender and adaptation.

Ask a "how to" question about your practice and watch how it propels you into another "how to" question and from there into an adaptive response. Notice how the mind takes over and exploits the gap of time between reflecting on the question and applying the answer. Now ask a "what" question that takes you directly into the experience of the event. What is this? What is happening? What am I? These questions do not send you into thought but focus with interest upon the nature of the experience. Entering a "what" question requires surrendering all noise and just seeing.

As confusing as all of this may sound, it is important to understand and act upon this logic so we know how not to proceed. This is an example of a valuable spiritual directive: that we learn what is true by perceiving what is false. This directive becomes increasingly important as we approach the formless paradigm of the heart. We often learn the orientation we need to take by seeing how not to progress. In fact, there are many more false paths than valid paths, and if the sense of self is left in charge, we can be sure we will go the wrong way. The mind is as clever as a tax attorney, and all loopholes must be sealed or they will be exploited and will eventually circle us back to the safety of an adaptive response.

Awareness is not adaptable. What this means is that awareness does not adapt to what is arising within it. It just reveals what is arising. When a sound arises, awareness holds the sound but will never adapt to that sound. No matter how long the sound continues, awareness will continue to know it is arising. This means that all adaptation occurs in the mind. When we know where any process is located, in this case adaptation, we can then decipher whether this process will be helpful as we journey out of the mind and into awareness. Obviously any process that originates in the mind will take us only partway before we have to abandon it altogether as we shift into a new paradigm.

Discovering whether any trait, quality, or process originates in the mind or is an intrinsic part of awareness is a wonderful way to flush out mental imposters posing as awareness. For instance, earlier in this chapter I stated that fairness was mind derived, not a facet of nature. Be quiet for a moment and see if that is true. When you directly perceive nature, you will immediately understand that fairness is a mental construct that has nothing to do with nature. Once this is understood, you will no long allow the concept of fairness to haunt your spiritual path. Now ask whether adaptation is intrinsic to awareness or to the mind. Does awareness adapt? That is, do the sense impressions of hearing, seeing, and so on eventually fade away because awareness tires and listens to something else, or does awareness continue to hold the sense data regardless of their duration and quality? If awareness is continuous and never flinches from the sound, then adaptation must be coming from the mind but not awareness.

We have now unlocked the mechanism through which the formless paradigm works and provides the necessary shift out of the consensus paradigm. In doing so we have unlocked the very mechanism of surrender through which the passage is made. The movement out of consensus reality needs to be fully understood or we may find ourselves halfway in and halfway out with no clear idea how to resolve the issue.

6

Crossing the Divide

Your hand opens and closes and opens and closes.
If it were always a fist or always stretched open,
You would be paralyzed.
Your deepest presence is in every small contracting and expanding,
The two as beautifully balanced
And coordinated as birdwings.

—RUMI

In 1980 I was a monk in Thailand visiting a branch monastery where Westerners stayed under the tutelage of Ajahn Chah, a famous Thai Forest Buddhist master. I had recently traveled from Burma, where I had ordained, and had come to this monastery to evaluate the method Ajahn Chah taught, which emphasized a full embrace of life, against the intense and subtle focus of mind that I had learned in Burma. During a brief exchange with Ajahn Chah, he asked what I had learned and how I had practiced in Burma. I enthusiastically gave him a detailed account. He nodded and inquired how I would like to practice now. I told him I thought I would isolate myself and continue to explore the fine distinctions within my mind. He looked at me rather sternly and said, "Do you think subtlety ever ends? You have already seen it, isn't it time you moved on?"

Like many meditators, I had become enamored with the magnification power of my mind, and Ajahn Chah was poking at this attachment. There is a tendency within some Buddhist traditions to search for transcendence within the nuances of form. As the mind focuses and quiets, very fine distinctions within the various expressions of mind become apparent. If the retreat emphasizes strong concentration, this focused attention seems to be able to access the quantum field of reality. Form is seen as enigmatic, transitory, appearing and disappearing in random and chaotic ways, and utterly unreliable. The immediate effect of this on the practitioner is disenchantment with appearances at the gross level accompanied by a disengaging energy from form itself. In my experience this disillusionment continues throughout the afterglow of a retreat but eventually wanes when the student returns to his or her normal activities.

I have been curious why this divestment of energy from form does not establish itself more firmly, and I believe it is because concentration lures us into a world vastly different from the one we know. The world of subtlety becomes so fascinating that it assumes its own worth and value, and though there may be disenchantment with the gross forms of reality, the practitioner may become captivated within this subtlety. The student may believe this refined world is a more legitimate expression of the truth than the gross world because some of Buddhism's fundamental teachings seem more easily accessible from this vantage point.[1]

As the power of magnification increases and form is experienced as porous and insubstantial, the sense of self, the expression of self in form, follows this subtlety in lockstep. We perceive ourselves as we perceive the world, and the meditator experiences firsthand that he or she is insubstantial as well. This conviction of insubstantiality perfectly conveys the Buddhist teaching on the nature of self and world, and it seems that it is only within this level of magnification that this truth can be fully realized. We are convinced that we are aligned with the words the Buddha is reported to have said: "Whatever exists therein of material form, feeling, perception, thoughts and consciousness, he sees these states as impermanent, unsatisfactory and non-self. He turns his mind away from those states, and directs it towards the Deathless."[2]

Explore the words of the Buddha by investigating what it means to turn your mind away. If we simply turn away, that is an aversive response that has us avoid form. The Buddha is likely suggesting that we release form by thoroughly exploring the value and limitations that form offers. Once we have realized the limitations of pursuing forms, form no longer holds our attention and there is an organic release from form.

But concentration is also a conditioned state and therefore "impermanent, unsatisfactory, and nonself," and so it too waxes and wanes, moving the student back and forth along a continuum from a gross to a refined sense of self. The student often leans away from the gross appearance of self toward the more refined state of self because it is a less persuasive expression of the ego, and egolessness is often mistakenly thought of as the fulfillment of the spiritual journey.[3] We must remember that in the quote above the Buddha asks us to turn our mind away from these conditioned states (see sidebar), which include concentration, and redirect it toward the deathless.

If we attempt to fulfill our practice through the subtlety of form, we have merely substituted one transient world for another, and appearances, gross or subtle, have not fully been turned away from and adequately understood. The sense of self will arise corresponding to whatever thoughts are still believed, and as the refined state of concentration diminishes over time and the subtlety is lost, the sense of self relocates back into its grosser expression of life and we are left feeling that nothing has changed.

This world of refinement is often paired with an accompanying belief that if we could just stay here long enough, we would break through this quantum field into something unconditioned. There may be brief moments in which the unconditioned is known, but there is always the return to form. These "unconditioned breakthroughs" can further support the world of subtlety as the only doorway of passage to the unconditioned. Since concentration experiences need very protective and exclusive environments that cannot be maintained within the turbulence of normal activity, students who feel that the enhancement of concentration is their only gateway often lose their intention to know what is true once their focus becomes less refined.

The point here is that seeing the emptiness of self is not the end of self or even the beginning of the end. In fact, the leaning toward egolessness or subtle appearances assures the continuation of the self. Experiencing the empty nature of ego still has someone who is experiencing it, and ultimately this someone will evolve into a more gross display. We need to understand how the self is formed and what it feeds upon to limit its influence, and experiencing it as empty is only a baby step in this direction. When the sense of self is not thoroughly understood, the ego will seek form to maintain itself. After an intensive period of meditation, the sense of self then goes in reverse and renews its egoic life through its spiritual gains or the wisdom accrued or the disenchantment felt. It springs back in full regalia with anything that can stimulate its rebirth.

The reemergence of the gross sense of self may result in feeling as if everything gained on the retreat had been lost, but that is because we usually think of ourselves as a fixed point on the spiritual journey always moving in a progressive direction. We may believe that with more practice we will be continuously mindful, have sufficient concentration, and be kinder with more integrity. However, much of the spiritual journey is like a rolling wave in a closed tank, lolling from one side to the other in constant movement. When new territory is seemingly acquired, we turn around and are right back where we started. Our understanding may grow accordingly over time, but even our wisdom will have periods of progression and regression. To the sense of self this may feel as if we were treading water or drifting in reverse, and it can take a long time for these reversals to be understood in a positive light. As our understanding starts to incorporate the history of these backward and forward movements into its overall knowledge of the spiritual journey, we no longer feel defeated when reactive patterns reemerge, our mind becomes noisy, or our hearts close down in vanity and selfishness.

What is helpful throughout this process is to see spiritual growth as a continuum, a continuous sequencing—sometimes progressive, sometimes regressive—within distinct extremes. The extremes establish a direction with a view and intention, but just like a rolling wave, there is no fixed position anywhere on the continuum. Even though it sometimes feels as if we were relapsing in the opposite direction, spiritual movement is a little like the circuitous route that water takes to find the lowest level. It is seldom, if ever, a straightforward linear advancement from one end of the continuum to the other.

Even the lapses of mindfulness we struggle to resist have their own value on a spiritual journey. The darkness of forgetfulness feeds the light of remembering like winter feeds spring. As we begin to move outside the strongly conditioned self-reference model of events, where each experience implies something about me and what I need to do about it, into a more universal understanding of how reality operates on its own, we see there is nothing missing or out of place. From that view the absence or presence of self-awareness is simply the current configuration of reality, and any tension we exert to correct it sustains the dichotomy of "the aware me" pitted against "the unaware me." Remembering chapter 3, we see this is a resurgence of the divided mind, and any force in either direction ultimately obstructs unification. Relaxing and accepting whatever reality presents is the only way to heal that rift and end the egoic notion that we are in charge. We have to turn our life over to the dharma, which means the complete disempowerment of the interfering "me."

There are forces that will act upon the gap of inattention that have nothing to do with ambition or willful effort. These forces come from outside the egoic structure, are intrinsic to awareness, and are the organic pull of life to know itself. They form themselves in the mind as a strong intention to awaken or a thirst for completion. This intention is a very simple and straightforward drive to end suffering, but when the sense of self remains in charge we prolong the journey with countless spiritual distortions until we tire and concede the point that we are helpless in our quest for freedom.

Does this mean we can do nothing to nudge our spiritual journey along? The answer to this question lies at the very heart of wisdom, and cannot be answered outside of the individual who is asking the question. We apply the amount of effort we believe is needed until we see the limits of its usefulness or evolve out of its power. Almost all of us start with willpower, biting our lips to restrain from unskillful speech, or disciplining ourselves to sit every day. For most of our early years of practice our minds have blind inertia and are impervious to insight or reason. As the practice develops, the "I" centered thoughts slowly change in direction to more inclusive "we" thoughts, and effort changes accordingly. Heart energy now takes over mind energy, and we could now unthinkingly run a mile to help a dear friend or find ourselves in a deeply creative flow that is not willfully induced. At this point effort becomes the expression of a full heart.

At a certain point in practice this heart energy becomes completely unhooked from the sense of self, but that does not infer that awareness becomes inactive. Not at all; in fact, awareness becomes more vigilant, but this does not occur through our wanting it to happen. As awareness increases so does our understanding and wisdom. Deeper questions about the nature of life arise naturally, and the pendulum swings from the brute force of will to the light touch of awareness and discernment. For example, we all start with self-centeredness, because a life lived within the sense of self is all we know. As we apply additional effort to resolve our tension we realize that this effort is tying us in a tighter and tighter knot of struggle. The harder we try to end our suffering the more tension we feel. It gradually dawns on us that we cannot struggle our way out of suffering. A new model begins to form from this realization, and our strategies change accordingly. Now we want to learn about ourselves, and we ask, "Are we really what we have believed ourselves to be?"

This question leads us to a deeper understanding of the transient nature of the self and confirms that the spiritual journey travels right through the middle of our self-assumptions. This has tremendous implications for our practice because continuing the same dialogue with ourselves even after we have realized the truth of our centerless existence keeps bringing the center back as if it were real. Once centerless existence is seen, many of us do return to thought for our description of reality and to our emotional life to establish our current disposition, but it is here that spiritual resolve has its place. We have to hold ourselves accountable to what we know is true and not fall back into the patterns of our self-centered habits. Here we take a stand and ceaselessly question the conclusions of self.

If we live in another culture, the way into that culture is through its language. Without the language we are merely seeing the foreign country through the filter of our own societal norms. It is the language that offers the nuances of the customs and behavior of the people. So, too, does the language of "I" hold a view of the world that is untenable once we have seen reality as it truly is. We cannot in good conscience keep reasserting the old worn-out view of ourselves as separate from the world in light of these new revelations and are forced to examine our thinking so that every recurrent thought of "I" is seriously questioned.

We can no longer maintain the old model of separation as the gauge of how well we are doing and what we need to do. We have to let our thoughts become aligned with the new paradigm of nonseparation. That means we have to take ourselves out of the equation, not just in theory, but also in fact. The fact is that we do not exist as something separate from reality, and once we have finished trying to force our ideas upon reality, there is just reality. The spiritual journey is learning how to concede that point.

What are the implications of that fact on a practice that references everything through the filter of "me"? What does this mean even to the concept of spiritual progress? Contemplating and working with these questions begin to mature our orientation toward the new paradigm.

Notice that when you use effort, you bring yourself along within that exertion, and the sense of you remains very strong throughout the task. Now notice that when you learn about something, "you" are considerably diminished, because when you learn you are receiving life and are not forcing your way through. Bring these two strategies into your practice and see which one opens you wider and allows more inclusivity.

Each of us has a unique way forward that is not dependent upon what others have done in the past. For some, the life of a monk or a nun has perfect resonance, and for others, the lay life is the precise form for awakening. Only when we step out of our intuitive resonance into someone else's path do we go astray. The opposite is also true. If our intuition tells us to do something and we do not do it because it seems too difficult or we are frightened by the consequences, we become lost. One path cannot be compared with another, but both paths may be perfectly aligned with the results.

THE FIRST CONTINUUM

Suffering to the End of Suffering

A continuum is a kind of story about the spiritual journey, a partial tale that provides a context for understanding the map and terrain that we cross. Myths are built from continua and are the human expression of the problems and difficulties encountered along the way. The extremes are the starting and ending points. In his first sermon after he awakened, the Buddha started the narrative of his teaching. He said he taught only suffering and the end of suffering.[4] This is the birth of the first continuum: from suffering to the end of suffering, and his entire teaching fits between these two discrete limits. He taught for more than fifty years but always remained faithful to the continuum of his first sermon.

Why did the Buddha say he taught only one thing, when his teaching expounded upon many topics and was broad and expansive? By narrowing the definition of his teaching to one essential subject, he kept us alert to this essential continuum no matter what topic he was covering. Everything we do has to be monitored by the direction we take relative to suffering and the end of suffering, and this becomes the underpinning of our entire journey. If we are contracting, recoiling, protecting, resisting, or exerting ourselves in the name of spiritual progress, the scale warns us that we are moving toward the wrong end of the continuum. The question foremost in our thoughts is "In which direction is this action taking me, toward suffering or toward the end of suffering?" If our effort is causing greater struggle even though the effort seems to point in a wise direction, then it must be reexamined in light of the Buddha's continuum. Struggle usually indicates a reversal of the person's relationship to the scale, where we are pushing something away or embracing it too firmly. Such resistance moves in service of our self-centered needs but away from the fulfillment of the journey.

You can see from the scale on page 100 that self-centeredness is equated with struggle and rests firmly on the far left side of the scale, while nonseparation is paired with the end of struggle and sits to the right. The assumption here is that believing in the sense of self creates all the struggles we will ever encounter in life, and nonseparation ends all suffering. As we will see, nonseparation is more than the understanding of no abiding permanent self, but for now we will focus on understanding the nature of the self as the end of the continuum.

Since this book is based upon the supposition that suffering arises simultaneously with the sense of self, I would suggest that the reader test this proposition for him- or herself. You are not a person who is suffering; you are arising within the struggle. First begin to notice the state of struggle: what the mind and body feel like when you are struggling and when you are not. See the resistance that arises and how resistance leads to self-inflation. Notice that the greater the resistance, the more you struggle with your thoughts. Now notice how the pitch of your thoughts increases when there is further self-inflation through your complaints, reactions, blame, and emotional volatility. These are not separate events; as the struggle increases, your thoughts increase, and you feel more defined. Now notice the opposite. When there is no struggle, your thoughts are less urgent, your mind becomes quieter, and you are less defined. Where have you gone?

If all struggles are self-inflicted, then the thorough understanding (not the elimination) of self is the cure. Why is the cure not in the elimination of self? Because it cannot be done, nor does it need to be done to end struggle. There is a functional necessity for the self to be present when we apply the knowledge we have to any given situation. Knowledge and the knower arise together. When we are navigating harmlessly within the world, the knowledge that we are different from the doorway brings forth a remnant of self. This remnant is not the conviction that we are separate; it is more like the vacuous wisp of a self that settles without self-centeredness.

Understanding offers the cessation of belief. As we see how the self arises within circumstances—when a thought is believed, there is a thinker; when there is something functional to do, there is a doer; or when there is an invested emotion, there is a reactor—and it all happens within the formless embrace of awareness, then there is no more belief in self even though the self is arising. That may seem paradoxical until it occurs to us that history is full of the same revelations. For example, to accept Einstein's relativity, we had to abandon the certainty of Newtonian absolute space and time—the certainty that space and time are separate from each another and concrete certainties in themselves.[5] This realization altered and traumatized the world of physics even though most physicists were not able to embody that truth.

Over and over again history has shown that what was once relied on as hard fact proves at another time to be false, and that has always brought us to a better understanding of reality even though it stuns our system while the shift is occurring. The revelation of centerless existence will shock the system as well, but the real impact comes in the embodiment of the truth, and that is where science departs from a transformative spiritual tradition.

This is not a call to master the equations and learn the science. Realization is seeing without protection, but the self tries to dominate by mastering the details. If we are gaining power and therefore egoic definition through our efforts, then it is likely we are attempting to overcome what we see. Realization requires an equal and loving relationship with both the subject and the object. Remember that separation is thought created, but the sense of self takes separation as real and then attempts to resolve the difficulty by working only on the problem and leaving itself unquestioned. To avoid this dead end, the solution must be bipolar by including both the subject and the object.

Divided Mind   **Unified Mind**

Struggle   End of struggle
Self-centeredness ———————— ▲ ———————— ▲ ———————— Nonseparation

           False Nirvana   Paradigm Shift

Like a cursor that moves ever so slowly from the left side (divided mind) to the right side (unified mind) of the continuum, let us make the journey from one end to the other, examining the obstacles along the way. The first five chapters of this book have set us up to understand the transformative qualities of this passage, but we may want to review and draw from that understanding as the cursor moves from left to right.

Moving from the Left Side (Divided Mind)

Progressing on the continuum begins with a life lived within a very protected paradigm, where the sense of self is the cornerstone of existence and everything else is peripherally separated from "me." All the senses and all the information come into the master control center, where they are thought about and reflected upon by "me." The controlling "I" likes the distance this reflection gives because we can then consider our options, but here at control central we also have the burden of being the owner and operations manager of the entire organism. That makes it a lonely position with enormous responsibility when something goes wrong. However, one of the reasons we maintain our position is that we get all the credit when the organism is running well. The truth is that sometimes it runs well and sometimes it does not, and our moods go up and down with the general well-being of the organism.

One of the ways we keep ourselves entertained on the job is by seeking pleasant experiences to offset the pain of our position and attempting to steer away from uncomfortable circumstances so that conditions will always be to our liking. When circumstances cannot be controlled, we get upset, argue, and demand our own way. Eventually the situation passes and the organism resumes under our control. We have been at the controls for so long that the organism pretty much runs itself, and we can nap for long periods of time. Days are tedious and routine, and we do not feel very alive or creative, but we like the fact that the organism can run on cruise control.

This is the view from the far left side (divided mind) of the pathway. It takes an extraordinary amount of inward tension to distort the truth, and the left side of the scale lives within that stress. But it is this distress that motivates us to move toward the right side, or unified mind. Ignorance, with its ensuing struggle, is the problem, but it also provides the impetus to move to the right. As the spiritual journey is pulled to the right side of the continuum, our consciousness becomes more focused. With this sharper perception comes clearer seeing and less distortion. With less distortion we see that the genesis of our suffering, which we have long ascribed to others, is really our own. It is self-generated and cannot be blamed away, and this makes us more accountable. The more accountable we become, the less we struggle, and now we are beginning to see the relationship between facing the facts before us and the easing of our self-induced misery. We are no longer prone to imagine our way out of situations or pretend life is against us. We have a growing need to stay the course and see what life brings and an accompanying belief that life is workable. All of this adds to a gathering curiosity about other ways we may be misrepresenting life and a growing resolve to discover our false views.

FALSE NIRVANA

Many of us begin our spiritual journey for the purpose of resolving a central issue, and that issue, of course, differs for each person. The pain of self-hatred drives some of us, others are driven toward more intimacy, and still others attempt to satisfy their wish for a quieter mind and a less stressful life. We all have an agenda and measure the success or failure of our practice against the resolution of this central issue. The practice is under a great deal of pressure to pay off, and we may stay with the meditation only as long as we see some progress toward that end.

For those persistent enough to stay the course, progress does become apparent. We soften and relax and are willing to face the difficulty we avoided for years. We discover a growing confidence and at-easeness through our willingness simply to see and understand the problem. A huge emotional and psychological weight is often lifted, and we may sense a lightness we have never known. This may be accompanied by a cathartic release of energy that is disorienting and otherworldly, and we may harbor the secret belief that we have touched the liberation spoken about by the Buddha.

Every continuum contains a false nirvana, and many of us easily succumb to its allurement. A false nirvana is a partial relief from the burden of our central issue that can be mistaken as a complete reprieve from the burden of suffering. Though we have traveled further to the right side of the continuum than we ever imagined possible, there remains a lot of distance yet to traverse. Whatever we ultimately want for ourselves we will find, but the end result will still hold a residue of struggle that cues us that this false nirvana is not the ultimate end. This partial release may be satisfying enough to arrest our journey for a while, but the reappearance of a lingering sense of incompletion can often encourage us to continue. We may fight the conclusion that we are not fully transformed because egotistically it is very satisfying to think that we have arrived, but eventually we can no longer deny the struggle that remains.

When we quiet down from the initial euphoria, we sense that residual incompleteness, and a deeper level of intention may arise to resolve it. As we journey through the false nirvana, we become less reliant on experiential goals to compel us forward. Yes, they are nice, but something else is catching our eye. Until now we have been using time and distance as a valid way to proceed. "I am here and need to be there, and I would like it to happen soon." At a certain point on the continuum, we understand that thinking in terms of time and distance moves the sense of self right along with us on the path. Our intention to practice changes accordingly, and we start accommodating this new observation. The new intention that arises can no longer be governed by egoic satisfaction, and we are forced to look deeply inside to see what we really want out of this journey. Though this questioning has moved us through the first false nirvana, other false nirvanas are waiting as the scale becomes more nuanced.

Where are your false nirvanas, the places of extreme contentment and ease on which your journey rests? What provides the motivation to continue when you have achieved what you thought you wanted? Look deeply inside and see if struggle remains. Can you sense a more subtle level of intention that pulls you through and beyond this comfort level?

The more refined pathway, depicted on the diagram as self-centeredness to nonseparation, now comes into play. It is still guided by the encompassing grander scale of suffering and the end of suffering but is subtler and no longer entrapped within the pressure of time or the pursuit of a goal. Whether our intention at this point is liberation or an astute attempt to circumvent the self we do not like will be revealed as this cursor moves a little more to the right. In either case emptiness is the predominant experience as nonseparation begins to be realized.[6] But emptiness can be a false nirvana when it is embraced as an aversion to being someone. Again all the euphoria can be present and once more there can be a feeling of an enormous burden being lifted. "Thank God I do not have to be who I thought I was" may seem like the voice of wisdom, but it is not. Wisdom lives everything and avoids nothing. Wisdom fully embodies the person with all of his or her flaws even as it simultaneously knows the person's inherent emptiness.

The treachery of a false nirvana is proportional to its subtlety, and the scale becomes far more nuanced as it proceeds toward nonseparation on the right side. False nirvanas are numerous as they follow the refined grasping of our motivation, but one of the most difficult is attachment to emptiness. When emptiness is embraced as a refuge against form, there are few ways to reach the person who has become deeply protected within his or her philosophy. Stating that there is nothing to do and no one to do it thwarts all attempts to point in a new direction. The saving grace, if there is one, is the residue of suffering that continues within this pattern, which may shake the person to reconsider his or her position. But even the suffering can be met with the obstinate refrain "I am not suffering because there is no one to suffer."

No one has the ability to move us out of the comfort and logical certainty of a false nirvana until we have the desire to move. What makes it nirvana is that a deeply wounded place within us is temporarily eased, and for once in our life we are no longer under the pain of its oppression. Though it is not the end, it is a safe harbor, and a resting place can provide the healing time necessary to observe the pain closely so that we have the energy and stamina to move on.

SHIFTING PARADIGMS

Strange and sudden surprises fill the pathway from one side to the other. We begin to realize through direct observation that our perception of reality is relative. Before we began we likely believed in a strictly defined and clear-edged world that was one way or another, but soon the spiritual path begins to reveal the indeterminate nature of the reality, that it is relativistic and dependent upon the quality of the observation. We form the world by what we bring to it, and the world forms us through the memory that is imparted to the world. This is also the nature of the world according to science. The physicist Brian Greene puts it this way, "Quantum mechanics describes a reality [that] hovers in a haze of being partly one way and partly another. Things become definite only when a suitable observation forces them to relinquish quantum possibilities and settle on a specific outcome."[7] He also says, "The act of measurement [observation] is deeply enmeshed in creating the very reality it is measuring."[8]

This "Alice in Wonderland" reality only becomes more eerie as we progress down the continuum, and though at first we try to protect ourselves from the implications of what we see, eventually we surrender and relish the potential it is revealing. As we relax deeply and no longer struggle with the strangeness we are confronting, we suddenly and unexpectedly enter a new paradigm that abruptly shifts the figure/ground of our life. Where we have always been front and center, with the world funneling through our reasoning, now we see ourselves being birthed moment to moment by the infinite, held by the infinite and an extension of it. We immediately understand that the sense of I was always and only an idea believed—an idea arising from the infinite. Once this is seen, there is no debate, no argument that counters the realization. We know this is how it has always been, and more to the point of the continuum, in the moment seen, there is no suffering.

This cosmic shift can actually occur at any time throughout the continuum completely serendipitously. I believe this realization is much more common than we imagine, but having this recognition is not an end; it is how fully we allow it to transform us that is the key element for reaching the end of suffering. If we look at the diagram on page 100 we will see that this shift does not end the continuum. At this point, though there is nothing more to do, there is more to understand, and the spiritual path changes accordingly.

There are two insights that occur during this shift that give us a remarkable boost in confidence and energy. We no longer believe in the self as a solid and permanent entity, and we no longer doubt where we are going. But given this, we still have to allow ourselves to be affected and changed. Even though the old view of self and other usually returns in a less convincing manner and the ego may pick up life as before, our consciousness has been irrevocably altered; yet it still needs our consent to complete the journey.

Though this paradigm shift may or may not have happened to you, get a sense of how straightforward your path would be if you no longer believed in the thought of "I" or had any doubt about the fruit of the path. Be aware of how the persistent sense of I drains your energy and motivation, especially when you hold only a vague idea of the end point of the path. It is extremely important to move forward despite this waxing and waning of energy. Moving forward regardless of doubt will begin to weaken its control and influence.

NONSEPARATION

This shift did not just affect the idea of who we are; it changed everything. This is not a process of adapting to this new view but a complete and utter surrendering to its truth, and that consumes the rest of the journey. First and foremost we have to drop the certainty of separation that our eyes may still perceive. The brain has long been organized within the view of separation that it is reluctant to relinquish—remember from chapter 2 that our survival once depended upon that perception. We are up against a genetic predisposition, and that belief system is not about to let go. When separation is our active view, it keeps us in survival mode by efforting, forcing, overcoming, and confronting. These strategies become untenable to the awakening process, which is not organized for aggression. The actions and thoughts of our system have to change in accordance with this new realization even when the revelation is no longer directly perceived. The ongoing perception or nonperception of the shift in consciousness has nothing to do with the expression of certainty that the realization entails. That remains without question and is acted upon accordingly. The action within that certainty is nonseparation.

Nonseparation is not merely having the experience of selflessness or perceiving the truth of our empty nature; it is seeing the self in proper relationship to the infinite universe. It is seeing that we are not merely empty but also complete: that our legitimate place is with the arising of all form, bathed in the formless, complete in our emptiness, complete in form, undifferentiated until we are called to differentiate. Nonseparation is the embodiment of nothing and everything without distinction. This requires everything from us, a complete paradigm shift of the heart.

Now let us attune to the residue of the suffering that remains before and after the paradigm shift occurs. This is earthwork, body to the soil, eyes to the ground, and bare observation of pain, nothing majestic or esoteric, no Ouija boards or séances. This is dealing directly with the history of our life and the struggles that persist into this moment, yet it is absolutely essential for the completion of the continuum.

7

The Buddhist Continuum

Suffering and the End of Suffering

The meditation of my heart
Shall be of understanding

—PSALMS 49:3

A paradigm shift will force us to look at what we have realized as opposed to what we have been taught. As we move toward the right side of the continuum, our path becomes more demanding and our attention more focused. We know what we are about, and the necessary sincerity arises that allows us to align our worldly and spiritual intentions. We return to our practice with the intention of further integration, since we now understand that the completion of the spiritual journey depends upon the total assimilation of reality. There arises a deep and compelling need to know what is true, which is a sure sign that we are indelibly altered and transformed.

This insatiable interest in what is true begins to supplant our usual overriding need for pleasant experiences. We usually think that the pursuit of pleasure is an inalienable right and maintain that bearing years into our spiritual journey. I have seen many long-term practitioners guard their right to pleasure as indisputable even after they have explored the roots of suffering. Something is not being understood, and it is common on a meditation retreat for students to complain about environmental sounds, annoying participants, or any number of irritants, never realizing that these are the very rubs we are here to explore. Blindly following this urge for pleasure creates a very different intention and direction for spiritual practice and is only a half step from looking to God for a safe haven against pain. Interestingly enough, we do look into the pain and find God,[1] but that comes only after we have abandoned our pursuit of an eternally pleasant heaven on earth.

Pursuing pleasure keeps us superficially entertained as we move from one desire to the next, but the pull to know what is true takes us to the fundamentals on which the organism is based. Here we get firsthand lessons on the operating system: what we are, how it all works, and the forces that compel us forward. It is like being invited behind the curtain in Oz, a place where few people have dared to go, and we see the machinery of life as it is being lived. It is all there: nothing is hidden, nothing has been kept from us, all the facts were simply waiting to be observed.

As we move along the continuum, suffering is still accompanying our journey, but the gradation and definition of suffering become much more refined. New questions about the nature of suffering arise from behind the curtain. Questions such as: If there is no abiding self, what is accountable to the pain? What is behind the pain driving it forward? And is suffering the pain itself, or is the contraction around pain the suffering? From here we see the strong conditioning that has kept us bound and contracted and how we have been working our whole lives to avoid these questions. It dawns on us that we have to learn our way through our difficulties and that can be done only by entering the struggle, not by avoiding it, and by moving into those very places the sense of self resists going. This is counterintuitive to our conditioned response, which is to place distance between ourselves and any difficulty.

When I returned from years of travel through Asia, I decided to fast one day a week. I did this to reacquaint myself with the degree of suffering I had observed in all the countries that were less fortunate than ours. The raw human condition was so apparent that it felt important to stay in touch with the plight of half the world's population. In this country we often attempt to buy our way out of pain by eliminating irritations and by tempering unpleasant environments. Under the influence of that conditioning, it is of little wonder that our spiritual journeys look very much like our worldly lives when we approach our mental and physical difficulties.

Where we hide is where we are unconscious, and as we will see in the next chapter, the continuum from unconscious to conscious overlaps perfectly with the scale of suffering and the end of suffering. Being conscious means waking up to the causes and conditions of struggle by facing difficulties head-on. I often hear students say they know all about their struggles but still their struggles continue. When we really know all about our struggles, they end. Students may have an intellectual understanding of why they contract, but Buddhism is not a system of beliefs about pain. I find that students are more reluctant to go into the emotional experience of the struggle because their emotions seem to incriminate them in ways the intellectual understanding of their pain does not. Emotions are also seen as a messier and more muddled area of the problem. Let us look and see why this is so.

First let us understand how and why emotions arise at all. When there is contact with an experience, there arises a conditioned psychic leaning toward or away from that experience. In traditional Buddhist language this is called the feeling tone of the experience.[2] Feelings in this case are different from emotions and cue a conditioned reference for that experience. They are our first taste of an experience, and this small opening to the past is quickly flooded by memory that can then fill the brain with massive dialogue.

The brain aligns the feeling tone with an expectation of what is about to follow. As the feeling is invested with a personal narrative, there arises an attitudinal disposition to the experience. Once the words are believed, an accompanying emotion corresponding to those words follows. Now the emotions and the words play upon one another. Often the words are attempting to justify the presence of the emotion: "He did this to me, so of course I feel this way." Sometimes the emotion infuses the words with exaggeration, increasing the tone of the drama: "How could he have done that to me!" There can also be a secondary emotion that tailgates the first emotion. For instance, anger may arise within a deep sense of guardedness. Let us say that historically when our father was angry we got hurt, so when anger arises in us it arises with that memory and an accompanying fear that is now paired with the anger. The physical posture contracts and the mind begins to defend against the assumed onslaught. The intensity of our inward narrative is anxious and cautionary as we wait for the angry shoe to drop.

More often than not, we try to off-load an emotion onto some cause or condition that allows us to rationalize its appearance. We analyze our emotions to give us a rationale for why they are occurring. Without that justification we feel implicated by the emotion as if each emotion said something secretive and devastating about us. Tucked into many recurrent emotional patterns are very durable self-beliefs that carry much of the fear we ascribe to the emotion. These self-assumptions are often introduced into our psyche at a very early age, before we have the maturity and power to understand the circumstances in which they were implanted. If not caught fairly quickly, this self-talk forms into an attitude and then cements into a belief. The belief gets hardened and encrusted over time, and since we believe it to be true, it is never reexamined or questioned. It remains dormant until conditions arise that in some vague way correspond to their induction when we were young— perhaps someone yells at us, we make a mistake, we fail miserably, or we get ridiculed—then out pops the belief, its rationale, and all the accompanying emotions fully intact. The little girl who was severely judged for her mistakes now becomes the fully mature woman who fears all forms of criticism. The man who was on his own as a child feels that every problem is up to him alone to solve.

We try to compensate for these assumptions with an action that attempts to repair the damage. Perhaps we feel inadequate, so we compensate by becoming a perfectionist. In that way when someone examines our work, the person will not see the personal blemish that we feel is so obvious. The root systems of these assumptions are intricate and complex, but we can trace much of our current behavior to a core belief. We would much rather act these assumptions out than look at them because the core belief holds the seed of so much of our personal pain. In fact, the fire of our personal suffering cannot be stoked any hotter than the burning coals of this belief. The core belief is what we do not want to be yet believe we are. In this culture our core belief usually centers on some form of unworthiness.

The reason we say we know all about the pattern is that we have lived with it our entire life and the behaviors we emit from these self-assumptions are well known, and the emotions arising from the core belief are also very familiar. "I know all about that," we might say, but there is just an intellectual understanding of the pattern, not a real knowing. We have intentionally shielded ourselves from experiencing it because it is too painful. As with Rip Van Winkle stirring from a twenty-year sleep, the emotional assumptions and conditioned volatility are pretty much as they were before the slumber. Emotions can only mature through direct experiential contact, and that is where we fear to go.

We may believe that if we exposed ourselves to this pattern without our usual defenses, it would be unbearable;[3] however, when the emotion is exposed to the present, the past assumptions have a channel for healing. At first the emotion carries the heaviness of its own assumptions and the burden of its memory, but as it meets the light of the present, it becomes modified by the truth of what awareness sees. Awareness sees but does not reassert the strongly held assumptions on which the pattern is based. In fact, awareness discerns that these assumptions, so long believed, are not true. But for that to be known, the patterns have to be exposed—completely exposed to awareness—not just the emotional state of mind but the accompanying words embedded within the emotional memory at the age in which they were first introduced. That may mean we will feel the disempowerment and utter dependency of the little girl who is looking out upon the adult world, but we do so from the maturity of an adult's awareness. The little girl's understanding can quickly mature to the adult woman's wisdom, and the pain healed.

Be willing to trace an emotion back to whatever self-assumptions are behind it. Experience whatever thoughts support the emotion and affirm its core beliefs. Almost everyone has core beliefs that define his or her sense of self. It is the darkest and most protected belief you have. When the self-belief arises, you will find a compensatory action to avoid or offset what it is saying. Suddenly you are daydreaming, blaming, or exerting the opposite influence. If you find yourself compensating for a mistake or feeling as if you were a mistake, deeply burdened, or inadequate, stop, sit down, and place your ear to your heart. Tune yourself in and quietly listen to the emotion. Usually your energy goes toward trying to offset your self-assumptions by deflecting attention away from them. Instead, bring your attention into the emotion itself and just listen to what is arising. Listen with more subtlety and you may find refined words or images releasing within that state of mind. It is very important not to invest any additional reactions or words back into the pattern. Stay with the emotion until it becomes quiet and has nothing else to say. Sometimes an uninhibited writing down of whatever is occurring, or allowing yourself to speak uncensored from the emotion, can aid the process.

It is as if the present, with its formless awareness, offers the healing and we offer the courage of exposure—and there in one brief moment is the continuum of suffering to its end. The present never reaffirms or supports any conditioned response, and that is why suffering can come to an end. Without our reaffirming reactions to this emotional pattern, it is simply stilled within formless awareness. Our conditioning, in the form of this pattern, was maintained only by the infusion of our unsettled reactions back into the emotion, and within formless awareness these are quieted and dispelled.

Since formless awareness does not hold the past as something separate from itself, the pattern has no other time frame to seed and cannot turn to the past or the future for confirmation. "I really was that bad in the past," says our memory, but that statement is impossible to confirm in the present. Conditioning requires that we believe in the sequencing of time and needs the past to verify its existence through memory, a sense of self where it can feed and gain energy, and a future where it can reappear. When conditioning enters formless awareness, it goes through the present but has no life outside the present. Formless awareness is all-encompassing and stationary, and therefore nothing can take root or arise from outside it.

> To get a feeling for how formless awareness encompasses all experience, do not move or make any deliberate sound, simply listen to what is already present. What is arising and passing away in this moment? Is the moment the content that is passing through this time frame or the space that holds the content? Get a feeling for each of these. The content is the experiences that are arising: the sights, sounds, smell, tastes, physical sensations, thoughts, emotions, and states of mind—all in movement, luring you into the future through their story and emotional charge. We talk ourselves into the future. The space is the formless awareness of the content, and the space is not in movement. The space heals the content because it will not move with the content and therefore does not encourage a personal narrative. Once the narrative ends, so does the conditioning.

ENDING THE VOICES OF SEPARATION

What is so interesting about this complicated and twisted internal language and the ensuing emotional turmoil is that they were birthed from the simple flash of a feeling (pleasant, unpleasant, neutral) that was projected from our minds onto the experience. The experience did not contain the feeling; it was our conditioning that contaminated the experience. The whole thing begins and ends with us, and we are like the artist who paints a lifelike tiger, puts it away for a few months, then opens the door where the painting is stored and is frightened by what we see. We think the world carries the charge, but all emotional investment comes from us, the artist. When the projection is believed, we extend the painting forward and fear other animals that might also be lurking in the closet.

Let your eyes light upon something appealing and feel the pleasant quality emanating through that experience. Ask yourself whether the pleasantness is coming from you or from the object. Now look at the same experience and own that pleasantness as belonging to your mind. Look out upon the world with that recognition that nothing contains the attraction or aversion that you give it. Furthermore, the thoughts you give it, the value and corresponding meaning you assert, and the image that you hold of it are also from the mind. Reality itself contains none of that. Does this change your relationship to external objects?

It is impossible to relax and allow an authentic connection with the world as long as we believe that external conditions are responsible for our problems. As we learn to see the world as mind created, projected out from our internal world of thoughts and emotions, the cursor begins to gently move to the right side of nonseparation. We move through the obstructions of blaming self and other into a new arena of accountability, where all thoughts and emotions are held as conditioned internal responses. These responses are not the truth of the experience but, rather, the projection of our internal narrative upon the event. Realizing this fact helps us understand that neither the world nor the self is separate from the other, and they are codependently arising.

Basing ourselves within this accountability, we are now prepared to question the reliability of thought. As mentioned in chapter 2, thought directs and limits the stream of consciousness to just what the words mean. Self-beliefs are usually thoughts that labor under the additional burden of unpleasant memory. We have formed the image of ourself and believe that image because of the memories we selectively choose to invest in from the past. At some point what we choose to believe is referenced through our self-assumptions. For instance, if our root issue is unworthiness, no matter how often we are told that we are doing well, we listen only to the convincing voice of our own authority because no one else knows us as well as we know ourself. All other opinions are rejected as dishonest flattery.

If we are going to free ourselves from thought, more understanding is needed. As we move to the right of this continuum, something begins to occur that helps us considerably toward that end. We move into more psychic space (awareness), and space shows us thought in relief. Space arises when experiences are no longer feared or possessed and therefore increases as our personalization of thought decreases. This means that thought no longer fills the screen with only what it is saying and is now heard in the context of the space that holds it. Before, we might have been innocently walking in the beauty of a spring morning listening to the singing birds when suddenly the space that held the singing collapses around an intruding thought. Once again we believe that the thought is more worthy of our attention than the singing birds. Once we have moved a little further down the continuum, the birds frame the space that thought arises within, and the space, the birds, and the thoughts are all included in consciousness.

When you are relaxed and at ease, begin simply to listen to what the ears hear and sense the space around the sounds. You will lose that space as soon as you think about what you hear. After sufficient practice, you will begin to hear your thoughts just like you hear the external sounds, as words held within space. From here you will be hearing the thoughts, not thinking them.

From this space we can question the relevance of thought and its appropriateness to the situation at hand. Suddenly the space offers a perspective that thought alone never did, and with that shift of perspective comes quiet and discernment. Discernment will be thoroughly explored in chapter 9, but for now we need to know that discernment is born of awareness and shows us the limitation of thought. We once believed that thought was the only way to navigate the world, but now discernment proves far more reliable and far less noisy.

There is a growing sense that we can release the noise of thought and trust the quiet of discernment, and this speeds the movement of the cursor to the right side. As thought is questioned for its relevance to the moment, there is less suffering and a greater sense of nonseparation. Opinions are hardened thoughts infused with an emotional stance, and opinions can be more difficult to release. But space also provides wisdom, and we begin to see that every opinion is equal to every other. It is only the self's assertion that it knows what is right for everyone that confuses this understanding, but as conceit lessens, so does our righteousness. With the abeyance of the separation that opinions create, life becomes joined in a way that thought could only suggest.

The continual pain of our self-beliefs will throw most of us back into the consensus paradigm of separation well after the paradigm shift on our continuum. We may be feeling spacious and connected when someone says something unflattering, and suddenly we become lost in our historical issues. We move to the right side of the continuum only to be spun around and forced to face the left, and either we keep getting disoriented and dizzy or we get honest. We realize we have to face this lifelong pain if we want to abide in the sacred for more than a few moments. Now, and perhaps only now, are we willing to take on the firestorm of our self-assumptions.

As mentioned in the early part of this chapter, this requires diligent work. But here is the key: almost every interaction provides the opportunity to work on this struggle because there is almost always a contraction within an interaction, and that contraction signals that the assumption is still active. These are usually minor bumps on an otherwise fairly smooth playing field and often go unnoticed. But to the shrewd eye, the body represents an arena that clearly reveals the arising of these beliefs. Tightness, tension, contraction, knotting, flushing, restlessness, and many others are all bodily sensations that signal that the assumptions are functioning. Let us take a fictitious scenario and apply this method.

> Bob and Bill are longtime friends who meet once a month for a spirited game of handball. Bill won last month's contest, and Bob is very aware of wanting to even the score (contraction in the belly accompanying the thought "I never win at anything"). Bill is the better player, but Bob refuses to acknowledge that and blames his losses on his worn-out gloves and his slightly arthritic knee (chest tightens slightly as he rationalizes away his feelings of being the inferior player). As the game gets under way, Bob has the early advantage and feels self-satisfied (his chest expands as he holds an air of confidence that attempts to offset his real assumption of unworthiness). Soon, however, the game turns the other way, and Bill once again dominates. Bob not only loses the game but becomes mired in a self-defeating narrative that lasts all day (his body slumps, his shoulders round, and he feels the old familiar feelings of self-contempt). On his way home he lashes out at a group of schoolchildren

that is crossing the street too slowly and finds himself irritable with his wife (since it is too hard to accept the feelings of self-dislike as his own, Bob projects those feelings onto the innocent, deflecting them from his self-image).

The point is that Bob does not have to wait for events to cascade from his handball loss to the overwhelming feeling of self-dislike before he addresses this pattern. At the point of severe self-criticism, the attitude is usually too engrossed in the story, thought is too all-consuming, and the mind is too hardened within this belief to allow the nimble and flexible awareness to reveal what is truly occurring. It is within these minor transgressions, before the fully embodied unworthiness has taken hold, that much of Bob's work can be done. However, during these minor bumps, the pain may not be severe enough to warrant his attention, and he can easily ignore the symptoms for the sake of keeping the belief suppressed and undisturbed.

Connect with your body during your next conversation and notice whether there are minor moments of tightness, stiffness, or tension. These physical constrictions are emotional bumps that indicate active self-assumptions. First, are you curious and interested in learning all about the pattern? If so, incline your mind toward understanding it. Listen deeply to the troubling voices even if they are modest and temperate. Sense the pain behind the narrative. Let your awareness gently rest upon the voices and emotions that emerge. Add nothing to what is arising but relaxation and surrender.

ENDING THE LOGIC OF SEPARATION

There are many self-induced arguments that keep us contained within the view of separation. They have a tenacity and conviction that are born from our cultural imperatives and are usually induced at an early age. They hold us to a logic that is unassailable from the position of consensus reality. By drawing us back into their suppositions, they keep us cornered on the left side of the continuum. Let us examine a few of these arguments and expose their faulty conclusions. This list is by no means complete, and I encourage readers to expound and investigate their individual beliefs that have arisen from the culture's logic.

The Need to Worry

I was having a conversation with a friend whose daughter was having financial difficulties. The friend said she worried night and day about her daughter's welfare. I asked how worry helped the situation, and she replied that her love needed her worry. This is a good example of how our culture confuses love with guilt. Somehow the mind has paired love with worry, and we believe that authentic love requires the anxiety of worry; otherwise we may doubt that we really care. The thought that we may not "really care" is so abhorrent that we force ourselves to worry so that we have tangible proof that we do love.

But the language of worry actually detracts from the experience of love. Love arises from and within the moment and cannot be found even an instant later. After the event we have a memory of the experience, but that is the remembrance of love and not love itself. It is important to distinguish the left-sided caring of the mind with the right-sided opening of the heart. There is the mentally shaped love found within our thoughts and images that is possessive and individuated, and there is love within awareness that is quiet and blankets whatever it sees. Since the mind relies almost exclusively on thought and emotion for its sense of connection, it is of little wonder that we mentally attempt to prolong love through worry. Worry tries to perpetuate love through thought and thereby give it a reassurance that love is still around. Anxiety cues us that we must still love the person. Why else would we be anxious?

Worry says that now is not safe: the present represents chaos and the future embodies the hope for a resolution of that chaos. The fear of chaos fuels the desire to know the outcome, but since the outcome is unknowable, worry sets in. Worry is followed by a fix-it mentality that involves extensive planning. The assumption is that given enough willpower and determination, any problem can be fixed, but worry is about a future problem that has yet to arise. When we worry we are often trying to work out the problem in advance of the problem's occurring. In my friend's case, her daughter was not failing, my friend was just afraid that she would fail. Finding a solution to a future problem keeps the problem from being understood and resolved sanely. Like love, understanding can arise only from contact with the actual problem in real time.

We actually believe our worrying works and are afraid to stop worrying partly for that reason. Thinking "I have the sole power to correct this impending disaster" is a form of self-affirmation. When we know "only me," we believe in "only me," and that thought forces us to loop back to the left side of the scale. The thought that we are needed for the world to function must be experienced emotionally because it is likely arising from our historical pain. Emotional narratives like "It is all up to me" can have their origins in a history of abandonment and if not addressed will form the way we see the world.

Worry demands that you work endlessly toward the resolution of a problematic future and sets you up to see problems as an imposition with a correctable alternative. Observe the sense of power you derive from worry, how the future needs your involvement. Test the accuracy of this claim by surrendering to the unknowable future without worry. Let the results unfold as they will without leaning into the future with anxiety. Whenever you find yourself worrying, simply say, "This is out of my control," and feel the love that comes with that acceptance. It may or may not turn out as you wish, but either way, you can work with the results, and the love will remain undisturbed.

Living an awakened life provides less room to maneuver as an egoic identity. Each time the ego arises, we feel the edginess and tensions of its manifestation. The ego "shoulds" and "musts" its way through life carrying a tremendous burden of responsibility wherever it goes. We feel the hidden tension that comes with the worry of caring and the heaviness involved in attending the world through the image of self. This weight of self-responsibility applies to almost everything we do. We say, "I have to"; "I should"; "I must"; "I will disappoint"; "I need to uplift, to care more, to worry about, to protect and defend"; "They need me. . . ." But since life is an indivisible whole, it cares for itself perfectly. The more formless we become, the more we join that caring; and the more formed we are, the more caring is felt as an image we must uphold. We surrender the burden and tension of being responsible. By getting out of the way, life has free claim to move us as it wishes. We do not become irresponsible by worrying less; we love more by worrying less.

How much of the day do you spend fulfilling the responsibilities of your image? Like the Boy Scouts' pledge, we try to live up to our ideal expectations by being kind, cheerful, and caring. As we age we assume more roles and responsibilities that become incorporated into our posture and manner. But what and where are we in all of that? Is this smothering or helping us? Sense the space (awareness) available when living quietly and free of an image. Test this out in action and see if a natural caring arises within that space that is not "yours" to project. Perhaps the responsibility of living up to our image actually deters this natural kindness.

Only My Will Can Motivate Me

I hear this often: "I do not want to be passive to the injustices around me, so I have to remain angry to stay motivated." This is a left-sided argument where the egoic center is closing off all avenues to the right side. As we become more conscious, the injustices of the world increasingly affect us, and we feel a growing sense of pain for the underprivileged. Our righteousness and anger may have motivated us before our practice began, and we may even concede that without anger we would not have had the passion to involve ourselves as we have. But now this logic has linked our heart's decency to our anger and has falsely ascribed anger as the driving force behind our love's involvement.

The problem with the left side of the continuum is that it trusts only the view of separation and does not believe in a force outside its own will and volition. From the perspective of the left side, the right side of the pathway may look too tame and disconnected—a sort of backing-off mentality within a far too passive "letting be" philosophy. This projected passivity is unbearable to a heart that is increasingly feeling the sorrows of the world but is still held within its old motivation of reacting to injustice. This logic can easily freeze us in place, and our present passion can feel so undermined by the projected passivity that we refuse to move to the right side.

There is an undeniable risk that we will lose the directed passion and incensed motivation behind our actions—even though history is replete with examples of world leaders such as Mahatma Gandhi, Martin Luther King, Nelson Mandela, and Vaclav Havel, who were both conscious and passionately engaged. The question we will all have to confront is whether the duress of separation, motivated by anger, the very emotion that has driven the species toward near destruction, is worth continuing, or whether we should try another way to heal social inequality. Knowing that there is no way to be absolutely certain that injustice will be addressed as we move to the right side of the pathway, we move on faith alone.

Though we may not engage life as we did when we were mind driven, the right side is not passive or without passion. As thought becomes less intrusive, the heart becomes more exposed, and the heart is the seat of passion. We are affected more, not less, and action arises spontaneously and appropriately to meet the injustice. Such action is not confused or weak but holds the steady conviction of the ground we stand upon and the confidence of the earth's solidity and core. This is the "no of love" that will not compromise the truth of nonseparation for political position or personal reputation, but it needs to be trusted and tenderly nourished.

The Need for Opinions and Judgments

In contrast to our cultural understanding, a view is not a simple abstract collection of thoughts but a charged interpretation of experience that has a strong pattern of identification and intensely shapes and affects actions of body, speech, and mind.[4] The Buddha called such mental fixations "the wrangling of views, and the jungle of opinions,"[5] and as we pay more attention to our views and opinions, it is clear that there is more here than the arbitrary ideas that fill our day. Often our personal image is so entwined within views and opinions that we do not know who we are without them. We often believe our personal reputation is at stake when our views are threatened, and we are willing to struggle deeply to convince others of their correctness.

Drawing from our earlier discussion on the struggle within our reactions, we can see that anytime we force our identity within an idea, that idea will be as strongly protected as our egoic image. In our culture the more opinions we have, the clearer we are seen to be, but as we move to the right side of the scale, just the opposite is realized—the more opinions we hold, the more confused and separate we have become. The culture reinforces the certainty of position that opinions seem to offer, but right-sided movement empties us of content and disengages the mind from fixed assumptions. It is only when we have slipped the moorings of our ideas and conclusions that we float free of form.

This is a major hurdle for even the most serious spiritual practitioner. Our practice shows us *directly* what is occurring in the moment, and we find we have little time to waste in philosophizing reality. Since our minds are still ripe for ignorance, we can easily form an opinion about the truth we just saw, and insights can quickly form into a judgment about what others are doing. The problem is that we know we are right because we have seen it for ourselves, and the seeing of it has doubled the ferocity and strength of our view. It is not a belief; it is the truth! What we have seen may be relatively true, but we are missing a deeper dharma point. We are missing the fixation that is arising within our certainty, and the fact that the fixation has increased our suffering. When our struggle increases we are looping back to the left side of the pathway.

Let us look for a moment at the self-assumptions that are buried within views and judgments. As a view is asserted, a personal position and painful assumption is appearing. We argue our view in order to elevate our current status above those opposed. We would not need to argue if we were comfortable within our own skin, but because the pain of our inadequacy is activated, we need to defend our position and thereby protect ourselves from others seeing our deficiency. Being right is how we compensate for feeling insufficient. We are no longer interested in what is true; we are now interested in concealing our pain from others.

Again, views, opinions, and judgments can all be distilled down to the contracted pain we have historically lived with. We can quickly lose our orientation to the inward struggle by focusing on the external conflict. Remembering that the Buddha taught only one thing, suffering and the end of suffering, can help us refocus on the area that will be of greatest benefit to our growth.

The cultural imperatives we've just discussed do not form an exhaustive list by any means. Freeing ourselves from culturally distorted perceptions becomes our work in moving toward the end of struggle. The logic of the culture is deeply ingrained in our patterns, but almost without exception we can feel the suffering associated with following those dictates. Because we are interested in freeing ourselves from all forms of struggle, we expose the pain that arises within these cultural imperatives and remain connected to the self-assumptions that perpetuate that pain.

This is not to imply that uncovering and working with emotional self-beliefs ends all self-assumptions. The "I" thought itself is a self-assumption that has a resilience that far exceeds all the others, but the emotional self-beliefs are often the hardest to acknowledge and address. Within each line of inquiry, another layer of pain is exposed, until the residue becomes transparently empty and both the suffering and the person suffering end. When thoroughly examined, suffering ends in the formless. The task does become lighter and easier once we have framed the spiritual journey as the end of struggle.

Working on our self-assumptions is working toward nonseparation by releasing the narrative that keeps us separate. This practice can accommodate all settings at all times. Self-assumptions do have an end, but when first exposed it may seem they are never-ending. To arrive at the end of a self-imposed belief is to arrive at a cliff without an obvious path down. We got what we wanted—the end of that expression of suffering—but we are not sure who we are without the belief. Those beliefs have fed our individuation our entire life, and though it has been painful, at least their exposure was worth the noble effort that ensued. But now what? We no longer have the noble effort nor the definition the self-assumption offered us.

It is here at the edge of the cliff of our suffering that we either leap across the abyss into emptiness or remain and turn back to struggle. This is a solitary decision that each of us will face in one form or another. Accompanying this decision there can arise a sorrow and grief that lament the choice we have to make, but ultimately there is no choice at all; we jump because our heart demands it.

Let us now fit the continuum of struggle to the end of struggle back into a more generic set of pathways that may speak directly to each of our particular concerns. We will not lose what the Buddha taught as we expand the definition of suffering to include other synonyms for struggle. Personalizing the path in this way can keep us within the Buddha's teaching as it directly aligns with our practice perspectives.

8

Other Continua

Quietness is the surest sign that you have died.
... The speechless full moon comes out now.

—RUMI

I have found through teaching over the decades that offering students different perspectives on truth can loosen the certainty of what they are doing and open them to new insights. Each new perspective can change our preset assumptions and allow a refreshing new direction for inquiry. A rigid map of awakening can create its own obstacles as our minds conjure up an image of what that path must be like while we attempt to mold our journey around that idea. Unfortunately, the mind is incapable of imagining any dimension beyond its own making and fails utterly in this task. By changing perspectives we soften our reliance on forms and techniques, allowing the practices to be secondary to the formless truth that is the end of the path.

I have seen many well-intended students flounder by grasping a set of practice instructions too tightly, much as a drowning person would clutch a life preserver. The mechanics of a practice seem to become a salvation unto itself, where just the doing of the method becomes its own reward. Like endlessly repeating a rosary, we think all we need to do for repentance is mouth the words of forgiveness.

Lost within the dependency on any structure is the sacred formless, infinitely available once form has been released.

All practices are a kind of ritual that allows a rite of passage through the different experiences promised within that structure. Each spiritual structure has its own progression and accompanying experiences that seem to indicate where we currently are within that path, but those progressive experiences change depending upon what system we are using, indicating that none is an absolute or the "only way." All structures have a life span, allowing them to work for a while before they cease working. As we saw in chapter 2, form is only half of the story, missing the formless pairing, and therefore partial and incomplete, eventually working against the very process it was meant to accomplish. I am referring now to every known system, including all meditation structures and trainings, as well as every tool and practice that aids our awakening, such as the guru and *chela* (disciple), teacher and student, monasteries, retreats, all spiritual lineages and traditions, and all forms and expressions in between.

Reflect upon all the spiritual forms you rely upon and feel their value, how they serve the spiritual map you travel. Now see if you can gently sense their limitation. Practicing meditation, for instance, may rely on your assumption that you need something from it—quiet, calm, stability, clarity, mindfulness, and so on—but remaining in the new paradigm requires ending all lingering self-doubt and sense of incompletion. If meditation fosters any form of dependency or conclusion that something is missing, then at some point it will become an obstruction to abiding within this new paradigm.

Why is this so? There is no bridge between form and the formless, and all form can ever do is establish a readiness to surrender to the formless. As we learned in chapter 5, form does not evolve into the formless. The formless takes the shape of form when seen through the mind, so it is a complete surrender of all mental attachment to form that is the real work. Many techniques promise a fruit that is impossible to accomplish through any practice structure. When a structure (form) holds the promise of a formless truth within it, we can be certain that the promise will be unfulfilled. What the form will do is keep *us* formed and endlessly attempting to effort our way out.

The sense of self loves to believe that if it works hard enough within a formed structure, one day it will find itself miraculously in the formless. That never happens for two reasons: First, the sense of self often evades moving in the direction of the formless as a destination, since to do so would eliminate egoic control. The ego claims it needs to do other practices first to be adequately prepared, and somehow it never gets around to the real work. Second, even if it does acknowledge that practice is meant to move us into the formless, the sense of self tries to get there through its own strategies and will. This ties the process into a knot that tightens around form even as the self is attempting to escape that very thing. What the sense of self loves to do instead of moving toward the formless is polish the structure it is already in, and here again we go astray. "I can do this better," "I can find a better way of doing this," or "I need to be better in order to do this" are closed loops of form entrapment.

A polished form can look pretty sublime, and an inspiring appearance can easily take priority over transformation. Form entrapment does not allow us to step out of self-deception and subtly works to maintain the hold the self has over our lives. The "improvement" yardstick the self uses to satisfy its objectives is a left-sided ensnarement on the continuum pathway. The problem is that we are never finished polishing, never finished improving, because the standards we are using are coming from the paradigm of separation, and that paradigm never feels complete. Those very strategies force further effort, and that is the hallmark of all form: it is perpetually moving toward completion. To be eternally complete would end the paradigm, so to keep the paradigm of separation going, we find a temporary completeness, one that is based on the "feeling" of being complete. That feeling is a temporary abeyance from the pressures of a time-oriented future when we can be better than we are now. This feeling is a false nirvana, because soon the feeling changes, and we are off scurrying after another temporary fix to a psychological problem.

> Reflect for a moment on the last time you felt complete and content. How long did it last, and what was it dependent upon? Ask yourself in this moment if you are content, and if you are not, what are the qualifying reasons for being discontented? Form will rest only momentarily, if at all, before it will be in search of a more perfect feeling of contentment. To find the formless within this restlessness, we must call it forward: ask, "Where is contentment in this moment?" That question reframes the problem. Now we are no longer bent on finding provisional contentment but are seeking the contentment that holds whatever the mind is doing, whether it feels content or not.

We take the polished form to be a statement of advancement and growth, but growth toward what—a more refined display of itself? We are called here to think out of the box, to apply a little spiritual logic. Is our present spiritual form ever going to let go of us? Will it ever say, "Job well done, you are finished and ready for the formless," or is that readiness going to have to come from us—with the understanding that the "feeling of readiness" may not be part of what it means to be ready?

COMPARING CONTINUA

The key points of all continua are illustrated on the scale on page 131 that was introduced in chapter 6. This is a depiction of the Buddha's continuum "from suffering to the end of suffering." The left side is the contracted way we begin, where we know only the world of form and our personal place within it. This is a tense existence that can hold only a self-centered perspective because life is formed around the idea of separation and individual identity. Looking at the left side of the diagram, we can see that struggling to get away from or out of this vantage point sends us further to the left side (struggle) of the scale and increases the hold this perspective has on us.

The horizontal line of the scale is not a time line, though from the perspective of the individual, it may seem like it is. Many events take place on the horizontal line, and it can take a considerable amount of time to cross from one side to the other, but there is actually no separation between the two end points of the pathway. The mind fictitiously creates the time needed to cross, but the objective is always at hand. Let me explain.

One of the paradoxes of any spiritual journey is that the infinite (the far right side) is always embracing the limited (the far left side), but the limited cannot feel that embrace. The sense of self wears the blinders of its own thoughts, and that prohibits the wider gaze necessary to see the infinite. The path provides the opportunity to see the infinite by refocusing the individual's attention away from the all-consuming narrative that defines and limits his or her life. Suddenly the sun bursts through the clouds (paradigm shift), and the direction in which the path leads becomes obvious.

The continuum delineated above suggests that we monitor whatever actions we are taking in body, speech, and mind in relationship to the struggle we bring to those tasks. Struggle or suffering is the surest sign of left-sided dominance and the most obvious way to know when we are under the ego's influence. I label this on the graph as "counterinfluence," which means that at this point on our journey we understand that the intrusion of the ego's will on the direction we are heading is no longer useful—it is counterinfluential. This is a huge shift, since until now we have been governed by our volitional efforts. Now we realize that any willful force that we think moves us toward the right side adds to the overall struggle and therefore ultimately moves us to the left.

The sense of self in some form or other follows us pretty much to the end of the continuum, and having a foolproof way for its presence to be known can be very helpful. Struggle in all of its subtlety provides just that. Effort, surmounting problems, framing the path in terms of distance and time, and all forms of egoic intervention are seen as adding struggle to the path and thus moving us in the direction opposite to the desired ending. We could say we learn how not to use ourselves in order to advance. We do not mind when the ego appears; it just has very limited use in directing us toward the end of suffering.

Our Buddhist practices need to have an orientation to suffering from the very beginning. What is essential is to keep referencing our destination (the end of suffering) to what we are bringing to the path and then adjusting these strategies so they work in cooperation with the final direction in which we are going. The means we use must be aligned with the ends we seek or we will find our path reinforcing the sense of self.

This may sound like a contradiction to the statements earlier in this chapter about the struggles of any goal-oriented practice and the limitation of form. We may rightfully ask, "How is looking toward the end of struggle not a goal?" and "How does this continuum free me from the future?" and "This just seems to compound the problem by thinking I should be somewhere that I am not." Let us keep those questions in mind as we discuss the right side of the scale.

The difficulty comes in trying to interpret the experiences of the new paradigm with the language of the old. As we cross this field from suffering to the end of suffering, we do not remain within the same paradigm. Everything changes in the crossing. This pathway is not the crossing of a "who" that is currently suffering into a "who" that has ended his or her suffering, because the "who" arises within the suffering. No suffering, no who. The end of the path is nonidentification with the who, and any residual identification with the who means that you are suffering and are back within the old paradigm of time, space, and distance.

At some point the end of suffering is not a future prospect but an immediate possibility. It is not something we are working toward through practice but is directly accessible. If we happen to be staring at the clock on the wall and miss the hummingbird fluttering outside our window, our visual neglect of the bird does not make the bird any less immediate. So, too, once we have crossed into the new paradigm, both paradigms are still immediately available. When we are lost in thought, formless awareness has not gone anywhere; it is just not being attended to. When formless awareness is not attended to, there is some residue of struggle, and that pain eventually captures our attention until we release the struggle. When we release the struggle, formless awareness reappears. Suppose you wanted to see the bird and know what time it is in the same moment. If both were suitably arranged in space, you could watch the bird and the clock simultaneously, thereby relieving the pressure of seeing one exclusive of the other.

At this point, journeying on the path is not a struggle because we are not bringing time into the equation. It is really a releasing of the narrative that binds us to one or the other paradigm and is not a progression of moving somewhere else to find the missing piece. Even the previous sentence is too strongly worded because at some point we realize (counterinfluence) that we are not able to stop ourselves from suffering. In the end, awareness ends suffering without any intrusion of ourselves into the process.

This is the perfect transition point into other equally valid continua. The main point in all that follows is that everything going forward will be aligned with the Buddha's first sermon, where he outlined his continuum of suffering to the end of suffering. In fact, we should be very careful that the words we use to define the end points are spiritually synonymous or quite likely we are betraying the Buddha's message. The mind can easily create its own scale that stealthily curves our direction toward pleasure and comfort seeking, and since pleasure seems like the antithesis of suffering, we can convince ourselves that we are headed in a wise direction. As we go forward, we will occasionally look up from whatever line we are drawing and ask pertinent questions that authenticate our direction.

As mentioned in the opening paragraph of this chapter, we are forming these alternative pathways because at various stages on the path different ways of speaking about the journey may resonate more deeply with our hearts than simply stating it as suffering to the end of suffering. It gives us a fresh perspective, a novel approach that can renew our interest and add momentum to our questioning. It can also add a dimension of wisdom by expanding our understanding of the problem and its resolution. We can get stuck in working in the same old ways from the same fixed ideas about what we are doing and why we are doing it. The path, like any activity, can become habituated, where we no longer show up completely for the practice because we have already seen it over and over from that perspective.

The first continuum that appears to work as a complete embrace of the Buddha's path is from noise to stillness. Let us explore the scale below and see if this pathway is a well-suited replica of suffering to its end, keeping in mind that each pathway will have its own false nirvana and ultimately its own paradigm shift. If this is a mirror of the original teachings of the Buddha, then the path must lead to an identical ending point, with the only difference being the perspective we take on the problem and the solution. The first question we need to ask is whether noise is the mirror image of suffering and stillness identical to the end of suffering.

Let us define our terms. *Noise* is defined as identification with thought. The more we think of ourselves as the thinker of the thoughts, the greater the attachment to our inward narrative, and the noisier our minds become. This also parallels the belief in the self. When we affirm the story of our life, we confirm the storyteller— and the more oppressed we feel when the story does not go our way.

We see from this brief description that identification with thought is the reason we suffer, but the Buddha said we suffer because we want something immediately unobtainable (Second Noble Truth). How do these two come together?

Identification with thought is also dependency on time, and time is created by thought. Our thoughts generate the past and the future from memory formed into expectation. Within the present we may remember something that this moment could contain that would make the present more complete. The thought of that desired experience is projected into the future, where it can be procured. That creates resistance between the future, when we will have the experience, and the present, where the experience is missing. All of that, from beginning to end, is attachment to thought, formed into a desire that is very noisy and full of the tension called suffering. There are other forms that suffering can take, but all require identification with the thinking mind (noise).

Let us move along this pathway and see what occurs as it unfolds. As we move from noise to stillness, we discover a growing urge to be quieter. Simplicity follows quietude, and quietude leads to more simplicity. We find that the simpler our life becomes, the less cluttered and dramatic we make it. Renunciation, or the willing relinquishment of a noisy internal and external life, is the product. This is identical to the path of suffering and the end of suffering even though we are not framing this current journey in terms of those concepts.

But here the counterinfluence shows itself. Since the self is very much alive and active throughout this phase, it tries to control the degree of mental quietude. It attempts to set up the right environment, the best practices, and the wisest methodology to quiet the mind, all the while keeping a firm hold on the outcome. Remembering chapter 3 on the divided mind, the sense of self is most comfortable being noisy, since noise gives it position and definition. What the self has been doing all along is talking back to the mind, trying to keep it in order while maintaining its own noisy location. At this point we recognize that the sense of self is feigning quietude but does not actually want to move in that direction, and we can no

longer comply with its authority. The only solution is to understand our way out of its control, and to do so means we thoroughly
examine what the self is until we are no longer influenced by its
voice.

Our minds become quieter when thought is less employed as a
resource for overcoming problems, defining our opinionated positions and judgments, and when the sense of self no longer feeds off
its image, or tries to establish control. This quieting inevitably leads
to a false nirvana when we prematurely believe this end has been
obtained. One day we glance up and our mind has been transformed
into the quiet that we have always wanted. Often there arises a sense
of elation as we ponder the implications of coming to the end of
struggle, but this is an emotional high that will shortly be followed
by the loss of this relative quiet.

What is conditioned into the mind can be taken away, and this
quiet, as consuming and contenting as it is, is just the absence of
noise. Noise can and will return when the conditions are ripe for
it to return—when we lose our job or receive a terminal prognosis,
when our spouse dies, or any number of events that spike our
emotional reactivity. Conditional quiet can feel like stillness to the
mind, and we can get caught in trying to replicate the conditions for
its reoccurrence when we mistakenly believe it is the end. The end
point of each of these pathways is not conditioned or it would
merely be a point on the continuum. The end of suffering, or stillness, is unconditioned, unaffected by conditions, which is why it is
the end point.

Along the path a paradigm shift does occur through which an
abiding stillness is entered. When this happens, we can no longer be
fooled by the conditioned quiet of the mind. This stillness is not
dependent upon noise or its absence. It is still because it says nothing
to or about the noise that does arise. We have been calling this by
various names—formless awareness, the infinite, timelessness, the
end of suffering, the deathless—and now we call it stillness. We will
give it other names as we explore additional continua, but let us be
clear that on each pathway we are referring to exactly the same unconditioned end.

ADDITIONAL PATHWAYS

Let us look at some of these pathways, remembering that their numbers are endless:

> From suffering to the end of suffering
> From form to formless
> From noise to stillness
> From self to selflessness
> From divided mind to unified mind
> From unconscious to conscious
> From relative to infinite
> From denial to surrender
> From contraction to love
> From restlessness to absolute contentment
> From separation to nonseparation
> From morality to basic goodness
> From knowing to not knowing
> From doing to nondoing
> From then to now

We cannot cover all of them, but let us pick a few and see where they take us. Since we have talked extensively about the first five, let us look at the sixth, from unconscious to conscious, and set up our now-familiar scale:[1]

Unconscious to Conscious

A very good way to comprehend the Buddhist path is to see it as a shift from unconsciousness (ignorance) to full consciousness (wakefulness). Again we have to define our terms. The unconscious mind is the product of conditioning and is essentially running on self-determined information. Self-determined information is facts that are filtered through the lens of self. Such facts are driven and interpreted by and for the narrative of "me." This unconsciousness is extremely well defended, using all of the defense mechanisms to keep contradictory information at bay. Denial, a simple turning away and pretending the fact does not exist, is one of the most common defenses used. *Conscious,* in this context, refers to complete wakefulness, where nothing is denied, imagined, defended, or protected.

What are the chief characteristics of this pathway? The most obvious is that we are willing to look where we have not been willing in the past, and that keeps us on an important edge that might be missed within another continuum. We can see that one of the values of switching pathways is that each emphasizes a different attribute that may be subtly avoided within the pathway with which we are currently aligned. "Am I willing to look at this?" becomes the overriding question that governs this path, and that eventually leads to, "Am I willing to look at what I am?" which takes us to the counterinfluence of this pathway.

If you believe that all facts are friendly, you will find yourself undefended and willing to look. When resistance arises, you are questioning the benefit of that fact. Are *all* facts friendly? The absolute right side of the continuum suggests they are. Ask yourself, "What am I afraid of seeing in this moment?" Write down all the implications that that fact has on your life, and then decide whether, when it arises in the future, you will remain unconscious to it.

The counterinfluence is the force of embodied willpower that will look at whatever arises regardless of the timing and consequences. This may again sound like wisdom, but it is really ego strength, and though it feels as if we were at the top of our game, we are actually moving to the left side of the scale. Wisdom will always consider the complete picture, including the usefulness and timing of looking, and the readiness to look, at issues that may currently overwhelm us. The hallmark of the wisdom within this pathway is usefulness and timing. Is this "need to look" being led by curiosity and interest or by dogged determination?

We can be sure that such ego strength is being controlled by fear, and perhaps what we most fear discovering is our own impotency on this spiritual journey. To counter that fear, we overreact and assert our discipline and force of will. As the sense of self is understood, this exertion of control will temper and soften.

The false nirvana occurs when we have looked in every direction and nothing currently scares us. We feel we have conquered the mind, have sought darkness wherever it appears, and there is nothing left to do. I fell under the sway of this false nirvana after I had been living as a monk in the forests of Thailand for a few years and had to renew my visa in Bangkok. My mind was so calm and tame I felt my worldly impulses were gone forever. The first passenger to enter the train once I was seated was a man holding two live chickens. He sat beside me in cramped quarters for the entire duration of the six-hour journey, his chickens squawking the entire time. The trip to Bangkok destroyed my serene image, and my nirvana was lost. I was left feeling humbled about how completely mistaken I had been. My serenity was contingent upon the circumstances of living in a quiet and secluded forest. With a change in environment came a dramatic change to the mind.

As mentioned previously, the paradigm shift can come at any time but tends to reveal itself after the major obstacles on the continuum have been at least partially addressed. Once it occurs, gone is the fear of fear. Though fear may still arise, it cannot contract the mind back to the state of unconsciousness. Since the self is understood, nothing the mind brings forth has personal implications. We now understand that this journey is not under our control and is not derived from our will. The fusion of darkness and light comes together in its final stage when darkness is no longer being forced into the light, and when we, the forcing power, are seen as the very darkness we have been trying to overcome.

Contraction to Love

Instead of repeating the scale with each new pathway, let us simply substitute these two poles on the scale we mentally know so well, so it now reads: Contraction ———→ Love

There are many reasons we are drawn to a pathway of love. Some of us have Christian backgrounds in which love was a dominant influence, and others simply resonate deeply with the word. It is comforting to know that love works equally well across traditions, but before we get too far into this pathway, let us define our starting and ending terms. *Contraction* is the state of guardedness and resistance, and as mentioned previously, it is a self-centered state in which the world is funneled through our desires and fears. It is the same state as suffering, separation, and noise, which were the beginning points of other continua. *Love,* on the other hand, is inclusive and open-ended, without boundaries or demarcations. Love does not look like the romanticism we have come to call love but is the complete validation of life as a whole.

> Feel the air around you. Notice that the air places no pressure or force on you. It wants nothing from you and allows you total freedom here and now. It simply surrounds, envelops, and holds you timelessly within itself. Now substitute awareness for the air and allow the feeling of being unconditionally held to replace the sensation of air. This very roughly approximates unconditional love.

As with all the other pathways, only our intention moves the cursor from left to right. We feel a need to be more loving, kinder, and more open, and we commit ourselves to those qualities. At the beginning of this journey, the sense of self is very much controlling the process, but even under egoic authority, we sense the increased availability of our heart as we allow ourselves to soften and relax. We realize that baring our heart means being vulnerable and exposed, feeling and being affected by the world. As we allow life in, warm-heartedness becomes the unmistakable hallmark of this pathway.

Since a warm and kind character feels like a valid self-image, the ego has allowed this to happen. But as the pathway moves toward greater vulnerability, the ego becomes concerned that we are exposing too much and are too defenseless and starts weighing in on the risks of continuing. "I can't live in the world this way; people would constantly take advantage of me." "What if I start feeling so loving that I take the destitute home with me?" "Baring my heart is too much for me to stand." These mental objections can easily stop us when there is insufficient wisdom, and we learn that wisdom is a necessary companion to the heart's journey. Wisdom reveals that the true heart is not tentative, and many of these questions fall gently away as the path steadily unfolds.

The counterinfluence arises when the sense of self repeatedly argues for caution and keeps interrupting the pure intention of the heart. We realize that we cannot listen to the ultimatum voiced if this path is to move forward. The clever guardedness cautioned by the sense of self cannot coexist with the determined resolution of this opening. The only way to advance is to thoroughly understand the ego by using love, the very ends and means of this path, to overcome the obstacle of self-restraint. For the path to continue, we simply have to love "ourself" to death. What that means in practical terms is that with mercy and kindness we open to self-understanding.

The false nirvana is the power of love itself when it is subtly possessed within the film of self. The film of self is a tattered remnant of the full egoic expression we know through our self-definition. The "I" thought is active and engaged, but the "I" thought points to a much more spacious center. Though much of the overbearing nature of the self was explored and understood as the counterinfluence arose, there remains a film of possessiveness that still points to a center. That center now has what it has always wanted, to own love and be recognized for that fact. Many spiritual leaders in all traditions have stood on this ground and proclaimed they are love. It is a hard ground to dispute internally when we sense our own radiance, but this proclamation is a false nirvana, and only sincerity moves us beyond it.

Ask whether love acts as a motivating force in you or whether it arises as a spontaneous response. Notice that most of your actions have a motivation behind them—some altruistic, some not. Motivation is a cause that spurs an action, but motivation is also sequential in time; the motivation happens and then you respond. From chapter 2 we remember that time lives in awareness (another name for love), awareness (love) does not live in time, and therefore unconditional love has no cause-and-effect sequencing. See if you can get a sense of this when you feel loving and aware.

If we have not halted our journey at the many irresistible rest stops and rest homes that love offers, we will eventually pass through a paradigm shift, an alteration so profound we will sense we are continually birthed from love, held by love, and unmistakably safe within it. Though the path continues after the paradigm shift as new obstructions arise, we work with the remaining conditioning. The end is never doubted, and as the sages have proclaimed since time immemorial, we discover that the essence of all form is love. Love reclaims everything until nothing else remains.

Morality to Basic Goodness

Let us look at one more pathway, with the intent of preparing for our individual quest within our own continuum. The pathway from morality to basic goodness seems at first glance to be very ordinary and relative. We all know our own tightfisted moral and righteous mind, so we probably understand the starting point, but what is this basic goodness? Is this pointing to anything other than just being "good"? And being good feels like it is taking us back to morality.

Basic goodness is a term coined in Trungpa Rinpoche's w.. though my own definition will be applied. Basic goodness is the freedom to move without restraint within the warmth of awareness and the view of nonseparation. At this point I am using terms like the *"warmth"* of awareness and the *"view"* of nonseparation, but the warmth and the view are not recognizable within awareness, any more than generosity is recognizable as the motivation for listening to someone you love. Love and awareness do not act from motivation; if they did, they would be tied to the world of form. Basic goodness, then, is an attribute of formless awareness.

Basic goodness is different from wanting to be good, in the sense that wanting to be good is an effort toward rightness and righteousness and is an egoic attempt to hold us in check with forbiddance and punishment. Within this pathway, morality is the starting position and needs to be explored thoroughly. We may begin by wanting to be good but quickly discover that there is tension in that wanting, and the wanting polarizes the world into our fears and desires. We realize that the world looks fractured and divided because of the way we hold it internally. This polarization provides a firm and righteous position for the sense of self, but the mind remains divided and ill at ease within that division.

The counterinfluence comes into play when we see that the sense of self is prohibiting further advancement on the pathway through its position on morality. When the self surrenders its position on all polarities, the unified mind arises and basic goodness appears. We understand that we can no longer listen obediently to the positions taken by the self or we will continually separate ourselves through this polarization. We are now willing to investigate the nature of the divided mind much as we did in chapter 3.

The crisis of the false nirvana occurs when there is a strong felt sense of goodness but it has not yet culminated in basic goodness. As we incline our mind toward goodness, goodness appears, no longer as morality but as the heartfelt ease and joy of a tensionless life. We want to believe that this harmonious life is all there is and we are at the far right side of the pathway, but time will show that deeply polarized issues remain. Until then we are called to go deeper and

uproot the troubling way the mind continues to divide the world
and us within it. When the paradigm shift does occur, the ease experienced within that harmonious false nirvana becomes coupled with
the basic goodness of the new dimension and life assumes fluidity
never experienced within positions of morality.

Being good and morally upright is a deeply ingrained principle in
this culture, and it is almost heresy to suggest an alternative. But we
have to release this logic of thought to discover the basic goodness
that resides within nonseparation. After the paradigm shift, our heart
is bare and our vision is clear. We see the truth of nonseparation
and feel deeply the pain of immorality. Actions now come from nonseparation, and we no longer attempt to find nonseparation within
our moral compass. Trust and faith in the new paradigm alleviate the
tension of trying to be anything at all, including being good.

You have now moved in and out of several pathways and
perhaps have a feeling for how they unfold, the obstacles
you will be confronting, and the starting and ending points
of each. Remember as you construct your pathway that it
must overlap and perfectly represent the Buddha's teaching
of suffering to the end of suffering. Do not allow your scale
to have a false nirvana as an end, which will be some permu-
tation of pleasure and a closed loop unto itself, feeding off
the sense of self. The beginning will be your present state,
and the end will be a paradigm shift within an absolute that
is without limits and outside of form. If constructing your
own paradigm seems confusing, pick one of the already described pathways for guidance.

Sometimes the end point on your continuum may seem
confusing, as one conditioned state of mind after another
captures your attention and engrosses you within its story
line. It can be helpful to call forward the end point on your
continuum and prove to yourself that it is much more available than the engrossed state of mind would seem to indi-

cate. If, for example, you have chosen the path from contraction to love and at some point you feel hopelessly distant from love, lost in irritation and divisive thinking, sit down and call love forward by asking, "Where is love in this moment?" Now, if you are going to call it forward, you must be willing to allow it to be revealed. To do so you have to be still and see if love is there. See if it is in fact there in the *midst* of these other states of mind, not in opposition to them. See if love is holding the other states within its wide and infinite reach.

Aligning our spiritual journey along a pathway allows us to have a sense of where we are going and how to get there. It provides a view, direction, and orientation to an otherwise mystifying journey out of self-deception. As the continuum unfolds, surprises, obstacles, and deviations occur all along the way. Sometimes we move backward and sometimes forward, often carrying our sense of self along with us even when it is an obvious obstruction to do so. We do that because the self is familiar, and at times we need an imaginative companion to counter the shocks and fears that all paths contain. We need our old grumblings and ruminations, our irritations and annoyances, our pleasures and reminiscences, to give a vague terrain a little security and us a little confidence. Soon enough all that will go, but there can be a wistful turning back to our image to wish it well one last time.

Now that we have a sense of the topography of our spiritual journey, the key moment on that pathway is the paradigm shift that occurs somewhere along the continuum. Exactly when or where is anyone's guess, but with honesty and sincerity it will happen. As mentioned previously, that shift is a complete reorientation of perspectives. A question might arise as to what awaits us once that shift has occurred. What are the qualities of awareness that allow our body and mind to remain functionally in the world even as the consensus paradigm is pulled out from under our feet?

9

The Discerning Power of Awareness

Real questioning has no method, no knowing—just wondering freely, vulnerably, what is it that is actually happening inside and out. Not the word, not the idea of it, not the reaction to it, but the simple fact.

—TONI PACKER

In chapter 5 we explored the mechanism through which consciousness evolves from the old paradigm of form into the new paradigm of formless awareness. Instead of adapting our story and staying within form, we surrendered our separation by releasing the narrative that bound us to form. Our story gave us our image and individuality, but it shielded us from the field of awareness that is our surround. Surrender is the doorway through which our consciousness has to pass to access formless awareness, but we have to be willing to give up the narrative that keeps us in form and within our history. Similar to an opening to Harry Potter's Hogwarts School of Witchcraft and Wizardry, this access point closes up very quickly to anyone who believes a single thought upon entry.

This is not all that surprising when we realize that thought is the first expression of form. Thought holds the image and invites the recognition and memory forward, forcing the experience to be what we say it is, but surrender reverses this process. It releases the narrative and allows the experience to be what it was before we embellished it with thought. We surrender the noise of our thoughts into silence, adding nothing to the experience.

> Engage the phrase, "Add nothing to this experience." This includes the need to think about or inflate the moment in any way. See if you can be present without adding a single thought to the moment, as if you were speechless and experiencing the moment not through words but directly for the first time. What is the bodily felt sense of the moment when you add nothing to it? Do you sense that the stillness holds something other than the absence of noise?

But what makes surrender possible? It cannot be an act of will, or the very effort we exerted would keep us formed as the self that is surrendering. Willful effort is a further adaptation of our story, where "I" am going to surrender away "my" separation. This does not work, and using surrender in this way holds us in place. To use a play on words, any act of will keeps us informed (in form) about our needs, goals, expectations, and journey. We are making effort for a reason that is directly related to our story line, and any extension of our story is an extension of self. Remember that the story is an adaptive response that perpetually keeps the sense of self alive and active and the formless at bay.

Surrender is not an adaptive response; it is a release into stillness. What happens in that moment of release? Surrender is actually a response from wisdom. In chapter 5 we saw that the strategy of adaptation maintains the sense of self and keeps "me" adapting but never allows the sense of self to end. The mind knows no other recourse, has no other tool or method, so it keeps on adapting as if it were being directed by wisdom, but wisdom sees that we cannot adapt ourselves into the formless, and becomes still. This is not a forced

stillness or a trying to be still, or it would be an adaptation. This stillness comes when there is nothing more to be said.

Surrender provides the only access to stillness from the noise of
form. Surrender is the transforming element, the paradigm shift itself. The sacred is entered through surrender. Surrender is the most
helpless experience we will ever feel, which makes perfect sense, because the protective defenses that have historically formed us are
now completely silenced. We drop our guard and life enters on its
own terms. The sacred comes in when we are not.

We have come to the point now of asking, If surrender arises
from wisdom, where does wisdom come from? This takes us to the
formless. Wisdom comes directly from seeing what is true, and that
pure seeing is awareness. Now stop for a moment and feel the sheer
beauty that lies within this sequential unfolding. Life provides the
instrument to escape from ignorance. What I have been calling
formless awareness is unobstructed life and from life arises wisdom
that provides the pathway of surrender that frees us from perpetuating our narrative. Life turns back around to meet itself and pull us
through the ignorance that our minds have created.

> Get a sense of how surrender and adaptation play through
> your spiritual practice. You will find yourself adapting when
> you are not completely convinced that you need to give
> something up, but surrender knows that there is no recourse
> but to give it up. Only wisdom can establish the certainty
> that something is not needed when your story will always
> tell you that it is.

Let us explore awareness and see what it offers. First I would
recommend reviewing chapter 2 as a reminder of what formless
awareness is and how it can be understood. In the previous paragraph
I mentioned that formless awareness and life are one and the same.
Let me explain this a little further. If we started with dirty rinse water
and ran the liquid through a series of ever more refined filtration

systems, eventually we would arrive at absolutely pure water that looks very different from the way it began. So, too, if we filtered out all the external substances that are within life, all the objects, the particulate matter that we perceive, we would discover life in its rawest expression, we would arrive at awareness, simple and pure aliveness. Now, if you distilled out all the internal contents of your consciousness, including all thoughts and states of mind, you would again come to that same refined and simple state of being. This unprocessed sense of aliveness, both inside and out, is formless awareness. At some point form does not interfere with this simple state, but for now let us say that unadulterated life inside meets the same outside with only the imagined boundary of self between.

I have mentioned several times in earlier chapters that the end of struggle can be equated with formless awareness. Why is that so? With the removal of the boundary of self, all life, internal and external, comes back together. Simply put, formless awareness does not invest in the narrative that created the boundary and does not make up a story that is associated with the perception of any imposed border. It just sees—but there is more to seeing than meets the eye, because seeing lies within an infinite field of intelligence.

This intelligence is not yours or mine or owned in any way. This intelligence is intrinsic to life itself, and, I believe, is the basis for most of the phenomena we call instinct. Once the paradigm shift occurs, we move from our personal intelligence that defined the left side of the pathway and was filled with our personal commentary to the impersonal intelligence that is the hallmark of the right side. This universal intelligence is the knowing quality of our nature, or the "luminosity" often described in Tibetan Buddhism.[1] This intelligence gives us the capacity to see all aspects of experience, and from this basic seeing we learn what a particular form is, but the seeing is fundamental to that learning. As we move from the left to the right side of the continuum and we pass through the old paradigm into the new, the ground drops out from under us. This new surrounding has different playing rules and a different objective. The new emphasis is the simplicity of seeing (right side) rather than the objects of sight (left side).

Both the internal authority of our opinions and the external authority of what others tell us to do directly guide much of the left side of the pathway. At this stage we have not sufficiently developed wisdom, which can leave us dependent on counsel. There is some danger during this phase, since we could easily assimilate external authorities and directives as part of our pathway. Working our way through dependency is essential and calls upon us to consider whether our direction is coming from ourself or another source. We have to work on completing this developmental task, which has likely followed us since childhood, so that we can attune to a self-guidance that governs the remainder of the path.

As we move to the right side, we begin to feel a vague hint of appropriateness that is not based upon our opinions or what others are doing or suggesting. It is a little like going into several homes blindfolded, one of which is our own, and somehow being able to sense which house is our own. There is a subtle resonance with being at home that is not derived simply upon sensory input. This "felt sense" becomes more acute as wisdom is nourished and, when matured, becomes a dynamic that is not to be denied. We sense the rightness of our methods, of our direction, and of our teacher. Words that are in line with this felt sense move us; other words do not. It is not arguable or transferable to another person. Each of us has it uniquely to ourself.

Self-doubt is far and away the greatest obstacle to this felt sense of being aligned with our hearts and it blocks the relaxed confidence that is essential for alignment. Self-doubt is a persistent pattern in most Westerners that is a consequence of a deeper sense of personal inadequacy. We have not learned to trust ourselves sufficiently, and the longer this patterns endures, the more we are at risk of losing our way. It is most helpful to address self-doubt early on and often throughout our spiritual journey.

PASSIVE DISCERNMENT

Wisdom begins to arise from observing experiences free of personal identification, and as wisdom filters out more and more of the subtle expressions of thought, it eventually merges into discernment. Discernment comes from the intelligence of awareness itself, and unlike the left side of the continuum, the right side uses discernment, or pure seeing, to advance its cause. This is a living wisdom, part of the fabric of awareness, not directed or reasoned. It arises within the moment and is accessible only when there is complete abiding.

See if you can get a sense of the discerning power of awareness, perception in the absence of judgment, as opposed to opinions, which is perception with judgment. Can you feel the source of intelligence that is giving rise to discernment? If you can learn to trust that discernment more than your opinions, you will find it guiding you unambiguously.

In a famous sermon known as the Satipatthana Sutta (The Four Foundations of Mindfulness), the Buddha lays out the course of practice when observing the mind. He says,

And how does a monk remain focused on the mind in and of itself? There is the case where a monk, when the mind has passion, discerns that the mind has passion. When the mind is without passion, he discerns that the mind is without passion. When the mind has aversion, he discerns that the mind has aversion. When the mind is without aversion, he discerns that the mind is without aversion. When the mind has delusion, he discerns that the mind has delusion. When the mind is without delusion, he discerns that the mind is without delusion.

When the mind is constricted, he discerns that the mind is constricted. When the mind is scattered, he discerns that the mind is scattered. When the mind is not scattered, he discerns that the mind is not scattered. When the mind is enlarged, he discerns that the mind is enlarged. When the mind is not enlarged, he discerns that the mind is not

enlarged. When the mind is surpassed, he discerns that the
mind is surpassed. When the mind is unsurpassed, he discerns that the mind is unsurpassed. When the mind is concentrated, he discerns that the mind is concentrated. When
the mind is not concentrated, he discerns that the mind is
not concentrated. When the mind is released, he discerns
that the mind is released. When the mind is not released, he
discerns that the mind is not released.[2]

There are several points in these passages that are worth elabo-
rating on. First, the Buddha is not suggesting changing the mind at
all nor having the mind one way as opposed to another. He is essentially including every possible state of mind within these two paragraphs, with his only instruction being to "discern" what is arising.
This is a very pure and simple instruction that undercuts a lot of the
counterbalancing that most of us engage in throughout our practice.
We usually counterbalance one state of mind with another when we
are unsettled by the state that is arising. We attempt to modify our
mind by taking the edge off through any number of adaptive methods. But here the Buddha is not trying to offset any state of mind
with another, more-preferable state. We are simply allowing each
state to be seen (discerned) exactly as it is. What is the point and
purpose of this instruction?

Practice pure discernment in your meditations. No matter
what the mind brings forth, your job is simply to observe
(discern) and let it be. Do not interfere even when the mind
is lost in thought. Just let yourself be lost in thought until
you return. The resolution of your intention to be awake
will determine how long that will be, not your personal effort. Notice that the less interference within your meditation, the stronger the discernment; and the stronger the
discernment, the less substantial the sense of self appears to
be. The Buddha seems to be showing us that the way to dis-

solve ourselves is through noninterference, by turning all control over to discernment, but we have to prove the truth of that path for ourselves.

In the Four Foundations the Buddha seems to be moving the practitioner from form to formless awareness. He starts with the instructions in the First Foundation to explore the body thoroughly, the most personally identified expression of form. He then moves us into the Second Foundation, which is an investigation of how the sense of self is formed, the very way all form comes into existence. The Third Foundation, from which the quote above is drawn, is an attempt to allow the sense of self to disappear by eliminating all interference. Finally, the Fourth Foundation, building upon all the previous foundations, is the paradigm shift where the formless is discerning form.

We could spend much more time on these foundations, but I want to limit the discussion to the Third Foundation. The Third Foundation is the crossover foundation between the old paradigm and the new. It is the working edge where many experienced practitioners find themselves. We relax into the moment and feel ourselves dissolving into awareness with only a film of self remaining, when suddenly something shakes us back into full embodiment. Again and again this division between the arising of the sense of self and the empty and relaxed attention seems to move us back and forth across the boundary of form and formless.

The Buddha is suggesting that if we are willing to observe this boundary thoroughly without doing anything about it, it will disappear on its own. Since it is a product of form, it arose through the mind's desire or fear and will relapse back into nothing when we are silent. All boundaries will dissolve on their own when we are no longer fearful of being unprotected. Discernment sees the need to be silent and surrenders all resistance, and form falls back into the formless.

Drawing from the divided mind in chapter 3, we see that surrender heals the rift between the two hemispheres of the mind by releasing the need to pit one side (me) against the other (the object of my dislike). We can now see the confluences of healing the divided mind: surrendering, nonseparation, and leaving the mind completely alone as suggested by the Buddha in the Third Foundation of mindfulness are all one and the same event. Each offers a slightly different perspective from the vantage point of the self but is precisely the same from the view of discernment.

How does noninterference resolve problems? Life will continually present challenges whether we abide in form or the formless, but a problem—defined in the dictionary as "a situation regarded as unwelcome or harmful"—does not transfer into the formless. This is because a situation can be "unwelcome or harmful" only when it is resisted within a divided mind, and the formless holds no divisions. When a "problem" is lived rather than surmounted or overcome, it manifests as part of an abiding moment of life itself and not separate from it. From the unified mind the flow of life is uninterrupted when a challenge arises within the moment.

> Notice how your resistance to an experience defines that event as a problem. You may be afraid to release the resistance because from your vantage point the problem would then overwhelm you, but for this exercise, risk being overcome. When an experience arises, say a problematic emotion, pause and drop your guard. Do not separate yourself from it in any way. Do not judge, argue, or resist it. Simply leave it completely alone. Ease yourself back into the moment and coexist with the experience until there is just now, and nothing to get over.

The wisdom within discernment keeps awareness unfixed and unformed, and the mental formations quiet down on their own without suppression. The Buddha is saying in the Third Foundation that the expression of mind is not important. It may feel more pleasant to have the mind cohesive, focused, and concentrated, but if our effort becomes seduced by that pleasure, we will create a schism between what we have and what we want, forcing the mind to divide. There is no way around this except to surrender to whatever happens within the mind, thereby allowing it to unify. Unification is the end result of all the continua of practice and is synonymous with formless awareness.

The Buddha is pointing to a deep acceptance of our humanity. He is saying there is nothing wrong with us except our desire to be different. He is pointing back to self-formation and asking us to check our egos at the door. However the mind is, let it be—we have no problem to overcome, no argument to cast, no side to take, no dispute to nourish, and no comparison to make. All we can do is surrender our resistance and be completely self-allowing. "Is there space for this too?" is a perfectly aligned mantra that can keep us directed toward the right side of the continuum.

ACTIVE DISCERNMENT AND THE POWER OF QUESTIONING

As the sense of self becomes less substantial, other forms become equally transparent and awareness brightens considerably. A threshold is reached when the energy we were giving to our opinions is transmuted into the discerning power of awareness, allowing more clarity to arise. This discerning power uses the mind when needed for the memory it offers to navigate the world of phenomena. Sometimes experiences pull us back into form as we work and deal with the issues at hand, and at other times the sense of self is but a whisper of form within the clear expanse of awareness.

Discernment has two ways of dissolving form into the formless. The first we have already mentioned: patiently surrounding form with pure awareness. Since form needs our investment of words to sustain it, silence slowly dissolves form back into the formless. There is nothing we need to do except be willing to see without words. The simple seeing of "just this" does it all and is the essence of practice within the right side of the continuum. But there is a second expression of discernment that is active, though its force and energy are not self-driven. Active discernment has an innate curiosity that is not often recognized.

There is a primary curiosity of the heart that is the force of life attempting to complete itself. In its purest form, primary curiosity transforms all expressions of ignorance into truth. But interest can easily be corrupted by the mind into intellectual curiosity. Intellectual curiosity is the mind's attempt to understand through language and reasoning what life is about—as opposed to the primary curiosity that is attempting to silently merge life into itself. The mind's curiosity builds a body of knowledge that can become a source of self-esteem and personal power that is strongly tied to the image of us, the knower. Meanwhile, the primary curiosity of discernment moves toward absolute contentment and stillness.

Our personal interests are often examples of active discernment. Though much of our interest is intellectual curiosity, we can often find a hum of the primary interest running through intellectual inquisitiveness. For instance, we may have an interest in astronomy that when fully mature merges our mind with the wonder and mystery of the universe; or we may delight in cooking, and that taps our creativity, spontaneity, and self-appreciation through the actions of preparing food. Following the thread from intellectual curiosity through the primary interest of wonder and contentment (or any right-sided ending point on a pathway) allows us to be uplifted into the joy of the heart as we travel our continuum.

> List four or five of your most passionate interests. Spend time with each one and see if there is a link between the interest and the right side of the continuum you are practicing. Encourage that thread forward. For instance, if you love photography, ask what it is that you love about it. Perhaps it is being in nature or being creative or looking at the world free of assumptions. These are all links back to your spiritual

life and can be consciously intended within your photography so that the spiritual life grows alongside your passions.

Interest is where we are most strongly connected to life. It is where life is feeding us, touching us with wonder, and encouraging us beyond our assumptions. The fascinating enchantment of interest is life meeting itself, life delighting in its own recognition. The best quality about interest is its proximity. It is literally as close as what draws and holds our attention. If we were willing to pursue our primary interest into a full-fledged inquiry and move wherever the investigation would take us, we would reach a point where we would have to relinquish our form and merge into the formless. By necessity the inquiry would pull us beyond ourselves into a stillness without individuated things.

Curiosity from active discernment is the heart's attempt to understand and connect. Curiosity reaches out to explore what is keeping real interconnection at bay. Active discernment appears in the mind as a question when it encounters an obstruction. Questions such as "What is going on here?" "What is this?" "Who is feeling insufficient?" are all arising from discernment.

What makes questioning such a perfect spiritual companion is that it moves unconditionally across settings, never dependent upon the rarified environment of a retreat or obscured by the full impact of our daily life. Its thirst knows no bound and is equally at home alone or within a crowd. It will travel anywhere and is only limited by our fear of asking the question.

The key to a discerning question is that the question looks behind us into areas where we are normally unconscious. We ask questions about those areas of blindness that we have been acting from and want to move into the light of awareness. "What is going on here?" is a question that reaches back into our unconscious patterns and places the difficulty in front of us where we can see and deal with it consciously. The question does this on its own, and no other impulse or effort is needed. The very willingness to ask exposes us to the unconscious. The following sections discuss a few more of the benefits of questioning.

Questioning empowers us to look critically at what we have been told.

When I was an undergraduate psychology student, my girlfriend was a friend of the most prominent psychology professor on campus. The professor was retiring and invited my girlfriend and some other students to dinner, and I was allowed to tag along. At one point during the meal the professor engaged me with questions that could have drawn out either my intellect or my intuitive heart. I went with my intellect, and he quickly reengaged with another person. In that brief exchange he suggested that if I wanted to understand psychology, I should free myself from other people's knowledge. After dinner he took us out to his flower garden and spent most of the time until we left sharing his love of plants.

The professor was suggesting that being a student was more than regurgitating the words of the teachers and texts that we had been studying. His definition was more demanding. This professor was asking us to look critically at what we had been told and use our wisdom to accept or reject the premises on which the conclusions were based. I was fortunate to have taken a course from him, and he changed the way I learned, and his teaching has stuck with me throughout my spiritual journey.

At one point I realized I knew almost nothing for myself. I was full of knowledge, but it was all secondhand. Even my spiritual insights had been emphasized and defined by others. "See everything as impermanent" was the constant refrain from my early years of practice. Where was my intention in this instruction, and did I even care about impermanence? Would these insights even be significant if my meditation teachers had not repeatedly emphasized them? How was I to make this practice my own if I simply looked in the direction that other people were pointing? What were my own questions, what was important for me to see, and did I even have a bearing on that?

I learned I did have questions, and I also learned that asking them was a journey of complete aloneness. My questions arose from my own inward terrain, from my needs and interests, concerns and limitations. At first I felt the burden of questioning and a nagging doubt about my ability. But I had no choice because I was getting nowhere working my spiritual journey as if it were a school class-room that is dependent upon the teacher. Once my doubt subsided, the questions started to arise quite simply and naturally from what-ever I was dealing with in the moment. I chose to remain with a question until there was a fully realized embodiment of the answer. I would then open myself to the next question, and the questions have never stopped.

Questions show our pattern of dependency.

As mentioned above, questions reveal our insecurities, which is the reason that many of us do not ask them. There are few times in our lives that we are as sequestered as when we ask relevant questions. Our world closes down around us, and we are driven by the yearning to know. Questioning requires a laser-beam focus of our intention and passion. What blocks this total participation in asking a question is the belief that we are insufficient to answer it. Who are we, the perpetual C student, to ask a question of this magnitude? Questions like "Who am I?" and "What is this?" are better left to the wise and judicious. Once more, self-doubt prohibits further progress on our continuum.

We feel vulnerable when we do not have the answers, and ques-tioning takes us deeply into that display of insecurity. Usually when we are vulnerable, the most painful expression of our psyche be-comes exposed. It is not surprising that questions most frequently reveal our inadequacy, because unworthiness is an epidemic in the West. If our continuum from suffering to its end is clearly estab-lished, then the arising of these painful facets of our psyche are not intrusions or distractions but become the very focus of our current questioning. Our energy moves directly into the difficult state of mind and we ask, "What is going on here?" Experientially we move into the thoughts and emotions formed within this pattern of mind. "Are these thoughts true?"

Nothing is beyond questioning, and it becomes intolerable for active discernment to meet a defense mechanism that denies access to an obstruction. For example, we might use the defense of denial and refuse to question our mortality. What discernment does is show us the denial until we are willing to address it. Discernment never forces anything; it is just unremitting in its presence. It is impossible to shake the knowing of what we observe—we see our resistance, we see our not wanting to know—and even when there is resistance, the knowing wins out and we concede the process to discernment.

Questioning focuses the mind with interest and opens the heart.

I love watching Tibetan Buddhists engage in dharma combat. Usually within a large sangha gathering an inquisitor hurls difficult dharma questions at a responder, who must answer quickly to the satisfaction of the attending crowd. Although this sounds fierce, within the context of a serious exam, it is actually quite playful and there is accompanying joy and laughter throughout the process. This is combat of the heart, and the Tibetans are masters of this form.

When the Buddha chanced upon the heavenly messengers (an old man, a sick man, a corpse, and a wandering ascetic),[3] he dove headlong into the questions that such encounters bring. If they are aging, tired, sick, worn out, and close to death, what about me? Am I, too, subject to such conditions? Suddenly everything the Buddha had spent his life doing was called into question, and once his basic life assumptions were questioned, everything became a question. These new questions that arose carried an importance and focus he had never known before and ultimately led to his awakening.

Whether it is a Zen koan[4] or a dharma inquiry, whether it is logical or nonsensical, makes no difference; the questions pierce and open the heart to wonder and mystery. Questions are a juxtaposition of silence and thought. It is as if discernment were using the best the mind can offer to unify itself, and the best the mind can offer is a

question. Discernment adeptly plays between the question and silence, skillfully moving the mind from the question into wonder,
where the mind quiets and stillness descends. There comes to pass a
beautiful symmetry between form and the formless, between self and
awareness, as form attempts to resist the wonderment by finding an
answer, while the formless relentlessly questions. This play between
thought and stillness uses the power of both, playing one against the
other in perfect balance within the delight and wonder of the heart.

Questioning shows the limitation of knowledge.

Questioning is fed by the impulse to be free, and seeing the limitations of knowledge helps access that freedom. There is a wonderful
opportunity when you misplace something to feel the forces that are
aligned against not knowing, and they are considerable. We can feel
the tides of our evolutionary past fight the chaos of not knowing.
Forget where your car keys are located and all sorts of self-incrimina-
tion, blame, irritation, and confusion reign. We are so unsettled in
that instance that all of our energy goes toward moving consciousness back into the position of certainty. Nothing else matters except
finding the keys.

How does it feel not to know? Do you think not knowing is
a reflection of your intelligence? Notice that when you are
certain of something, knowing fixes that form in consciousness. That form cannot be anything other than what the
mind says it is in that moment. No wonder or mystery is
accessible. Notice when there is a lapse of knowing that
nothing is fixed and the world is wide open with possibilities. This feels chaotic because the mind is an organ of security built upon knowing and defining. Reflect on whether
the consciousness of knowing or of not knowing is closer to
the formless.

As mentioned in chapter 1, just below the surface of our knowing perspective lies a world of chaos and mystery. Here we enter the world of quantum reality, where subatomic particles are in random disorder, they appear and disappear without cause, one particle can be in two places at the same time, and it is impossible to determine both speed and location. We could not navigate through such a reality, so we layer this fluctuating world with consistent thought that holds each thing stable and momentarily secure. From this stability we know what to do with objects, how they function, and their exact placement, but knowledge also alters reality and blocks full participation. Here we have formed a safe and protected layer of concepts upon the raw, exposed consciousness we call life. In doing so we have lost access to the wonder of life and have gained the certainty of knowledge.

If the particles that compose the universe are in commotion and disarray, then we may be missing something fundamentally true by avoiding this confusion. Questions show us that universe by taking us below the conceptual level. When we question, we are not formed by our thoughts and are open and available to the sea of change that surrounds us. This movement from security to insecurity intimates the shifting of paradigms that our continua will encounter.

The means of questioning are the ends we seek.

Questioning may well be the most valuable tool we have to penetrate the old paradigm. Questioning is a little like peeling off layers of paint to find the unfinished wood. When asking a question directed at our unconscious, we usually have to go through all the old defenses and explanations that coated the answer. These are the illusions that kept the sense of self in place and worked perfectly as long as we were willing to remain unconscious.

For instance, suppose we have just told a lie and the mind begins to rationalize why the lie was necessary. But instead of remaining within our self-justification, we ask an authentic question, "What is going on here?" and observe the defense mechanisms and their commentary. We can now either remain in the lie or move with the wakefulness that exposes the lie. That is just one layer of paint, and there are many more to come. The point here is that a heartfelt question takes us through ourselves and exposes all the illusions we have placed between the truth and us.

To keep ourselves intact, we usually ask an intellectual question such as "How can I keep from lying so often?" This question not only keeps the ego in control but uses the sense of self as the final solution. The answer is always to work harder, to apply more effort, to be better, and to hold our temptations in check, all ways that deepen our self-illusion. An intellectual question evades the issue, which is "What is going on here?"

We might say that the answer to every nonintellectual question is the same. A question is a conduit for emptiness. Since it does not rest on previous knowledge or excuses, a question is the unformed mind. The unformed is a synonym for the unconditioned.[5] When we stop fleeing the content of our lives, existence reveals itself as a question. We start living the mystery before us rather than redefining the mystery back into our intellect. But the compromise is that we will never be safe in our questioning. If we want safety, we will have to go back into our intellect. By definition, questioning is accessing new and unexplored territory, and there is no defense against the unprotected answer.

We are now fully engaging the shift of paradigms that transforms our perceptions. We have seen how surrender is the key element for crossing over from the left side to the right of the continuum. What catches us as we let go of the self-centered left side of the pathway, passing through the door of surrender, is discernment. Discernment is not a thing but the abiding intelligence within formless awareness. But there is still a way forward that needs our discretion. We are putting the fundamentals in place that will provide a smooth transition along the pathway, and the next chapter continues that process by exploring the principles the shift of paradigms is based upon.

The Principles of Practice

To do nothing is sometimes the best remedy.

—HIPPOCRATES

One reason there is so little true spiritual fulfillment is that many of us do not have a clear idea of where all of this is headed and therefore use methods that are contradictory to the ends we seek. When we look directly at the end of the continuum, we may realize what a distance our methods seem to have taken us from a true, liberating freedom. We appear to be going in circles, because our thought-based actions are using the same paradigm principles that we are attempting to surmount. For example, we may intellectually know we are empty in nature because the texts and spiritual writings point in that direction, but everything we do all day long reinforces our central position in life, and we feel anything but empty.

Before we fully obligate ourselves to a view such as emptiness that may seem distant from our normal perceptions, we want verification that this understanding is worth our energy and pursuit. We talk to others, read descriptions, or may seek an experience that will reveal that fact. Certain concentration states may give us the experience of emptiness but will be received by a fully formed sense of self that will keep the experience distant. Experiences end up only modifying the tone and nature of the self and have limited value in shifting paradigms because they perpetuate the sense that somebody received something, usually leading to further thoughts and reflections.

Realization is completely different; we have to let go of the self for realization to occur. Realization is the direct reception of the information into the body of the organism and does not pass through the brain. Realization ends the separation between the experience and the person having it and therefore penetrates deeply into the body, changing the cellular makeup. The conduit for realization is surrender, and it is only through surrender that the abyss between self and selflessness is crossed.

If we choose to alter our course toward a more convenient relative goal than selflessness, we will deviate from the true intent of our pathway. This is the reason the Buddha stressed wise view as the first step in the Eightfold Path to awakening. The Buddha says, "Without Wise View one can aspire toward spiritual growth, but it is like trying to churn water into butter."[1] Wise view is what we know life to be and establishes the direction for our pathway. The view informs the spiritual continuum from beginning to end and keeps us properly directed despite the unpredictable variances of our desires.

Recently I enjoyed a hot air balloon ride, something I had always wanted to experience. What was remarkable was the complete change in vantage point the flight offered as the marvel of what we were experiencing began to affect our self-perspective. On the ground there was the ordinary viewpoint, but in the air, hovering a few hundred feet above the ground, lingering slowly and quietly over the landscape, not only was there a changed frame of reference to the earth, but there was an internal simplicity and stillness that accompanied the drifting balloon. My fellow travelers and I quieted down immediately, and even our sparse conversation assumed the spaciousness of the flight and held an ease missing on the ground. We became the wonder of the flight.

Unlike the balloon ride, our ego rarely allows a change of viewpoint. We have moments of amazement and mystery but always claim personal ownership of those experiences, which holds us within the egoic frame of reference. "Oh," we say, "I just had a moment of awe." We seem stuck within the same self-possessed view regardless of our experience and are held fast to a center that forces everything through the "I." This is the perspective of the ego, with its abiding sense of being cut off and distant from everything even as it perceives itself as the center through which everything passes. Like a downspout during a rainstorm, the world of the senses funnels its way into a central receiving point called "me," and all experiences seem to confirm our central place in life. Everything is understood and acted upon through the lens of "me," and since there is only one "me," everything and everyone is secondary to what the "I" wants.

Though this is the view we begin with, we have now seen, and science has corroborated, that the sense of self is a fiction and therefore has never been the force behind any change, adaptation, or construction of our lives. We give it a place of predominance that it does not deserve. Outside the mistaken belief invested in it, the actual sense of self has had no input into all that is or ever has been. Why? Because we simply have never existed as we have believed. How real was the dream we had last night? The energy of the dream, the realism, the actions taken, and the composition of the dream did not come from the dream state. It had other sources, and so, too, do our lives.

In addition, all forms of objective reality are equally as empty and are only disguised as objects having been shaped and molded by the mind's words and ideas. So there is nothing "out there" separate from "in here," only translucent images that appear and disappear on the screen of consciousness, all arising out of the unconditioned. The conditioned is ascending out of the unconditioned each moment, but it reveals itself only as appearances, while our words do the finishing work.

If there is no separation, then what is doing all of this? What force builds, creates, decides, and acts? What alien plot is going on all around us that makes it seem as if many separate actions were happening simultaneously? What does the world look like when we remove everything that is not real from it? It looks like Life meeting and moving itself. From this vantage point, nothing is or could ever be wrong or out of place. All things are formed from the same substance and are the play of consciousness without purpose or direction.

> Stop for a moment and reflect on the fact that your thoughts have never been your own. Every action you have ever taken, every impulse you have ever had, and every word you have ever uttered has not come from you. Your existence is based upon the incorrect assumption of a "you," which holds no truth whatsoever, but if you are not in charge, what is? Whatever is moving the entire universe is also moving you. The only way to know this is to join the movement by releasing the perspective of self-centeredness.

Even the spiritually adept rarely take their practices to the final conclusion. As our practices deepen, the spiritual journey keeps bringing forth different expressions of reality that when first observed from a mental vantage point appear like the summation of reality. Each facet seems complete in itself and the final destination of our journey, the place where there is nowhere else to go. These facets of reality keep transforming themselves into the next place where there is nowhere to go, and on and on until we suddenly realize there is no place to go, and that is the fulfillment of the spiritual journey.

These expressions of reality are like a deck of cards, each card complete in itself but also an integral part of the whole deck. In one moment we perceive the stubborn dualistic nature of life; in the next the dependent arising of self and object and the ending of that dualism; in another our complete aloneness in the universe; in the next the shared delight of interconnectedness. As the journey continues, we sense that there is nothing outside consciousness and in the next moment that everything is intrinsically empty and nothing exists. Then suddenly everything, including the sense of I, goes blank in objectless awareness, and upon reappearance the oneness of all things is seen. Finally we return to the street we are crossing with horns

Head in the Clouds,
Feet on the Ground

honking and sirens blaring. Somewhere between it is all one, it is all love, everything is empty, we are everything, and we are nothing . . . we have to buy groceries and pick up our children from school.

In the beginning our ego assumes apparent control and responsibility over many of these phases and almost all of our life in general. Through relentless questioning and insight we pierce a hole in the ego and see that the ego was born only within our imagination. Though the ego is not dead, it is mortally wounded and can no longer defend us from seeing what is true. Truth wins out, and slowly awareness shuts off the energy supply that fed the ego, and the ego relinquishes its control to formless awareness. To practitioners this transition feels like suddenly being born into daylight. The tight and cramped quarters of the ego give way to the wide-open space of being, and joy ensues.

The sense of self has now evolved into a different entity, an entity much more nuanced and spacious. Gone is the judgment-laden and self-critical commentator and in its place is a vaguely formed and subtle film of self. This film of self continues quietly self-referenced. There remains a very peaceful center to the circle of "me," and it is from here that the different facets of reality are discerned. In some traditions the self, with a lowercase *s,* now becomes the Self, with a capital *S.* "This is what I really am," we exclaim. It feels that we have finally discovered the heart of the matter, but "I am everything" or "I am nothing" is still "I" based. Even the sense of selflessness is based within the sense of self and can merely be a new description of an old experience. All experiences including "I am nothing" and "I am everything" need a center to receive them.

In a strongly worded sermon called The Root of All Things, the Buddha pushes this issue further by reframing each facet of reality without the film of self. In twenty-six slightly different stanzas, he refuses to allow any identification with any expression of reality. Here are three of the verses:

"He perceives All is All. Having perceived All is All he conceives himself as All, he conceives himself in All, he conceives himself apart from All, he conceives All to be mine, he delights in All. Why is that? Because he has not fully understood." The Buddha continues, "[She] perceives unity as unity. Having perceived unity as unity, [she] conceives [herself] as unity, [she] conceives [herself] in unity, [she] conceives [herself] a part of unity, [she] conceives unity to be mine, and delights in unity. Why is this so? Because [she] has not fully understood." And finally the Buddha reiterates, "He perceives Nibbana as Nibbana. Having perceived Nibbana as Nibbana, he conceives himself as Nibbana, he conceives himself in Nibbana, he conceives Nibbana to be mine, and delights in Nibbana. Why is that? Because he has not fully understood."[2]

This film of self has a functional role in consciousness. With the film of self we can navigate the world, find our way out the door, and distinguish this organism from the food it eats. The senses are tools of navigation and are organized by a mind that sees only in differentiating terms, and the film of self is a necessary remnant of that process. Our survival depends upon the film of self, but we do not have to give our power over to it. Spiritually we go beyond the identification with the film of self so that it cannot define our separation from the world. To do so we have to surrender everything into that spaciousness and then sense the distance that remains within all differentiations. Passive discernment of that distance eliminates the center of the film of self, leaving no position and no conclusions whatsoever. Now the energy comes from inside life, a total emersion of life back into itself without any subtle reference of a self that is seeing or being it all.

Take a moment and sense the distance between you and any object. Simply observe without commentary the interval that separates you from whatever you are observing. During this exercise do not focus on the object but on the distance or space between you, the observer, and the object observed. This perceived space is what creates the sense of being separate from. If you are quiet with the distance, you will undermine its reality, and the distance won't be sustained. Once the interval closes, watch how the mind reconfigures a new expression of separation through the thoughts it generates, and a new distance is created.

For much of our history we practiced as if we were a self on our way to becoming a nonself. We slow our transformation considerably when we drag ourselves along, believing we will eventually be worn away. Even though we may intellectually understand our empty nature, our actions confirm our real belief that we are somebody evolving into nobody. Our actions are the true indicators of the assumptions of our practice. In the Buddha's Eightfold Path, wise action is the essential link between belief and realization.[3] When we hold the thought of being "like this" on our way to being "like that," this very thinking prohibits any real change from occurring. Our current actions are governed by our immediate beliefs, and those beliefs assert that "at some point, I will be like that and then I will act like that." But the Buddha is asking us to turn this around and act in accordance with the end point prior to the change in belief. Essentially he is saying that just as actions follow beliefs, so too do beliefs follow actions.

What does it mean to act in accordance with the end point? This is a very important point, because later in this chapter one of the principles we will be talking about is "staying within yourself." Staying within yourself means living within your understanding rather than living a dharma ideal. Many people attempt to live dharma ideals prior to understanding the foundation on which those ideals are grounded. Such behavior will lead to moral judgments and unyielding righteous actions but will not end or reduce our struggles.

What we mean by "living in accordance with the end point" is testing the assumptions on which the old view is based and seeing whether actions aligned with the sense of unity work in greater harmony and create less suffering. Living in this way prior to the shift of our understanding that confirms the truth of this view is an experiment, and there is a healthy "I do not know" accompanying this testing. There is no image formation around this trial, no hardened opinion, belief, or egoic payoff. We are simply seeing if it works and adjusting our assumptions accordingly. Does some part of us get confirmed when we live within interconnection that is not fulfilled in self-centered living? How does entering this lifestyle change our worldly assumptions, and are those changes more in line with the way of the heart?

If we allow our practice to be directed by wise view, our actions will change accordingly and we will see the fallacy of our old conditioned past. For instance, we may wish to live in the world without harming others or ourselves because the view we use to guide our spiritual journey is nonseparation even though our thoughts and beliefs still operate from division. An interesting change occurs when our actions are aligned with not harming. We start having a felt sense of the truth of these new actions, and new beliefs around interconnection begin to form that encourage more actions in that direction. In addition, fewer thoughts from the old belief of separation pull us back into disconnected behavior. Though belief is not the same as realization, it is easier for realization to occur when that insight is aligned with our current actions than when it is at cross-purposes to the view we hold. Not only do our actions prepare the organism for the realization but also the body and mind are already compatible with the new direction of the realization.

Realization is independent of beliefs, but the ease of acting from a realization is vastly increased when the insight is aligned with how we are already living. Many people have had deep insights into their selfless nature, but selflessness is so counterintuitive to our conditioning that insight never shifts into action and is quickly forgotten. Realization is the full context and living expression of the insight, but unless the insight is brought out into the open and fully lived, it quickly becomes a memory without power or force to move us into realization.

The question might arise about how to act from selflessness when all we know are actions based within the sense of self that arise from old conditioning. As an interim step, center your actions on the view of being connected to all things rather than separate from them. Use the cues that normally turn you away from an experience to turn toward it. For example, when you are aversive, use the experience of aversion to cue you to move toward the aversive object rather than away. Hold the sense of aversion within awareness and do not allow aversion to set the course of action. Staying connected internally to the state of avoidance and externally to the aversive object, while you surrender the resisting narrative, is the overriding principle that allows this to work. After practicing this for some time, try this final step: Step out of all conditioning whatsoever, even the new cue of turning toward rather than away from an experience. Refuse to move out of any conditioned thought, state of mind, or impulse. Remain still until movement occurs by itself, and then ask, "How did that movement arise?"

Though we have been expounding on many different principles throughout this book, we will continue listing a few other principles that arise naturally from the new paradigm of nonseparation and convert them into tangible actions. The point is to live these principles. Remember that the mechanism that allows these principles to work properly is surrender, not adaptation. Adaptation is the key mechanism for the consensus paradigm of separation, and these two must be thoroughly understood and applied appropriately or we will quickly lose our perspective and orientation as we travel the new pathway. We begin by examining the principle that there is nowhere to land. Having nowhere to land reinforces the truth of selflessness that is the keystone of the paradigm of the heart.

NOWHERE TO LAND

When I speak about an end to the spiritual journey, as I did in the first part of this chapter, I do not mean a final product, place, or state of mind but, rather, an abiding formless awareness that embraces all form but rests upon none. Because formless awareness does not rest upon anything, it is at rest. Everything in life except awareness is in movement, but since awareness is not a "thing," it is not fixed or locatable. As our practice moves into formless awareness, consciousness becomes less established and certain, less of a thing in itself. Since settling means locating ourselves in time and place, an unfixed consciousness does not land and stays formless.

Now let us align our practice with the principle of a resting and unfixed awareness. All authentic pathways will be governed by this principle of not landing regardless of how we define the starting or ending points. Since formless awareness, which encompasses all ending points, is not locatable, it does not exist in time and place. This principle suggests that our pathway is not about the "I" landing somewhere and taking up residence anywhere on the continuum. The Buddha speaks of this in the following passage: "I do not claim to be All, I do not claim to be apart from All, I do not claim All to be mine, I do not affirm the All."[4] The Buddha is not landing on form, nor is he landing on the formless for any self-description. By our not landing anywhere, all things are allowed to be just what they are.

A life that does not land remains unformed as a ripe potential, while a life that does land becomes formed into a specific object. Life is transformed into a conclusion when we fixate upon it. The fixation creates the object. Before the fixation arose there were no objects or subjects. The sense of self lands and takes shape along with the objects.

This sounds more and more like the universe proposed by quantum mechanics, where subatomic particles remain a potential wave pattern until they are consciously noted, at which time they form a discrete particle.[5] When we understand formless awareness as the creative expression of life, we are seeing the mergence of science on the small scale with life on the large scale of the human domain. How could it be otherwise? How is it possible that a portion of life called "me" would not have to play by the same rules that govern the fundamental particles of the universe?

Knowledge is the key link that forms us as a separate individual.

In the Twelve Links of Dependent Origination (*patticcasamuppāda*), the Buddha lays out the series of conditioned events that gives rise to the view of separation.[6] Though an entire book could be written on this sequencing, for our purpose notice that mental formations set the stage for the conditions of knowing that propel us along the path of self and other creation. Mental formations are the impression created by previous thoughts, the habit energy stored up from countless encounters with objects. From that habit energy arises consciousness itself, with the recognition and formulation of the world as we have known it to be. Now the knowing subject stands confirmed against the world of known objects. We now land with a purpose and intention that belies our formless nature, and it is here that we forsake our open potential for the assurance of a closed and defined creation. We have landed and we take a stand.

One type of conclusion is an expectation. An expectation is the mental certainty that something will happen in the future and is a presumption about where the present moment is headed. This is an extremely elusive process of mind that needs to be met with the subtlety it deserves. When that future arrives as the present, the emotional momentum we stored within that expectation flows out as satisfaction or disappointment. Suffering results when that certainty is interrupted, life intervenes, and we are left with an unrealized goal. To the experienced practitioner, suffering is an indication of slipping into the old paradigm of time and thought, and with practice, suffering wakes us up to that slippage.

Begin to notice your expectations. What are you anticipating and what is your emotional investment in its deliverance? Search out the subtle thread of time that links the past, present, and future within an expectation. For example, when you turn on the hot water tap at your sink, you anticipate the water's being hot. What happens when it is not, and where did that expectation come from? You can see how thoroughly the past coats the present with expectations. What is it like not to land within an expectation? Of course you still turn on the hot water tap when you need hot water. You still hold the memory traces of the past, but the present encompasses the past and severs the reactive response when the water turns out to be cold.

Although it is a form of desire, an expectation is actually more nuanced than most desires. The thoughts around the expectation can be relatively quiet, yet there is often a desiring haze within that expectation that sets you up for disappointment. Disappointment may be an indication that an expectation has been operating below the surface of awareness. Trace your disappointments back to see if you were anticipating something that did not occur.

When an expectation is unnoticed but operating, a reaction will result when the expectation is unmet. The reaction lands and concludes that this should not be happening. When there is awareness of the expectation, curiosity plays forth and the question "What is happening here?" arises, but the question does not land or conclude and remains an expression of wonderment, charged with an unknown potential.

Curiosity meets the challenge of an unmet expectation and keeps it from becoming a problem even as it investigates the encounter. A problem is a disruption to a planned result, but wonderment does not allow a problem to form because it has no planned result. The reactive response (that this should not be happening) assures that a problem has already arisen and "I," the problem solver, must now tackle the difficulty. Curiosity never separates itself out from the challenge but moves into and through the challenge, always staying connected.

SIMPLICITY

Many of us derive satisfaction from a multifaceted and emotionally complex life. We like the drama life imparts, and the intensity keeps us on an edge that is expressively rich but psychically draining. The greater the emotional volatility, the more alive we feel, and the absence of emotional highs and lows seems to indicate a life not fully lived. As we enter the right side of the continuum, we realize that life does not derive its aliveness from emotions. In fact, the more we depend upon emotions for aliveness, the further from the formless we stray. This is not to suggest that emotions are unhealthy in any sense, only that aliveness is not dependent upon their presence or absence.

Simplicity is one of the guiding principles that help reduce mental formations and guide us effortlessly toward the formless. The more formed we are, the greater the identification with our self-image and the more complex is our relationship with life. As we allow formless awareness into our lives, our identification with our image lessens, and we become less complicated and quieter. Let us see why this is so and then shape our practice around this uncomplicated principle. Reviewing from an earlier chapter, form is defined by the mind, and the mind gives form meaning. Once the mind determines what something is, based upon its past usage and memory, it adds a layer of definition that was not fundamental to the form, and the form becomes more complex. As we tie a story around this history, the mind imparts an approach or avoidance to an object that keeps us relating to it through our past association.

Our narrative keeps us relating to the object as if its history were part of its essence. We lose sight of the fact that the history came from our memory and think history resides in the object itself. Once the mind is focused exclusively with the history of the form, there is no longer a tether from reality to the form. The form becomes whatever the mind says it is. The potential of the form is limited only by our imagination and can become the most feared or loved object in creation.

I once took an average-looking rock and placed it on a self-prepared altar with pictures of saints and other holy relics. I chanted and bowed to the altar on many occasions with the intent of seeing whether this once neutral object would take on new significance through association with the other sacred objects on the altar. After a number of weeks, a feeling arose about the specialness of this rock, with an accompanying story about how old and tested it must be and how it existed through much of the earth's early history. The bows became deeper as its privileged position grew. Though I knew intellectually that this was all nonsense, the feeling of its distinctiveness grew anyway. Finally I returned it to the earth as just another rock, and once I did so, I looked upon the other holy relics on my altar with a little more discernment.

The point is that when the essence of an object is mentally layered, it becomes more confusing and complicated to the person perceiving it. Since the confusion is coming from us, it is the confusion we are having with our own minds. We are now looking through the mind and have lost reference to what we are seeing. The projection is no longer owned as coming from ourself, and we can deny responsibility for the mixed feelings and reactive patterns that we place upon the object. We think our feelings are coming from the object, not from the definition we have given the object. We then use other objects with different definitions to intervene and help alleviate the complexity we gave the first object. For instance, we may pray to God to help us through the confusion of our difficulties, but what is the god we are praying to except another mind-created entity with its own layers of confusion projected by us?

All of this confusion signals that we are entrapped within form, and this cue can allow us to pause and question what we are doing. As we relax and take responsibility for the projections, the object simplifies considerably. We stop coating appearances with our mental formations, and they fall back into stillness. Even as it all quiets down, there is still a vestige of thought that continues to make something out of the nothing of the object. This thought can be as subtle as just wanting to see, understand, or connect, but that is just enough noise to cast a shadow of differentiation and create the sense of separation. This too must be patiently observed so that the mind-created something can return to its true essence.

Look into a mirror and acknowledge the reflection. Notice your comments, judgments, and criticisms about what is revealed in the mirror. It is just the appearance of you, as thin as the light that reflects off the glass. Notice the complexity of the emotions and the accompanying narrative that makes it so much more. Now pause, relax, and own those emotions and comments as coming from your mind and not being inherent in the reflection. The mirror reflects only what it sees, and you bring everything else to the reflection. As you become quiet, notice how simple the image becomes. It is not even owned or possessed by you. In fact, there is nothing there that is yours. You identify the image as being you, but can you sense the formless surround that cannot be reflected by the mirror? The sense of you and this image have been paired over time so that you are held within the image. The quieter you become, the less this pairing is confirmed.

STAYING WITHIN OURSELVES

Seeking has a natural time and duration within most people's spiritual journey. We sense that someone knows more than we do and seek this person's teaching to satisfy our thirst. Depending upon the sincerity of our quest, we will find teachers whose wisdom we can trust and whose encouragement moves us along. But seeking is founded upon the understanding that we do not have the same access to the truth and someone else knows better. It comes from a kind of self-uncertainty that seems true only from the left side of the continuum. Once the paradigm shifts, seeking becomes more disorienting than helpful. When we cross over into a new paradigm, we see the need to look directly at the issue of our uncertainty rather than seek in reaction to this uncertainty. The end of seeking depends upon the complete uprooting of our inadequacy so that doubt no longer compels us to search outside ourselves.

The principle that becomes obvious after crossing into the new paradigm is to stay within ourselves. It may seem paradoxical that we would stay within ourselves when there is no self to stay within, but in the new paradigm we see the utter futility of being dependent upon someone else's realization. Staying within ourselves means staying within our own understanding, what we have actually realized, regardless of how deep or shallow that may seem. We question every assumption that has conditioned our consciousness to seek truth within separation. The idea that the truth is outside us is a stubborn assumption, especially in a Western culture that is flooded with unworthiness, but it is here within this new paradigm that we become radically accountable and totally responsible to the assumptions on which our separation is based.

Recently on a month-long residential meditation retreat, one young participant was having a miserable time regardless of my guidance. He was trying to live my words and ignore the resistance he was having to them. His face and body were tense and his mind full of ideas about how his practice should be going. Finally I asked if the retreat was working for him, and after a prolonged discussion, both of us decided it would be better if he departed early. Once the decision was made, he completely relaxed. Noticing that his face was clear of the tension he had been carrying on retreat, I asked him what just occurred. He said he was no longer on retreat and could now relax. I said that was what I was looking for while he was on retreat.

This young man was obviously not living within his understanding and was making his spiritual life woefully difficult by attempting to think his way through his practice. He tried to tailor his life around every dharma point regardless of whether he had realized those truths or not. His efforts were followed by harsh self-criticism when he could not live up to these projected ideals. There was an obvious gap between his actions and his realization, which left him reeling under his self-created pressure.

Notice your tendency to move outside your own understanding and form a belief that seems true but is unrealized by you. How much of your spiritual journey is based within beliefs? Beliefs will create a conflict between your

assumptions and your actions. Can you feel the psychological pain, usually in the form of self-doubt, that encourages
you to believe in what is unrealized? If you question the
validity of the doubt rather than your ability to realize the
truth, you will stay within yourself and your practice will
deepen considerably. Earlier I spoke about living in accordance with the end point. How do you reconcile this statement with staying within yourself?

Each of us is asked to live our own understanding by thoroughly
exploring the obstructions that inhibit our continuum. Normally we
act as if the obstructions were true, which leads to a compensatory
action to offset the truth of the belief. All of this commotion takes us
out of ourselves, but when we are resolved to stay in ourselves, we
are forced to deal with the impediment directly as an assumption,
not as a truth. The question of what is authentically our own moves
us through everything that is impermanent and unreliable. Since all
states of mind are transitory, they are not authentically true, and this
search for what is authentic and reliable within us begins to take the
place of the earlier seeking and searching for external answers.

The last vestige of our personalization of life is always discovered
within a state of mind. Every state seems to tell us something about
ourselves and seems to indicate some valid point about our relationship to the external world. The final movement out of form is to
leave this chatter behind and sever all beliefs that hold us within our
narrative. Once that is completed, there is nothing that forces us
back into the story of our lives and therefore back into form. Now
the energy can move between form and the formless without any
inhibition or limitation on its governance.

DOING LESS

Noninterference with the mind has been a central theme of this
book, and doing less is a variation of that topic. This is such a central

principle in shifting paradigms that it cannot be overly emphasized. As we move from the left to the right side of our spiritual continuum, we become more willing to experience all mental activities and have less need to change them. We do not feel the need to defend ourselves from what the mind is implying or to blunt its impact. We also find that the less we alter our internal world, the more accessible awareness is.

We discover that formless awareness does not grow through our efforts. It exists independently of all things and paradoxically in the same moment is intrinsic to all things. We like to tie awareness to our efforts because it feels as if we can make it appear on command. Like a magician, "I will now be mindful of my breath," and voilà, we are mindful, but we actually have to step out of the way for awareness to appear. "Our" attempt to make it happen interferes with its arising. The reason for this is that the sense of self is a thought believed, and the "I" thought is lost within the image it is creating. The intention of the ego is to highlight the image and not the awareness. When the "I" thought ceases, awareness comes back into view, but we can no longer take credit for its appearance.

The next time you sit in meditation, notice how often you get lost in thought. What causes that drift into thinking? Did you deliberately try to lose yourself? If not, then getting lost in thought was not your responsibility. Now notice when you have awakened out of thought. You may take credit for waking yourself up, but the noticing you are no longer lost in thought occurs after having awakened out of it. You cannot take responsibility for losing yourself or waking back up. What really happens is a mystery.

The less we do to establish or cultivate awareness, the more it reveals itself. This principle guides our continuum from beginning to end and is perhaps one of the most important revelations, ultimately providing a passageway for selfless realization. We have very little real understanding of what is going on throughout our spiritual journey, and that is so perplexing to the ego that all it can do is continue to self-reference the process. The ego says, "I did this, I did that, and I need to do something else." If we ever understood the inherent mystery in the process, we might well be tempted to throw up our arms and quit. One of the true paradoxes of practice is that we continue to practice even though we cannot evaluate our effectiveness.

The question "How do I do less?" often comes from the sincerity of seeing how the sense of self inhibits its freedom, but it is a question that circles us back into ignorance. "How do I do less" is asking the self to do more and is therefore reconfiguring the challenge back within the old paradigm of separation. Doing less is possible only when we see the detrimental effect our manipulation has on emptiness. Mentally influencing experience is the reason experience appears to be something solid, separate, and tangible. As mentioned in chapter 5, we can try to adapt our way through this problem, which allows us to stay in the picture, or we can surrender ourselves up to the nothing that we are. In other words, we have to be nothing in order to do nothing. Anything less and we interfere with the outcome.

The Perfection of Imperfection

As mentioned earlier in this chapter, one of the perspectives the remnant of self likes to possess is the perfection of all that is. This is one of the facets of reality that have the most impact on consciousness. It is the complete resolution of all polarities. All things are perfectly themselves and are an emanation of the total perfection of life as a whole. This is not a philosophical point of view; it is a realized understanding. Though the sense of self may attempt to reference this perfection as its own—"I am God"—it is actually a perspective of life from formless awareness that has nothing to do with the sense of self.

As we cross over to the right side of the continuum and the new paradigm opens, our practice, if it continues at all, changes considerably. The sense of self is taken completely out of the equation. As mentioned in chapter 3, the unified mind now assumes the overview guided by discernment. Occasionally karmic tendencies reassert themselves as subtle judgments, assumptions, and expectations, but they are now incorporated back into the perfection of the whole, where nothing is denied and everything is accepted as inclusive of the whole. The practice can now be summarized as leaving the mind totally alone without division. Even the sense of self is left alone to manifest as it will within the whole. There may be moments of inattention, but nothing is acted upon or changed. In the absence of resistance, these moments of inattention cease without interference. There is not even an attempt to awaken out of confusion, as confusion itself is seen as part of the perfection. We are now abiding within the perfection of imperfection.

This makes sense when we remember that our continuum was never moving toward the perfection of form, and the formless was always perfect. We realize we will never solve the problems inherent with form because form by its very nature is imperfect. We feel a tremendous unburdening when this is realized and no longer worry about the displays of the imperfection of form. Form and formlessness become indistinguishable, and from this vantage point we see that the perfection of the formless includes form.

Nothing was, is, or ever could be incomplete. It is only the divided mind that establishes the assumptions where polarities exist. Heal the divided mind and those concepts are eliminated. But how do we live the truth of perfection? It is impossible to describe how to live this truth because every time we speak about it, we bring it within the imperfection of form, and something is left behind. If we were told to fully abide within the imperfection without thinking ourselves into an ideal, then that would limit the ideal we think about as outside the perfection. If we were told that this principle is lived by dwelling within the moment unobtrusively, then that excludes obtrusive living. Perhaps it is more to the point simply to say, as we expressed previously, there is nowhere to land. When we land, the perception from relative truth obscures the perfection of the whole. Although it is still a part of the totality, we cannot see it. So we resolve to be still and take no stand, and that brings it home. We realize we never were "out of place," and we cannot bring something that was never out of place back into place.

The Buddha ran into the predicament of not landing when a wanderer named Vacchagotta approached him and said, "Is there a self?" The Buddha did not answer. The wanderer then asked, "Is there no self?" Again the Buddha did not answer. The wanderer then departed and Ananda, the Buddha's attendant, asked the Buddha why he did not reply. The Buddha explains that if he had answered yes when asked if there were a self, he would have been siding with the eternalists and it would have been inconsistent with his teaching, but if he had answered no, he would have been siding with the annihilationists and a view would have formed about what the self was not. The Buddha continues, "And if, when I was asked by him, 'Is there no self?' I had answered, "There is no self," the wanderer Vacchagotta, already confused, would have fallen into even greater confusion, thinking, 'It seems that the self I formerly had does not now exist.'"[7]

Allow yourself to sit quietly for a few moments without changing anything, no matter what is arising in the mind. If you get lost in thought, fine, and if you are present and aware, fine. Allow the judgment to occur as it will and leave your reaction to the judgment alone. Nothing is to be added, modified, eliminated, or altered. Open a space large enough so there is no pressure or forced surveillance. All thoughts are perfectly placed. Try to sense how the whole of life works flawlessly in its own direction, with its own timing, toward its own end. Notice the awareness that perfectly holds the entire consciousness. Try moving this principle outward into your engaged life and sense the imperfection within perfection. A natural equanimity arises that both holds the perfection and responds to the imperfection. Notice how quickly this principle is lost when you become opinionated about the imperfections.

Guided by the central principle stated by the Buddha that "all things [form] terminate in nibbana,"[8] we can now select applications that move us in accordance with all the guiding principles. The applications we use need to be specifically aligned with these principles or they will distort the end result. With that caution in mind, let us look at how to apply ourselves to the resolution of our continuum.

II

The Applications of Practice

Besides the noble art of getting things done, there is a nobler art of leaving things undone. The wisdom of life consists in the elimination of nonessentials.

—LIN YUTANG

Traversing a continuum requires changing our view and intention long before the actual paradigm shift occurs. Unless we hold the view of where we are going and have the intention of heart to move in that direction, the mind will stubbornly refuse to surrender to a destination it may unconsciously be resisting. In some ways we have to live the truth we know prior to realizing that truth. Living it in body, speech, and mind begins to align both our psychology and our physiology with the outcome. The shift in paradigms is as much a neurological and biological alteration as it is a spiritual transformation; our body and brain actually evolve through the shift as new energy pathways emerge. For some this physical evolution can be rapid, dramatic, and painful, moving more quickly than our spiritual perceptions change, and for others it can be a gentle progression that is barely noticed.

Living the truth prior to realizing the truth may seem like a contradiction of the earlier chapters of this book that stress realization over an intellectual grasp of a subject, as well as the principle of staying within yourself from the previous chapter. Realization is essential for real transformation, but prior to that realization the body and brain can be prepared to accommodate what is destined to appear. The mind develops an orientation and openness for this new information that leaves us less confused and bewildered by the revelation when it does occur.

This, then, is one of the reasons we practice: to ensure an appropriate container for realization. The mind and body are being prepared during our spiritual practice to energetically hold the transformation the practice is directing us toward. The energy systems in the body and mind are vastly different before and after the paradigm shift, and it often takes time to prepare the mind and body for this alteration. There are, of course, other reasons that spiritual practice is important, one of which will be discussed shortly, and that is to begin to live within a view that is compatible to realization.

Recently at a Buddhist conference a fellow teacher asked the group how we worked with students who had a sudden realization of selflessness. He said he had noticed that a few of his students were so shaken by this disclosure that they temporarily lost their ability to function in the world. They could not return to their old view of self and were seemingly unable to move their lives forward without it. A few of us responded that the degree of disorientation might be caused by how we teach the practice. Perhaps if we taught selflessness from the beginning, our students would be expecting this revelation when it did occur and would have a context within which to hold this insight.

This question lies at the heart of the movement along any authentic spiritual continuum. The view of nonseparation needs to inform and guide the entire pathway. Not only is it important to learn about selflessness from the beginning of practice, but it is also crucial to develop our entire practice around that insight. When our perception does start evolving in that direction, our confidence will be reinforced by the strategies we have already assumed. When we are given sufficient preparation through techniques, exercises, and investigations, all meant to ripen our understanding, then even the most profound revelation will fit within the normalcy of our expectations.

Wise View

Essential to this outcome is the view we hold throughout our practice. The importance of wise view was mentioned in the opening of the previous chapter. The unwise view, what we currently take life to be, establishes our beliefs about time, distance, separation, and who we are as persons. Believing these assumptions limits our potential, and we stay entrapped within those beliefs for much of our lives. At some point we feel the need to break away from these boundaries and select spiritual strategies that promise to move us in an alternative direction. But all strategies will work only as well as we allow them, and if our methods are still directed by false assumptions, they will end up reinforcing our separation and individuation. The important element is not the methods we use— almost any method will work—it is the view we apply within the technique. The view we maintain, if not skillful, can hold the techniques within a perceptual prison that will not permit the transformation necessary.

Suppose, for instance, I am applying myself diligently to a system of practice that my teacher assures me will reveal the fruit of the journey. Now suppose I sit down and think about how "I" am going to master this technique, how far along "I" already am, how much longer "I" expect it to take, and what it will be like when "I" have shifted paradigms. We can see that we can apply ourselves diligently to the practice for a number of years thinking subtly in this way, but as long as we carry the central beliefs from the old paradigm along with our practice, we will be held within the logic of that paradigm. The logic of the paradigm is what prevents transformation. It is the belief in the thoughts from the old paradigm that entrap us within that view. We begin to notice that every unconscious thought, not just the "I" thought, is derived from that old view, and that nothing else needs to change except the invested truth we give thought.

If we started within wise view, much of this could be avoided. Essential to this undertaking is keeping the Buddha's teaching very simple so that the mind does not create a complex terrain to navigate. The teaching is pared down to the essential continuum of struggle and the ending of struggle (or an equivalent; see chapter 8), and all activities are gauged by their place along this continuum. We begin to notice, as we struggle less, that there is an accompanying feeling of greater space (less "me"); and as we struggle more, there arises a contracted sense of I, me, and mine. At this point we are beginning to understand that selflessness is equivalent to space, which also corresponds to nonstruggle.

We then gently reconfigure our life in terms of the wise view of interconnection even though we have not fully realized this truth. We do this in a number of ways, each of which has been explained in earlier chapters. First we learn to embrace all experiences regardless of their emotional appeal. This lessens our conditioned response to pleasant and unpleasant experiences and opens the world to be seen in a less possessive way. Next we become radically accountable for our projections, refusing to allow the external world to bear the weight of our internal reactions. This keeps us away from false blame and accusations that deny responsibility for our internal responses. We question the truth of our narrative that fixes us in time and makes it seem as if we were more substantial than what we are. Finally, we validate the formless space around the content rather than the formed content itself, which begins to open the new dimension of formless awareness. Practicing each of these begins to prepare us for the full impact of the new paradigm even as we dwell predominantly in the old.

When wise view is *realized,* it is not a view at all. It is not a way of defining and depicting the world; it is life unencumbered by thoughts of separation. We initially use wise view to counter our old dualist beliefs, but once deeply imbedded within the right side of the continuum, we leave the view alone and abide within the reality of nonseparation. The view oriented us away from our conditioning and toward something we intuitively felt was valid, but it was never meant to become an image that separated us from reality.

Wise Effort

Although we have been discussing effort throughout this book, a little more directed understanding is needed. We will now turn to the strenuous effort that dominates much of the left side of the continuum and begin to align that energy with wise view. For most people this is a challenging task. For much of our life we have known only one way to proceed, and that is through volitional control. Our efforts and willpower get us where we want to go and procure what we need along the way. But the journey along the spiritual pathway is different. If the end is formless awareness and volitional effort arises from a strong identification with form, then there is a conflict between the destination and the person exerting the effort. Effort has to be redefined so that it comes into alignment with the right side of the continuum.

Many of us find that our effort evolves along with our understanding of the nature of self. As we experience ourselves within a more porous and fluid perspective, our efforts lighten up accordingly. Time and time again, the old conditioning that everything worthwhile is accomplished through discipline, hard work, and force of will arises. The trigger of will always seems to be pointed at our practice, and we find ourselves again and again falling within its persuasion. When there is a strong belief about the value of effort, that assumption can inhibit the understanding of the nature of the self. The belief in effort can actually be a counterweight to insight and realization. Using the strategies of self, such as effort, maintains the definition of self and prohibits seeing its true nature. In other words, our use of effort may keep us within the force field of self, limiting what we see and how we interpret it.

Concerted effort early on helps us understand the difference between a thought and an experience. It establishes a threshold of steadiness that allows our attention to settle on an object free of thinking about that object. Since most of us have spent our lives within the force field of thought, the effort that we exert is to counter this conditioning. We believe we need to exert a strenuous force to break the bonding between thought and experience, but the bond exists because we like thinking about something more than we like experiencing it firsthand. Breaking this bond is then not so much a task of effort as one of understanding the value and limitation of both thinking and experiencing. It takes a while for this understanding to settle in favor of awareness free of thought, and at that point effort becomes effortless. Focusing on the question about the value and limitation of both, rather than trying to get over the thinking that we enjoy doing, can hasten this understanding.

We can now observe our experience without the accompanying thoughts that keep us reacting to the experience, and this begins to clarify what an experience is as opposed to what our narrative says it is. We also notice that any effort that remains slightly distorts the experience because the effort implies that we still want something from it, and there is struggle within every form of wanting. We begin to see that as we try harder, there is greater struggle (and more "me"), and as we relax and surrender, there is less inward tension (and less of a sense of self). Our use of effort is now monitored according to the tension produced and the self that is being formed from that tension. Once this is observed, we then keep adjusting our efforts according to the effect effort has on our continuum. For most people, monitoring effort in this way leads to an effortless awareness that remains unmarked by self-assertion.

Does accessing awareness require anything from you, and if so, what? It must preexist your formation as a self or the entire spiritual pathway would be self-induced. Awareness would then be artificially created through your efforts, essentially ending the spiritual journey toward the formless. If the whole continuum were self-controlled, the end would

> look just like the beginning. If the end is to be different from
> the beginning, somewhere along the line control has to give
> way to surrender. Surrender is the release of the self-image
> and therefore not a function of the self. Ask yourself what
> areas you need to further investigate and understand so that
> you can surrender more deeply.

Effort now becomes defined as the energy needed to stay connected (wise view), and the forces of aversion and grasping are always countering that energy. When we encounter any state of mind that seems to limit connection, we turn toward that state (in this case aversion or grasping) and connect with it. Paradoxically, turning toward aversion is the very application that keeps us within wise view even as the words of aversion are attempting to break that connection. Insight is possible only through the conduit of connection. Once we have connected, the natural next step is to explore the state that seems to want to disconnect. We learn to release all the words that impose a boundary between the experience and us.

Wise Intention

The formal environments of our spiritual practice are far less important than the intention we have to move to the right side of the continuum. At times retreats, monastic settings, or places where distractions are minimal can be helpful in establishing the stability of mind necessary for clear observation or to simply separate ourselves from the deluge of intensity that fills much of our lives. But as we move to the right side of the pathway, we have to bring our understanding out into the open, where the full catastrophe of life is being confronted. Unless we are careful, a specialized environment can become paired with our practice so that we associate practicing only with these rarefied settings. It is useful to remember that any form of dependency will ultimately inhibit our access to the formless reality we seek.

An essential element of the paradigm shift is intention. Once we have eliminated effort as the determining factor that moves us forward, we may be left wondering what does move us if not volitional will. Let us explore the question, What is behind the movement of life to complete itself? From a relative level, if we look externally, everything seems to be in movement and appears to be going somewhere. Galaxies are colliding, stars are being born and dying, and the universe is expanding, and it is obvious that it does not need our interference in order to move.

But what moves our hearts to seek completion? It is intention, the impulse to be free. Intention arises from the intelligence of discernment, but when it is captured by the mind, it configures itself into a desire—a wanting that uses time to seek fulfillment. This wanting can be gratified only by an experience. An experience is the outside world meeting the inside world, but it is not the merging of the two worlds. Experiences take on a disproportionate emphasis on the left side of the continuum because on the left side we still live in the view of separation, and experience is the most satisfaction that life can offer.

As we move through the paradigm shift and realize the true nature of self, we release the need to have a special experience. Experience was a way of communicating between things that are separate, but having an experience becomes less important as we realize the intrinsic togetherness of all things. The realization of interconnectedness is *living* fulfillment, not *experiencing* fulfillment. With this understanding there is less energy to pursue desire because desire does not resolve the problem of separation. Now intention returns to the heart and seeks fulfillment from the living reality of nonseparation.

Each of these issues needs to be fleshed out in more detail by each practitioner, but the point here is that there is a way forward that is in alliance with the freedom pointed to by the Buddha, as long as it is aligned with the paradigm of nonseparation. But the applications of practice must meet the challenge of that alignment on *all* fronts and in all actions of body, speech, and mind. This alignment may seem to take a long time because we can live in accordance with nonseparation in body and speech but not in action, or in action but not in thought, or any faltering combination. But if any step within the Eightfold Path is out of kilter, the light of freedom is refracted back into duplicity, and freedom is lost.

We are now moving through the paradigm shift and beginning to understand the principles on which this shift rests and the applications necessary to perfectly support all movement forward along this pathway. It is crucial that all applications work to integrate our lives within these principles so that there is an effortless transformation *into* the path we are traversing. We become the pathway and no longer practice in order to move somewhere or get something but to live the principle of the perfection that is the moment.

In this next section we will refine our applications to those that point directly at the nature of nonseparation, staying within the principles as outlined in the earlier chapters. These inquiries are examples of the active discernment described in chapter 9. These applications not only provide the optimum environment for the paradigm shift to occur by encouraging the formless forward but can also deepen the understanding of that shift once it does occur.

Not This, Not That

The key principle within all authentic spiritual continua is allowing phenomena to return to their essence through noninterference. Our applications, the techniques and methods we use to practice, must follow that principle throughout active and passive discernment. As explained earlier, passive discernment is allowing the object to return to emptiness by leaving it alone, which allows it to reveal its intrinsic nature. Active discernment is the engaged and curious exploration of an experience until it is thoroughly understood to be empty. If we find ourselves fixed within a narrative about something or someone, active discernment reveals our resistance until we finally surrender the narrative into silence. Both passive and active discernment end in stillness, which is the final result of all inquiry.

A technique that can be very useful in moving us toward stillness is a practice used in many traditions, but originating in the Hindu tradition, called *neti, neti,* "not this, not that."[1] This is a deliberate engagement of active discernment that looks at each area of our inward process until it is seen to be something other than we had initially thought it was. An early teacher of mine, Nisargadatta Maharaj, used a variation of this method for abiding in formless awareness. He would have his students question and release everything that was insubstantial and impermanent until we understood that anything in movement could not be our true nature because it was becoming something else. Whatever content the mind contained was negated (not this, not that) until we were left with what he called the "I AM," the very source of stillness and aliveness. He had us dismissing everything that was not the quintessential essence of being. Through a continuous systematic refusal to identify with any aspect of the mind by simply releasing it as secondary and returning to our sole expression of existence, we backed our way into formless awareness. This fundamental "I AM(ness)" is called by several names, including the formless, formless awareness, aliveness, presence, or simply awareness, but all the names point to the one thing that is after everything else is abandoned.

Sit down in a quiet setting and ask what the source of your aliveness is. As you do so, set the intention to discover the essence of being and release everything that is secondary to that search. The first object that needs your experiential scrutiny is your body. You have a body, but is it your essence? Feel the physical form and ask whether this is where aliveness dwells. It is obvious you could lose body parts and still be fully alive. Does aliveness reside in the mind? See if you can experientially find it in the mind. Sense whether your aliveness come from your thoughts, emotions, or any other mental formation. Does your essence depend upon any of these? Obviously it does not, because you are still fully alive even when your mind is quiet. Experience that fact. Does your essence reside in your personal story? Would you still be fully alive if you had amnesia? This is not an intellectual game but an experiential realization of what is primary to life. What is left when you have eliminated all the forms that you have identified as your life? What sees, smells, hears, and cognizes but is itself not the sight, smell, sound, or thought?

As this process continues and we sense a formlessness that surrounds form but is itself not a formation, we find that formless awareness is inseparable from aliveness. But even here we sense that formless awareness is but the first emanation of (not from) something irreducibly dark and deeply unknowable. Like looking back into a blackened cavern, we sense the ineffable unconditioned mystery that is. We sense the immeasurable, and we are but the thin film of a soap bubble that holds all of creation and precreation within it. This unknowable holds the answer to the question, What was there before, during, and after the Big Bang.[2]

Formless awareness is the first expression of the unconditioned and is the origin of the felt sense of aliveness. Form is composed of the formless, and out of formless awareness arises form. The senses are then created from form and bring forth the raw data that imprints upon our mind, and our mind reconfigures the data according to memory, belief, and expectations and manifests the world as we know it. Everything is created within the unconditioned well of being, forced into form through the attention we give it. Like a thought that dissolves when unattended, so, too, form cannot be maintained except through mental investment.

Form appears and disappears continually before out eyes. We call this coming and going impermanence, but nothing in its essence could ever change or fall away, be lost, born, or die. It is only the appearances that have altered. It is all different presentations of the unconditioned, which is the seat of aliveness and forever still.

An idea is placed over that aliveness and the sense of self deadens it with time and meaning, but even a concept, when seen within formless awareness, remains alive. The formless holds everything within its aliveness, and appearance is the mental display of that aliveness. Our spiritual work is to confirm the aliveness within all things by returning all things to the formless. The more we validate the formless source of aliveness, the less we are enamored by appearances.

We attempt to make appearances more important than the aliveness that supports the appearances, but the mental images cannot sustain our interest for long. Why? Because the images—from the view of self—are inanimate. They are not the epicenter, they are not the heart and do not capture the essence of life, and therefore they are peripheral to everything. They are literally an afterthought to creation.

The appearances of mind form our sense of self along with the world and provide enough distraction to arrest a deeper inquiry into the nature of conditioning. Once we realize the sense of self is only a diversion from the central issue, our interest and focus around the self begin to wane and we gradually concede our life back to its essence.

THE STORY AND THE STORYTELLER

The next variant of this theme of negating what is not true is the story and the storyteller, both central to the egoic life of separation. There is a specific application that allows the ending of the storyteller through the silencing of the story, but first we have to realize that the story and the storyteller are not separate from each other. The story defines the storyteller.

The story and the storyteller are different perceptions of the same event. One cannot exist without the other, and each fuels the continuance of the other. They arise together by framing the world in terms of a self that is driven by an inward narrative. The narrative contains the current disposition of the self as well as the background data that confirm how the person got there and the forces that have led this person to be what he or she is. The story unfolds chapter after chapter without a clear resolution, however it feels to the storyteller that a final solution is moving toward completion. The story, upon continual retelling, imprints itself on consciousness as an image, a sense of self. The nonresolution of the story translates as an incomplete image of the storyteller, and this drives the storyteller forward narrating more stories.

The stories are often molded around our defense mechanism and are projected externally. We believe we know how external reality is arranged and the forces that are aligned for and against us, and we fabricate a dialogue with reality that confirms our attitudes and assumptions. We begin to question these stories when we see how far the stories stray from the truth of the situation. How, we might ask, did we get from the grimace of a total stranger to the assumption that I am unlovable? We realize the entire illogical sequencing was filler for the narrative, which simply moved in alignment with our current mood and attitude, forming the perfect story to link those events. None of it was true, and all of it was painful.

In response to this pain, we begin to question the most illogical and insane monologues. We start with the absolute conclusions, the ones that allow no alternative to self-damnation. "I will be alone the rest of my life. I will never meet anyone like him," we might say after a breakup with our partner. The emotions conclude these disasters, but with training we can usually bring sufficient discernment to question the emotional statement. We start to wonder how close any of our stories are to the truth. Examining them with discernment shows us they are not close at all. We see our stories create a distorted reality that is warped and twisted to fit our emotional belief systems. The "I" believes in the assumption of its unworthiness and then looks through that assumption at the fact that my partner left me. What else could unworthiness conclude but "I will never find anyone else"? Discernment gives us the option of seeing without the overlay of unworthiness and to deduce that the narrative is false. After a number of story lines are seen as false, we become quieter, the stories become less packaged and continuous, and the sense of self becomes less formed and assured. The storyteller begins to fade away by seeing the falseness of the story.

By holding our story to a very high standard of truth, we cease telling ourselves the lies of our mind. "Is this true?" becomes our guiding principle. We are simultaneously looking at the storyteller with the same rigorous precision: "Am I true?" We discover that we are no truer than the story, since "we" last only as long as the story is being told. We also see that we are dependent upon the image the story is relating for our sense of position. Without the story, "I" have no position, no firm place in the scheme of things. In the moment the mind is quiet we are not, yet afterward we still claim the quiet as our own. "My mind was quiet just now," we might say as we scurry around to find a position. As soon as we have claimed ownership of the quiet (or any self-proclamation), we have generated another story and can feed again—story and self always arising together. After a number of encounters, we tire of both the story and the storyteller. Now, as we feel any movement away from that stillness, any sought desire or fear, we feel it as an imposition on the quiet and immediately cease the story.

Begin this exercise by becoming aware of your exaggerated and often emotionally charged story lines. Look for stories that hold no alternatives, such as "This should not be happening" or "I always . . ." From the quiet of passive discernment, sense whether this is true. Intellectually you may see immediately that this is not true, but emotionally you may be tied to enduring assumptions. Stay with the emotion until it extinguishes itself within discernment. Now ask again, "Is this story true?" Move on to other stories with more subtle beliefs and expose them to the living truth of passive discernment. What self-assumptions seem to make the story true? Sense yourself as the story of yourself. Look backward into your consciousness and see if there is any other you but the story of you. And finally, is that story of you true?

SEEING THE FALSE AS THE FALSE

We will review one final application that is in widespread use in Buddhist meditation though rarely pushed to its ultimate conclusion.

This is a very similar technique to "not this, not that," described earlier, though "seeing the false as the false" springs from the formal Buddhist practice of bare attention to mind and body, while the former is often developed through active discernment and inquiry. Like all the applications mentioned, the point is to encourage consciousness to cross over from the limited perspective of the consensus paradigm toward the limitless reach of its potential. We can do this by seeing the false as the false, which is meant to reveal what is both true and beyond definition. Through this method we remove everything that is circumscribed, and that reveals what is limitless.

The Buddha speaks about this application of seeing the false as the false in the Sutta-Nippāta as follows: ". . . what most [people] think of as truth, the [person] of wisdom sees clearly . . . as false. What the [ignorant person] thinks of as false, the [person of wisdom] sees as true." He continues, "[the ignorant person] sees substance in what is insubstantial [because] they [attempt to create themselves] in what is insubstantial. But whatever be the phenomenon through which they think of seeking their true identity, it turns out to be transitory. It becomes false . . . .[3]

Buddhist meditation practices attempt to find what is authentically true by closely scrutinizing every aspect of the mind and body experience. By stabilizing our attention, we develop a tool of observation called bare attention. Bare attention is developed by learning to be aware of an experience without an overlay of thoughts. Usually the experience and the discursive thinking overlap, so we do not know whether we are experiencing what is truly there or thinking about what is there. Bare attention sorts through this confusion by cleaning up our observation.

A clean and bare attention is focused on the activities of the mind and body. The point of the practice is to see whether the mind and body are what we have believed them to be. For instance, most of us have strongly identified with our bodies, but under closer scrutiny the body appears to be an object separate from "me." Physical sensations when seen without an identifying image do not form a recognizable shape. The shape of "body" is formed by ideas we bring to those physical sensations. The ideas we bring to an experience shape that experience to those beliefs. When we look at the mind through this insight, the mind is revealed to be very different from what we had initially believed. Looking closely at the mind, we see no ownership, no "I" other than the thought-of "I." The sense data are not even cohesively arranged until the mind coordinates the data to meet its view and expectations. It dawns on us that we are forming the world and the sense of self within our minds moment after moment out of the raw data from the senses that are strung together by organized thoughts.

One of the first revelations is that our reactions create the sense of separation. Experiences are believed as belonging to us only when we struggle with their appearance. The more we react to our inward world of thoughts and ideas, the more separate we feel from those experiences, and the world moves away from us. Conversely, the more relaxed and allowing we are with those thoughts and emotions, the more the world unifies the subject and the object. We discover we can arrest the reactivity by simply surrendering our commentary.

As we repetitively observe the mind, another revelation regarding our identification with thoughts and emotions dawns on us. We cannot be the experience we perceive. To see something objectively, meaning outside us, suggests that we cannot *be* that object in the same moment, and we are able to see everything of the mind objectively. This means we are not our thoughts, emotions, states of mind, physical sensations, or sense data. These have all been falsely represented as I, me, or mine. This insight weakens the identification we have with the mind.

Even the sense of self, the image of "me," can be perceived as an object of awareness. This revelation shook me when I experienced it years ago. I was living at a meditation center for a few years doing intensive retreating, and my practice began to bear the fruits of my sincerity. I began to observe the emptiness of all phenomena. At first directly encountering the Buddha's words about the nature of experience was exciting and joyful, but soon the sense of self fell under the same scrutiny, and I was startled to witness my own empty nature. This revelation was anything but joyful, even though intellectually

I knew selflessness to be the cornerstone of the Buddha's teaching. I felt that I had now wandered too far from home and could no longer return and was not at all sure I wanted to stay within this new frame of reference. I am not being overly dramatic when I say I sank into a period of intense grief, feeling I had lost myself for good.

As my own example illustrates, the revelation of what is false can be devastating when we have assumed its truth throughout our life. We can get a sense of this loss when we count on someone or something very important to be present and the person or thing is nowhere to be found. Since the spiritual journey is believing we are one thing, and wisdom showing us we are another, the whole journey can be wrought with grief as we continually release the form we thought we were.

J. Krishnamurti once said, "The understanding of the false is the discovery of the true."[4] What occurs through the systematic searching for our identity is a growing acknowledgment that we are not going to find ourselves. Between the understanding of the false and the discovery of the true is often a tortured time that Saint John of the Cross called the dark night of the soul. The dark night is the knowing we are not who we have taken ourselves to be yet not seeing any resolution to this confusion. This phase of the pathway is very important and cannot be hurried. The mind is attempting to relocate its origin and find another embodiment, and it cannot. After much searching, it comes to rest within this confusion by giving up all attempts to discover or recover a truer self. This is one reason it is important not to claim a truer self (Self with a capital S) beyond seeing the false self. The mind in its subtle desire for continuance would love a new and more expansive home, and if it can claim more territory within its new definition (I am all things), so much the better.

Now the paradigm shifts to formless awareness. What is seen as false is soon released, and once it is negated, our interest in it is gone, never to return in the same configuration. In the same way we would walk away from a desert mirage knowing it could never give us life-sustaining water, all energy is divested from the illusion of self. The energy that was falsely directed to the self is now free to be redirected toward the formless.

While meditating, observe your thoughts, emotions, and other states of mind. Sense that what you observe cannot be you, or you could not see them objectively. Let that realization season within your consciousness. You cannot possibly be any of the content that happens external to the observation. You are not your thoughts and emotions. You are not anything that arises in mind that can be seen, and everything can be seen. All mental occurrences are independent of you and have their own timing and duration. All of this has been falsely represented as you, and outside of these phenomena, you cannot be found.

Each of these applications is generic enough to be applied to every continuum. These applications are specific to temperament and character, but we can usually find one that resonates sufficiently to serve our needs. If the application feels right, use it; if not, leave it alone. Whether our pathway is from noise to stillness or from suffering to its end, each of us will likely reach a point where one or more of these applications may offer the impetus to navigate through an unconscious blockage.

All of these applications are variations of the overarching question of "Who am I?" that has been at the heart of spiritual transformation since time immemorial. The question may change slightly within each culture, but whatever form the question takes, the practitioner is asked to dive deeply within this penetrating inquiry and surrender to the stillness of its conclusion.

In the next chapter we will use the application of seeing the false as the false to align us with the paradigm shift of the heart. When we see a state of mind as false, it is no longer needed and we willingly let it go. This letting-go process that encompasses much of our pathway is renunciation, and we will now explore its implications and where it eventually leads.

12

A Paradigm's Shift toward the Heart

The minute I heard my first love story
I started looking for you, not knowing
how blind that was.
Lovers don't finally meet somewhere.
They're in each other all along.

—RUMI

Exploring the false as the false brings up the issue of renunciation, which I will define as releasing what is no longer needed. When we realize that an image is not an accurate depiction of the reality it is supposed to represent, we surrender the image and the accompanying story and feel the new expansiveness. Unfortunately, our culture has made renunciation into an austerity rather than a virtue, a contraction rather than a growth. The word has the negative connotation of self-deprivation and is therefore counter to our definition of success. It conjures up pictures of hermits, recluses, and darkened monasteries where the inhabitants have forsaken the world's pleasures in favor of isolation. Though this definition in special cases may have some merit, this is not how the word is being used in this book.

What does renunciation have to do with the Buddha's teaching on freedom and happiness? The Buddha, reflecting upon this very topic, said, "Even I myself, before my awakening, when I was still an unawakened Bodhisattva, thought: 'Renunciation is good. Seclusion is good.' But my heart didn't leap up at renunciation, didn't grow confident, steadfast, or firm, seeing it as peace. The thought occurred to me: 'What is the cause, what is the reason, why my heart doesn't leap up at renunciation, doesn't grow confident, steadfast, or firm, seeing it as peace?' Then the thought occurred to me: 'I haven't seen the drawback of sensual pleasures.'"[1]

The Buddha is saying that early in his practice, though renunciation sounded like a good way to proceed, he was not eager to release the world. He concluded that he had not thoroughly understood the limitations of worldly pursuits, and his desires were still active. Experiencing the limits of form is a good place for all of us to start. Applying renunciation before we have understood the limitations of desire will create an aversive reaction to the desire, as if we should not be having the desire. Forming a "should" or "should not" means we are not ready to release it. Renunciation is not a turning away but a natural letting go once something is thoroughly understood.

As mentioned in earlier sections of this book, the psychic energy needed to fix mental objects and invest them with desire prohibits us from sensing formless presence. Since the entire spiritual path is to do just that, we use renunciation to reverse this fixing process. When our minds no longer relish separation, the energy withdraws from objects and returns to the unifying source of life.

Renunciation now takes on a very different meaning from holding ourselves in restraint. When we realize the payoff of pleasure is not worth the pain of securing and protecting that pleasure, we renounce the narrative that binds us to that search. We are not turning away or pulling back but simply releasing the false story that keeps us recycling back into a pursuit that is ultimately unrewarding. Renunciation is the understanding that life can be lived only within the present and that desire is unfulfilling because it denies the present in favor of the future. Once this is understood, we are ready to face the forces of mind that enslaved us to time.

When I was young I owned a viewfinder that offered a series of pictures, usually of an outdoor park, on a single round card. I would place the card in the viewfinder, and with each press of the finger a new picture would move in front of the lens. The pictures would carry me to locations I had never been to but had always wanted to see. This imaginative journey was the next best thing to being there in person.

The mind depicts images and infuses them with stories similar to that circular series of pictures. Each state of mind captures a complete scene unto itself with its own mood, attitude, belief system, self-assumptions, and destination. Each state has a language and disposition all of its own, and each mental picture holds us within its spell of truth despite the fact that we may have experienced the opposite mood earlier in the day. All are tied together within the general narrative of our lives and somehow make temporal cohesive sense when viewed through the lens of the person who is identified with his or her mood. It is an absolute wonder that all of this coherent organization has been formed through the firing of billions of individual neurons that are seemingly unrelated.

At this point renunciation becomes very important. We begin to recognize that each separate frame of mind says nothing about the underlying "card" it is printed upon and cannot possibly be a true depiction of reality even on the most superficial level. The mind state creates a story, the story holds a mood, and the mood validates a self-image that believes in a series of assumptions that reinforce the state of mind. This circular trance of thoughts starts falling apart when any component of that process is questioned and discerned by awareness. It is seen and exposed as false from beginning to end, and because it is untrue, the state of mind is released from the words that distorted it. Once the words are renounced, the state dissolves and formless awareness appears. This in a nutshell is the essence of the spiritual journey.

How true can a mood be when it lives within a sequence of other moods that contradict each other? Write down the moods that arise during a single day with a brief description of the truth they contain. For example, "I am feeling really clear, buoyant, and alive." And thirty minutes later, after a disagreement with a friend: "I feel deflated and depressed. I am not very likeable." Notice how absolute and complete each state of mind takes itself within that frame of reference: "This is really what I am!" Look over your list and see how contradictory the moods are. Ask whether this mood represents anything more than the relative state of your mind, has anything to do with reality, or defines you in any possible way. A deeper inquiry is to examine what embraces all of those states of mind as they move through consciousness. What is the card that holds each picture in the viewfinder? What surrounds them and knows that they are even occurring? To move beyond the moods, you have to separate the story from the emotions the story asserts. Simply let awareness be present to the state of mind by seeing the narrative as a falsification of reality. Everything moves forward when we have seen the false as the false.

When we eliminate everything that is false within the consensus paradigm, we arrive in nonseparation. All we have done to enter this paradigm is negated the mind's perception of separation and all the accompanying logic associated with that false idea. By seeing the false as the false, we now allow reality to shine forth free of mental constraints. A crucial point is that the reality of nonseparation lies within the false perception of separation and is not a different perception. We have organized perception in a false way by assuming a stance (me) within it that is incorrect.

The path of renunciation is wonderfully expressed in the following sutta:

The Venerable Anuruddha went to the Venerable Sariputta and stated, "By means of the divine eye, purified and surpassing the human, I see the thousand-fold cosmos. My energy is aroused and unsluggish, my mindfulness is established and unshaken, my body is calm and unaroused, and my mind is concentrated and single pointed. And yet my mind is not released from the outflows through lack of clinging.

Sariputta answers, "My friend, when the thought occurs to you, 'by means of the divine eye, purified and surpassing the human, I see the thousand-fold cosmos,' that is coming from conceit. When the thought occurs to you, 'my energy is aroused and unsluggish, my mindfulness is established and unshaken, my body is calm and unperturbed, my mind is concentrated and single pointed,' that is related to your restlessness. When the thought occurs to you, 'And yet my mind is not released from the outflows through lack of clinging,' that is coming from your anxiety. It would be well if you abandoned these three qualities and directed your mind to the Deathless." So after that, Venerable Anuruddha abandoned those three qualities and directed his mind toward the Deathless and attained the final goal.[2]

What I appreciate about this sutta is that despite the extraordinary powers already attained by Anuruddha, he had not yet switched paradigms. Sariputta simply redefined his confusion regarding his lack of attainment and suggested that he release himself from his binding narrative of conceit, agitation, and fear. In essence, Anuruddha simply freed himself from a set of self-assumptions that had kept him entrapped. Sariputta then suggested a change of perspective rather than a new perception, replacing the self-centered focus around his attainments with a centerless refocusing on the formless. All Anuruddha had to do was to shift his perceptions so they became more inclusive. Anuruddha had much to surrender, since the forms he focused on were "exalted, purified, and unsurpassed." Perhaps we, less lofty practitioners, are fortunate to have taken a more mundane route.

Sariputta is not suggesting further mental development or offsetting the conceit, restlessness, and fear with other mental factors.

He seems to be suggesting forgoing the reactivity, leaving form alone, and allowing awareness to arise naturally around the forms. From here there is no "me" that is in trouble and no division between inside and outside the mind. The paradigm shifts for Anuruddha when he follows these very simple instructions.

Renunciation is the natural movement of the heart toward simplicity, and this is accomplished by releasing everything that is nonessential. By seeing all forms of identification as burdensome and untrue, we clear away much of the commentary and chatter that validates the consensus paradigm. New areas of our consciousness may now begin to appear that were obstructed by our narrative. For example, when we renounce self-indulgence, kindness appears. We do not have to cultivate kindness or train ourselves to be kind; it just appears when there is less self-centeredness. We might say that kindness becomes available when we get out of the way. Kindness was constrained within the consensus paradigm by our self-image, which distorts kindness like water refracts light.

FREEING THE HEART

The heart, as I am using the term, is formless awareness. I call formless awareness the heart to distinguish it from the mind, which is the seat of our narrative. The heart is the center of stillness and is associated with qualities such as patience, kindness, love, compassion, and generosity that are the terrain of the new paradigm. The heart holds the mind within it, but the heart cannot easily express itself within the cacophony of the mental noise. As we move along our continuum and get quieter, the mind goes into abeyance and qualities of the heart start expressing themselves through the stillness. This happens naturally, almost organically, when we are willing to see how the mental language we are using distorts love.

The new paradigm of the heart is the living expression of the wise view of interconnectedness that directs our continuum. The living reality of interconnectedness takes hold proportional to our willingness to see the falseness of self-centered living. Love is how life expresses itself within the paradigm of nonseparation. When separation ends, what is left to contest? The absence of dispute is the presence of love. Within the stillness, the newly awakened unified mind displays the full array of heart qualities.

Since renunciation is the entry point of the heart, the word *renunciation* inserts an uncomfortable question into our lives. Does our lifestyle take us away from what is important? Are we trying to be spiritual but give up nothing in return? If our intention is to shift paradigms, then we have to focus on seeing the false as the false and let our lifestyle form around that understanding. It is a complete surrender, a total release from the consensus paradigm into the new. What this means in practical terms is that all the noise we use to substantiate the consensus paradigm ends and the newly acquired stillness evolves consciousness into a completely new appearance. What was once full becomes empty, what was separate now becomes unified, and what was mind now becomes heart. Nothing changes, yet everything is changed.

Love exists because everything has always been unified. Love is not something that comes into being through the efforts of the individual consciousness. The best an individual can do is awaken to the existence of love that manifests when a small breach occurs in egoic consciousness. Often love is accessed during a moment of awe and stillness, a very common occurrence within ordinary living situations. When we see a startling sunset or enjoy the smell of a fragrant rose, we often awaken to a moment of tenderness and love. The quiet of our momentary rapture receives the love from the open heart, but the obstructing mind quickly moves on to more productive activities by relegating the experience to memory and reinitiating our narrative.

We have to open the door to love to let it in and receive it as we would a welcome guest. We cannot be preoccupied with other tasks and expect love to find us. Our daily chores of living often interrupt this receptive nature of love. It is possible to find love while accomplishing these tasks, but only if love takes precedence over the completion of the task. If the task is more important, then love will be excluded from the activity. To lead with love, attempt to understand the situation before acting upon it. For example, if you are a parent and return home to find your living room in disarray because of children's activities, there are two possible ways of responding. The first is to demand immediately that your children clean up the space. The second calls forth love by first pausing and feeling the parental love for your child before addressing the problem. The clutter is gone either way, but the effect on the child is vastly different.

These exposures to love are but a few of the many occasions throughout the day where the sense of self goes into abeyance and selflessness shines forth through the formless. As mentioned before, the sense of self claims ownership of those brief openings of the heart, thereby hiding the true source of the experience. "I felt such awe this morning while watching the sunrise; my whole mind was quiet." In the end we never acknowledge our absence, only our presence, distorting the actual origins of life. Years into our spiritual practice we may feel so distant from the emptiness that surrounds us that we unconsciously avoid it, when in fact emptiness infiltrates every pore of our body.

The heart also reveals itself repeatedly during moments of creativity. The dictionary defines creativity as "the use of imagination or original ideas," but that definition is what happens *after* the creative moment. It is impossible for the conditioned mind to think something original. It is discerning awareness that sees in a novel way, and when we look closely, we see that the actual act of creation is completely still, without thought. The absence of thought allows awareness to see, free from all constraints, but soon after, the mind possesses the creative moment and thinks about what just occurred. The person having the creative moment then claims ownership by believing he or she used his or her imagination to come to this insight, when the person was not even in the picture when creativity occurred.

The mind continually claims responsibility for everything the heart brings forth, as though it senses the limitation of its own range. Once the mind takes possession of an attribute of the heart, it distorts that quality by bending the experience through the lens of self. The self adds not only ownership to the experience but also a barrage of conditioning, memory, and words that warp the entire experience within its narrative. The experience now becomes so laden with personal noise it is almost unrecognizable as an emanation of the heart.

When the heart falls under the mind's influence, the mind organizes the formless nature of the heart into discrete qualities like generosity, compassion, and virtue, depending upon the context in which the formless appears. The heart actually does not hold attributes, but from the eye of the mind, "I" am expressing a compassionate response toward this person in pain. The heart, in this example, took the form of compassion when confronted by the suffering of another. We say that the heart "contains" compassion, but the heart holds only formless awareness, and formless awareness expresses itself in the form of compassion within the appropriate situation. The mind creates all the words we give the particular expression of consciousness.

We will look at three simple expressions of the heart and witness how formless awareness takes the proper shape necessary to express itself within each situation.

Love

Love in its truest sense does not look or feel like the love of romance or the giddiness of exhilaration. Does your body love your leg? The leg is part of the body and included within its totality, but there is no glowing amorous flirtation between the two. The body will support the leg, use it skillfully, remain connected, and care about it when it is injured, but it will not separate the leg out from the rest of itself for special consideration or privileged treatment. Love is simply the acknowledgment of unity and nonseparation.

Love is the first emanation when formless awareness touches form. Love in its purest form is warmheartedness, the simple joy of contact. It is as if formless awareness recognizes itself within the contact and responds with love. In this sense formless awareness is love and cannot be differentiated from love. The mind pulls the two apart when it claims to be "in love." When love is something we are "in," it becomes an object that is quantifiable. We feel separate from love, so we feel a need for it. "How much love do I have? Do I need more? How do I get it?" We yearn for the object or person that stimulates our love, not for love itself. The form love takes becomes more important than the love expressed.

Love is formless awareness, but the formless is invisible to the mind, so we look for love within objects. Mistrusting that love is in us, we look for proof of its existence, but all we ever see are the fruits of love. We see what love has accomplished, built, or produced, but love itself cannot be found within these statues, poems, or symphonies. We may attempt to bring the love we have for these objects closer to us by owning them or by copying their design, but the more we attempt to mimic the expressions of love, the further we stray from the love that created them.

We sense the power within love as something beyond us, something potent and unifying, but we do not know what it is or how to access it. We are often uncertain whether it is love or desire we are feeling. Love and desire get confused because both can arise together, as when sexual attraction becomes entangled with appreciation for the person. We can also desire the feelings of love, which creates further confusion. In reality the difference between the two is very clear, with love free of any possessiveness and desire defined by wanting to possess.

Sense the difference between desire and love. Desire attempts to bond by drawing something into your sphere of influence. Love does not try to possess but allows everything to pass through without distortion. Look at the loved objects in your life and see if you are attempting to possess them in any way. See whether love or desire comes forward when you allow something to be what it is without qualification. Desire makes demands on your partner to be the person you want him or her to be, but love accepts the person as he or she is. Feel the seeds of love within your personal relationships, and see how much you obscure real love through judgments stemming from desires.

When we first begin on the left side of our continuum, we usually have no idea what selfless love is. We begin by working with self-love, and eventually we discover love without self. We practice kindness and self-appreciation as left-sided preparation for right-sided formless love. We examine the mental obstructions that prevent us from making intimate contact and see them as false persuasions of the past. At some point fear blocks further progress, and we are unable to release our boundaries and make the genuine contact necessary for formless love. We would like proof that we will be safe without those boundaries before we trust, but trust must come before love. We must trust love more than we fear exposure.

The principle of renunciation states that we have to let go before we can receive, and love is no exception. No matter how much we prepare for love, how much we want it, proclaim it, and defend it, there is still the leap that is necessary for abiding within it. Trust is the bottom line for moving to the right side of the pathway, and trust has no real preparation. This leap of faith is required on all continua and settles in our heart as a certainty that we cannot continue to live under the laws of separation. When we sense that life is simply not worth living without love, we leap.

Appreciation

Appreciation manifests from formless awareness when there is the recognition of good-heartedness and is most easily accessed through tenderness, seeing the gentle side of life. In this unguarded softness, the heart is open and available, responding with appreciation when it sees uplifting qualities.

Sometimes people with early childhood scarring complain that they are unable to feel their emotions. We all have emotions, but some of us have learned to ignore them and turn away. I often suggest that those who ignore their emotions awaken to their emotional life through tenderness: looking around until something stirs their humanity, then resting their gaze quietly upon that. When they begin to experience a felt sense of beauty, they will also feel tender, open, and peaceful. Their emotions will begin to percolate through this process, and appreciation will arise within that tenderness. Appreciation is the quiet thank-you of the heart as it opens across the landscape.

Appreciation, gratitude, and thankfulness fill dharma practice from beginning to end. The heart just opens with a deep bow and a gentle acknowledgment of the greatest gift possible. The dharma demands everything from us and in return exposes our deepest vulnerabilities. When we feel the benefits of surrendering our image, we respond with an immense outpouring of gratitude. We realize this is a journey of love feeding upon love.

Appreciation is an often-overlooked treasure of the heart because the mind can contaminate the emotion so quickly. Appreciation can change into obligation and indebtedness by placing pressure on us to live up to the gratitude we feel, or we can burden ourselves with a moral imperative to pay back the debt. We may also give our power away to the person we feel gratitude toward and become submissive in his or her presence. But appreciation itself does not hold any of these features. Like all manifestations of the heart, appreciation is the simple acknowledgment of the intimate connection at hand. With gratitude we receive and from appreciation we act.

Look up from this book and pause. Let the fullness of life come in, with all the senses alive and awake. For this brief period of time there is nothing worth thinking about. Let your gaze light upon a tender experience, perhaps a spider spinning a web or the soft rustling of leaves blown by the breeze. Let your mind be soft and your heart relaxed, and feel the accompanying warmth that heralds appreciation. When there is awareness and the sensitivity of refined attention, appreciation is present.

Generosity

The attribute of generosity when filtered through the mind becomes owned and possessed by the sense of self. Once it arrives within the self's frame of reference, time, distance, and separation form the constructs under which it operates. When left alone, life establishes equilibrium; form flows from abundance to scarcity in the natural course of life's movement. As we enter the right side of our pathway, life becomes less self-centered and is replaced with a genuine care for others. The natural movement of material goods from formless awareness is from those who have to those who need, but when guarded by the forces of self, that same flow becomes arrested by personal possessiveness. We start giving with pride or regret. "I should be giving more . . . or less." While formless awareness moves effortlessly to fill the vacuum, the sense of self personally ponders the implications of the gifts. The image of self interrupts what was once an organic and spontaneous movement of energy by bringing in comparative giving. "How much am I giving related to others? Do they deserve this gift?"

The constraints on our ability to give are an important attribute of generosity and allow the state of generosity to be held within the practical realities of our lives. We cannot give away everything simply because our heart feels the pain of the world. Generosity considers the giver as well as the receiver. We can see how both the personal and impersonal sides of all issues of the heart need to be considered to work harmoniously in the world. Both form and formlessness work together to inform our lives, all within an actively engaged heart.

> Generosity is sharing some part of yourself with another. It could be time, attention, money, and so forth. It contains a no as well as a yes. The tension between the two allows you to care for yourself as you open to selflessness. Extend too far in one direction and you find yourself tight, self-enclosed, and contracted; too far in the opposite direction and you overextend and ignore the signs to stay within yourself. Work with this tension and explore both the yes and the no. A good direction for investigation is giving without regret. Too little or too much and there is a psychological tightening. How do this yes and no work in conjunction with the discerning awareness mentioned in chapter 9?

The mistake we usually make is to use the egoic state to determine the proportionality of giving. How much should I give and how much should I retain is a question better left to discernment than to self-centeredness. We often give from feeling disadvantaged, a kind of inward poverty that uses generosity to compensate for the sense of self-deficiency. Since only the symptoms of the pain, not the pain itself, are being addressed, the act of giving will not sufficiently address the problem. Though giving will give us a temporary uplift, it is a little like going on a shopping spree to offset feelings of despair. The despair will return as soon as the excitement of the shopping wears off.

This is an important point regarding all qualities of the heart. All attributes of the heart, such as generosity and kindness, usually bring forth highly regarded emotions such as intense feelings of goodness and joy. These are very uplifting emotions—especially when we have labored under our assumptions of unworthiness—and become an attractive alternative to seeing our unresolved pain. We can use these qualities to offset the negative emotions associated with our self-beliefs and lean on these attributes to protect us from our self-assumptions. We can become addicted to the highs of generosity and find ourselves needing the homeless, needing the destitute, the impoverished, and the deprived for a spell of relief from our pain.

There is a subtle mutual exploitation that occurs within all expressions of dependency. Dependency does not foster equality. Ultimately we give because someone is in need of what we have, not because the person is deficient is some way. When we are dependent upon someone being needy, we are working out of pity rather than generosity. Pity is a facsimile of compassion and generosity but is an egoic state of mind. Generosity is among equals. Subliminally we can pass on a message of inequality to those we help, diminishing them as human beings. We can hold them within a fixed perspective and refuse to allow the needy to grow beyond their need for us, because if they did, we would have no escape from our inadequacy.

One of the greatest gifts we offer is the gift of our time and attention. Time feels like the ultimate gift because of our limited time on earth. We have only so much of it before we die, so we try to conserve it like other limited commodities. We try to "save" time and avoid "wasting" time and attempt to dispense it with the utmost care. We think the proper way to relate to time is to be productive and busy, which then convinces us we did something useful within the time allowed. Form validates its existence by creating more form, and the formation of the sense of self is no different. We know we exist by producing something that we can see, hear, taste, touch, smell, or think about. Like a dog marking a tree to express his place within the neighborhood, we produce something to confirm our existence and give that existence a sense of meaning. We do this not only for the egoic reason of expressing our worth through the value of our productions but also because we hold an unconscious doubt about the reality of our existence. Production is our paper trail that proves we are alive and have a useful impact on life.

Being generous with our attention is not productive because it does not accomplish anything tangible. It does not dig a ditch or pay

the bills. All it does is connect. Our culture is so focused on the utility of what we do, on the forms we produce, that we give only passive credibility to formless activities such as listening, paying
attention, expressing gratitude, and being kind. In truth many of us
think these activities take us away from the immediate challenges
that need to be surmounted. We like people who are kind but may
hold a quiet opinion that such behavior is rather useless.

All of us have had the experience of being absorbed in someone's attention. We sense the healing within the attention, but we
cannot quantify it or prove its worth. The afterglow is that we feel
more complete and whole, as if we were held through the entire
conversation. When we offer our entire attention, we enter formless
presence and sanction the connection in ways that form is incapable
of doing. We authenticate the person who is speaking and say, in effect, you are worth my time and therefore worth being the person
you are. It is a validation for being an essential part of the world, a
world that frequently attempts to negate our place within it.

The paradigm of the formless heart works completely contrary
to consensus reality. It is not based on time, productivity, utility, or
accomplishment. Attention does not express its generosity in orthodox terms. Attention just hears, responds appropriately, holds without judgment, and moves on. Nothing special happens unless you
are the receiver of the attention. If you are, you feel special, as if you
were speaking to your best friend, who has all the time in the world
to listen. Attention serves to draw us in to the dimension of generosity, out beyond the world of separation.

SHIFTING TO THE HEART

The reason I am stressing the heart as a destination of the paradigm
shift is that the heart feels more welcoming, to most people, than the
word *emptiness*. They are synonyms, but in a predominantly Christian culture, where the heart of Christ is the symbol for much of our
religious activities, the word *heart* works in our favor. Many spiritual
people in our culture would like to be a loving somebody but are

hesitant to journey on a path to be a loving nobody. So we move slowly in conjunction with our spiritual continuum, freeing awareness until it consumes the image of us into love. We have to love ourselves so deeply we no longer want to suffer and are willing to give up even ourselves to end the suffering.

Most of us who enter the spiritual journey acknowledge the benefits of becoming a kinder and more sensitive person, but few of us realize that the person we are forming will eventually stand in the way of that very kindness. Every person on an authentic spiritual pathway will have to deal with this paradox at some point. We will all have to decide whether to deviate our journey away from this understanding or move directly through it, and that will force us to question the direction we really want to go. Do we want to stay within the known paradigm of separation and temper its coarseness by softening our character or switch paradigms and surrender our identity? This is perhaps the most perplexing spiritual deliberation we will ever have and ultimately is best settled through love.

Interestingly enough, this question is never really answered intellectually before it dissolves in the love of the truth. The beauty of the entire spiritual journey is that we never force any resolve. The journey from beginning to end is about learning our way, never pushing our way, through the process. Learning is synonymous with loving. When we learn, we are taking the subject in without judgment and receiving the information in its entirety. There is an intimate connection between the learner and the learned, and the two are not separate from each other. The internal narrative about what we are learning pulls us back from accepting fully what is being offered. When we intercede in the process, we are imposing our ideas upon the learning and have therefore stopped learning. As our spiritual journey gains momentum, we see this effect and train ourselves to stop believing in the thoughts that interfere with being fully receptive.

We can be as unsure about learning as we are about loving, and both are equally risky. Both expose us to an undefined intimacy. When we forgo our judgments and expose ourselves to new information, a sense of mistrust can ensue. We think that without our judgments we may fall to the dark side and be unable to differentiate what is best for us. Our ideas and opinions define who we are, and opening beyond a certain threshold seems as if we were moving too far and too fast into the selfless paradigm. So the crossroad between sustaining ourselves and opening beyond our self-definition is already at hand, but it is occurring within the love of learning. If we want to learn more, we have to surrender more of ourselves to the cause. If we pull back, we reclaim our self-definition but lose the learning. Love will eventually win over resistance, but the process works more easily if we surrender to the intuitive sense of where we need to go.

Observe the tension between loving and learning. You may have a love for self-knowledge, but learning about yourself opens you beyond your current definitions, and therefore could be risky. But love is endlessly curious and thrives in learning. Where do you resist further learning and close down to love?

Again, trust is indispensible on this journey, and as mentioned in chapter 9, discernment is waiting to dissipate our doubts. Discernment reveals what is beneficial and what is not. Discernment holds intelligence beyond our intellect, but it requires surrendering completely to access it. The only way into this new paradigm is to enter through the selfless door, and the only way we will ever inch our way toward that door is by trusting completely in love.

We now have an organized pathway, a well-defined direction, a passionate intention, and a clear set of principles and applications to begin the paradigm shift. The rationale for the shift is now obvious, as well as the need to align ourselves within the reality of the new paradigm prior to the shift's occurring. The success of all of this hinges on our sincerity, an intangible ally that becomes the sole reason we will move forward through the uncertainty and trepidation that all pathways present. Deep inside, something encourages us forward, and ultimately we are unable to resist its pull. This force does not seem to have a specific material reward; rather, it feels as if we were being pulled toward legitimacy, some sort of cleansing process, where we are washing away the tolls of an imagined life. It feels uncontaminated and spacious, as if we were suddenly born into a vibrant world of color. In the next and final chapter we will explore how to live within this new paradigm of the heart.

13

Living Nonseparation

Erring and erring
we walk the unerring path

—KHENPO TSULTRIM GYAMTSO RINPOCHE

We have now traveled the length of our continuum from beginning to end. We have noted the despairs and delights, the strategies and direction of our pathway, and we have observed that the path is all-consuming. We cannot be speaking from one paradigm and acting from another, holding the view of interconnection as we divide through gossip and complaint. We cannot mix and match according to our conditioned desires and hesitations. Ending the continuum means a total submergence in the heart and calls for a complete realignment from a life we have known into a life that cannot be known.

The journey invites us to give up what we are not but never asks us to become anything other than what we are. We might question the point of a journey that returns us to what we were before we began. What does the universe want from us that it did not already have? We are not being groomed to have a prominent place in the world but to be absolutely ordinary, without any pretension or hyperbole. We are not necessarily going to be leaders or teachers even within our spiritual groups. There is no egoic payoff of pride and power and no membership in an elite enlightened club that deliberates upon the conflicts of humankind. The sky does not part, proclaiming our saintly ways, nor does it give any testimonial acknowledgment of our freedom. This journey is a zero-sum gain, and from the consensus paradigm, that makes it useless if not worthless.

There is just awakening, and awakening does not even feel like home, since home infers a special affection and comfort level. It may not be obvious to others that we have changed at all. People are likely to see us moving through our day pretty much as we always have. We are different, not by what we have gained, but by what we have abandoned. There is no add-on, just raw humanity, the basic composition of living. We do not turn around in paranoia nor look ahead with worry. The moment is all there is for the simple fact that it *is* all there is. The entire journey did nothing but show this irrefutably. There is nothing else but the moment, and there is not even that. The moment is not something we live within because there is nothing outside the moment to give it reference, and there is nothing within the moment to give reference that we are outside it. Everything has always arisen together.

When we invest in conditions, we exist conditionally, arising within the longing for those experiences. We think that if we can get the situation to last, then "we" can last, but that is not the way of life. Life continually melts before our eyes, and we are constantly forced to resurrect a new present as the current moment recedes from view. We drag the fading now into the hope of a lasting future, but when the future arrives, it arrives as the flawed present. We exist now relative to what we want to become and are therefore trapped in time. But time is always within now—where else could it be, where could it go? To end time is to end the thought of anything's arising within another location. When nothing is outside of now, now infinitely expands.

Where does this journey go? It returns us to where we live. We thought our way out of our lives, and now we return to them. We arrive within a spontaneous and thoroughly unique presentation of being. We were never isolated nouns, but now we frolic in the verb of living. Perhaps this is what life wanted from us all along; it wanted us out from under the covers of deception so that full aliveness could enter our veins and offer itself back from whence it came.

Shunryu Suzuki recounts a Zen story called Half-Dipper Bridge in which Dogen Zenji dipped a full ladle of water from a passing stream and after drinking half, returned the rest to the source. Suzuki Roshi says, "When we feel the beauty of the river . . . we intuitively do it in Dogen's way. It is our true nature to do so."[1] So, too, it is our true nature to uncover our deception for no other reason than to recover our beauty and return what remains back to the living source. We pass through enlightenment to full awakening. To abide within our full potential is to be the exact expression of life needed in this moment.

> Do you truly believe you are outside reality? You may experience yourself as being in here and the world out there, but do you believe that is the fact? If you were outside reality looking at it, there would be two realities, the reality of you and the reality of what you are seeing. This makes no sense whatsoever. How could you be outside the only reality there is? This is the perceptual flaw that defines all spiritual journeys.

The Path and the Fruit

The spiritual path must be taken as seriously as we take the perception of separation or we will not work as diligently to understand this distortion as we do to reinforce it. A fully committed spiritual resolve is the only possible energy able to surmount aeons of trance-like thinking. The spiritual path must be embraced with the utmost conviction and resolution of spirit and framed in such a way that it extracts our deepest devotion and faith. It has to take everything from us so there is no possibility of renewing our image, and there has to be sufficient reward to warrant the toll of letting go of the conventional worldview. If the path is too easy, we may clearly overlook its value, and if it is too difficult, without sufficient payoff, we may give up in despair. The path has to be suitably wondrous to hold our attention and amply joyous to encourage us forward.

Even to begin the path, the best of us has to be reawakened. Much of our beauty has been forgotten or neglected. We have long lived within the gravity of our cultural despair, until there is very little resemblance between our original face and the one we see in the mirror. We are called upon to rediscover our beauty, worth, and intrinsic value but will often bypass this opportunity if the cultural and historical image of ourselves is too laden with shame. We will feel unworthy of this transformation and direct our efforts toward the hard labor of penance. But our efforts can turn this around if we are willing to restore our natural ease and well-being and ground ourselves to the earth. From there we can venture out to challenge the distorted assumptions of our childhood that can cripple us unless we give them the attention they deserve.

The spiritual path subsists on paradox and inconsistency because it must feign a direction before it reveals that it goes nowhere. When we concede the point that the destination is of the utmost importance, the landscape shifts and drops out from under our feet. As from a magician's hand, we pursue the appearance of the carrot even as the carrot disappears from view. To persuade us to make the journey, the path has to be disguised as a distance to be covered even when the end of the journey shows us the falsehood of this belief. We work within the braille system, faithfully feeling our way step by step from our present location toward an unknown destination. Once the step is completed, we sense the wisdom of having taken it, only to move beyond that calm assurance with the next uncomfortable step. There is no map or blueprint beyond a set of ill-defined terms such as *wise action* or *wise speech*. These are black-and-white terms that give a general pointing but cannot handle the gray of real-world living. The best we can do is to gather in groups and flounder our way forward. Groups give us a sense of companionship that delights our hearts, but the journey is really one of moving deeply into aloneness.

Inconsistencies flourish. What is right for us in one moment is not in the next, and what is wise for one person utterly fails those who imitate it. The contradictions include a journey that shows us our beauty as it takes the owner of that beauty away. The sense of self is first validated as worthwhile even as it is discredited as untrue, and we have to feel the full confidence and stability of our psychological selves even as we transcend the psychological as empty and story driven. The confusion only grows as we see that real movement is no movement and that to understand anything thoroughly, leaves its absence. All of this sounds like magical hat tricks meant to bewilder our intentions, but it is not. It is as accurate a description as language will allow, and it is up to us to muddle our way toward some sense of truth that holds these incongruities. When these contradictory facts fit our experience, it is a good indication that we are wisely aligned.

The journey entails endless mistakes, the most prominent of which is using our sense of self to advance forward. Everything we do is wrong until we learn how to be still. For the journey to be fulfilled, it must ultimately defeat us. We usually have to be pushed to the point of utter hopelessness, complete disempowerment, and near suicidal despair before we are willing to surrender our image. That is how much we value our thought-based life over reality.

The path could be defined as seeing our conditioned life as a failure, and to move forward we have to somehow find our way out of conditioning. But how do we move when everything we do, including the thought of "me," is conditioned? We make a lot of mistakes—that is what we do. One of the most conspicuous mistakes is weighing in on remembering over forgetting to be conscious. It is not the remembering over the forgetting, it is the weighing in that creates the tension. This switch will not happen just because we now want it. Forgetting will occur until the pattern of pitting ourselves against the unconscious has played itself out and is no longer needed. The understanding that the sense of self is the embodiment of the unconscious quickens this turnaround, but even this repetition of forgetting and remembering needs our patience. Forgetting is as equal a display of the perfection of the universe as remembering is,

and it works in conjunction with remembering to open to the formless awareness beyond both.

These in-and-out-of-awareness movements are not something
that need our struggle, although they do need our understanding.
These seeming lapses of awareness are occurring only from the
mind's point of view because it is selecting thought (form) over the
formless. In that moment we are assuming that thought has more to
offer than awareness. In order for thought not to be grasped, we have
to learn the disadvantages of thinking and the advantages of wakefulness, and that limitation has to be experienced directly, which only
remembering and forgetting can do.

This is just one example of how we learn our way out of conditioning all along the way, and that learning is the unfolding needed
to move our hearts toward completion. We see how we have trained
ourselves to stand in the way of this learning and obscure the information necessary to move forward. We try hard to overcome our
conditioning, and we end up reconditioning our way in the opposite
direction. Whichever way we turn, we condition ourselves further.
When we concede that our egos are useless in our journey to the
unconditioned, we begin to face in the proper direction of freedom.

Absolutes do exist on the path, because there is an unconditioned finality. The unconditioned negates all conditions where
relativity flourishes. The Buddha said it this way, "There is, O
monks, an Unborn, an Unbecome, an Unmade, an Unconditioned;
if, O monks, there were not here this Unborn, Unbecome, Unmade, Unconditioned, there would not here be an escape from the
born, the become, the made, the conditioned. But because there is
an Unborn . . . therefore there is an escape from the born."[2]

We do not like absolute statements because they pen us in without wiggle room. We like our options and choices, but absolutes are
unequivocal, and the dharma is full of these unambiguous statements
of finality. We could say, for instance, that growth is always inclusive, because to withdraw from the slightest detail is the very act of
separation. We could say that every thought must be discerned as
ultimately untrue because imagination thrives within any thought
believed. We could also say that all conditioned things are in transi-

tion, without exception, and because of this truth, everything passes away. We could go on and on, but the point is that this is the reason the dharma requires a total resolution of spirit; the old paradigm returns within a single moment of hesitation, and a single thought believed. The dharma is an all-or-nothing affair of the heart.

What do you know to be absolutely true? First eliminate everything that is not an absolute, which means anything temporal, situational, or impermanent. All forms of knowledge are relative, since they last only as long as the knower exists. The absolute must be outside of time and knowledge. An absolute cannot be discovered using relative methods, since techniques maintain the paradigm of time. How, then, can this be discovered? Start by exploring your dependency on the language of time. Time says there is a distance to be covered, something wrong with you that needs to be fixed, time to be served, and something to be known before you are whole. Drop all ideas about the path and ask whether this language is true. Ask where the self is located now and where it will be when the path is finished.

Each and every dharma truth holds us accountable because it is an absolute. We try in vain to temper the impact by misinterpreting the dharma as relative. We want it to be about our happiness, an easier way to live, and a brighter future, but the dharma does not invest in the relative. The dharma reveals the untruth of the relative, allowing us to pass through it without delay and abide in the unconditioned. It is asking us to look clearly at the relative and not be drawn in by the pleasures of its appearances. Abiding within the absolute while moving through the relative with nothing being denied is the fruit of the dharma. Here is how the Buddha summarizes this process: "So the holy life, bhikkhus, does not have gain, honor, and renown for its benefit, or the attainment of virtue . . . or concentration . . . or knowledge and vision for its benefit. But it is the unshakeable deliverance of the [heart] that is the goal of this holy life, its heartwood, and its end."[3]

The fruit of the dharma is the end of polarities, and the end of polarities is the completion of all skillful means, all practices, and all methods that were used to surmount ignorance. When ignorance is no longer pitted against wisdom, there is nonreferenced ease. This is the shift that so much of this book has been about. We have to extract the "me" from our salvation and prohibit identification with the self's return. Many people can understand selflessness; few can keep the self from meddling its way back in. This is not accomplished by force but through understanding. To understand exactly what the self is is to end the self. Once understood, it assumes its rightful place in our functional lives but never again assumes a place of power and authority. It takes just one polarizing moment that has gone undetected for self-centered living to resume.

Any experience that we believe needs our oversight and effort, such as continuous awareness, will ultimately be the rub that keeps darkness competing against light. The "now I have it; now I don't" mentality is the final tension that keeps struggle alive and the sense of self in place. Any area of spiritual journey where the sense of self still has a role to play will become consumed within the bifurcating divisions of thought. We will never find salvation in form, and any experience that is grasped by thought becomes formed.

Take any idea that has defined your spiritual journey, such as being interconnected, continuously mindful, totally equanimous, or completely spontaneous. You can usually find a quality by noticing any idealization of the end point on your continuum. For instance, if your continuum is from contraction to love, are you pitting contraction against love? Do you see them as opposites, or does love hold contraction? Can you sense how the self reaffirms its place within any opposition? You can now see how all forms of idealism must end, since ideals will always compete with the truth.

The formless is never in competition with form, but form can be in competition with the formless. As soon as we attribute qualities to the formless or make mental reference to it in any way, an edge is created. This sets form and the formless apart, and we begin to lean toward one side or the other. The formless, once grasped by the mind, becomes formed through our ideas about it. The Buddha called the formless the "unborn, the unbecome, the unmade" to keep it out of the reach of ideation. Once the formless is formed, the only way to surmount that edge is to see form and the formless as identical so the mind will not attempt to differentiate. We cannot pretend they are the same; we have to *see* that they are the same. And as mentioned in chapter 10, identical they are. Now the world of form merges with the formless into the unconditioned. The "Dazzling Dark"[4] of the unconditioned is the absolute end of all divisions. The unconditioned gives rise to the formless and the formless gives rise to form, but in the end it is all just appearances, nothing more.

The Buddha said,

So I tell you—Thus shall ye think of all this fleeting world:

A star at dawn, a bubble in a stream,
A flash of lightning in a summer cloud,
A flickering lamp, a phantom, and a dream.[5]

CONVERGENCE

Let us flesh out the details of this convergence a little more. On page 232 is the final diagram, which holds in its essential features a summary of the entire book. The far left side is the beginning of practice, with form confused with the formless, and the far right side is the fruition of practice, with form and the formless merged and understood as identical. As we have learned, most of us begin muddled and confused about where we are headed but tired of the conditioned tension within which we live. The beginning is the realm of practice, and slowly through the use of the methods and techniques, we split form out from the formless so that each can be examined separately from the other without interference. The two are disconnected in order to understand what each is without the influence of the other. We have to examine them sufficiently to understand their essence and how they fit in context within the whole spiritual path.

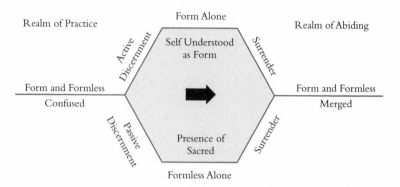

Though it is actually impossible to separate the seeing (formless) from what is being seen (form), it is possible to focus selectively on one and let the other go. As the diagram shows, the method for separating form from formless is active discernment, as described in chapter 9. As spoken about in earlier chapters, we learn to separate noise (form) from stillness (formless) by inquiring into the nature of mind. Form consists of all the objects of mind that can be perceived by our senses. How do these objects arise and what is their true composition? Does form preexist the mind's involvement, or does the mind make form what it is? Through investigating the mind we slowly begin to perceive the true nature of objects, and with that understanding comes the true nature of me, the subject.

We separate the formless from form by allowing form, through passive discernment, to be what it is without adding any thought to its presentation. There is no self-involved effort; we simply allow what is occurring to reveal itself within formless awareness, with our attention on the formless and less on the forms that are arising within it. At this stage, formlessness is understood to be the stillness that holds all form, and the presence of the sacred arises within that spaciousness. The formless is what has given us the capacity to see, hear, smell, taste, touch, and know the activities of mind, though it is not the objects of those sense doors. In the still and formless dimension we have lost time, distance, and separation. The sense of self is understood to be formed and cannot move into the realm of the formless through its volitional effort. All attempts to do so result in the creation of more subtle aspects of form.

Interestingly enough, neither form nor the formless alone can sustain the sense of self. Form without the formless is just shape, thought, and color, and the formless without form is still and unmoving. The sense of self needs the muddled confusion of the two, depicted on the left side of the diagram, to convince itself that it is real, and this becomes clear only after the separation of form and the formless.

Once the two are separated and understood, we can now allow them to return to their original union. When they merge, they do not merge as either/or; they merge inseparably as one and the same. When the moment is abided within, it carries both the translucence of the formless and the functionality of form. We walk through life never believing in one or the other exclusively but living both simultaneously. The Buddha said it this way: "But those beings who, having understood the nature of form, are well established in the formless and free themselves in cessation are the ones who leave death behind them."[6]

Surrender is the only response that allows the mergence of form and the formless. When the sense of self reemerges through identification with words, we surrender our separation and return to formless abiding. When lived, form and the formless are no longer in opposition to each other. When thinking is needed, the formless uses the mind, and thought informs consciousness but no longer directs it. It is tempting to say that the formless holds form, but it does not; they are one and the same. "Form is not other than the formless or the formless other than form."[7] They merge indistinguishable because the act of surrender is the release of all polarities, and it was only the mind that differentiated the two.

Let us walk through this diagram with a concrete example: Many of us are upset with this country's denial of climate change, and some deeply spirited people are so outraged by this denial that they cannot or will not allow their minds to work toward a more balanced perspective. We are now at the far left side of this diagram within the muddle and confusion of form (outrage) and simultaneously holding a deep love for the environment (formless). At this point love and its object are indistinguishably blurred together. Any threat to the object is a threat to love, followed by a reaction from the sense of self. We begin to investigate how the mind and the sense of self are caught in righteous anger. We inquire into the nature of reactivity and the formation of self and understand how the sense of self is formed within this reaction and feeds off the power the anger provides. The love is still acknowledged but not focused upon.

We begin to separate the formless from form by allowing the formless to hold the reactivity without adding further commentary. As stillness descends, love is clearly seen as separate from the issue of climate change and does not depend upon the outcome of the argument for its continuance. We also understand that until this point love has been confused with the reactivity from the sense of self. This is the middle section of the diagram, where form and the formless are perceived separately, and love, and the issues within love are clearly differentiated. With the end of confusion is the end of the problem but not the end of love.

We now surrender the need to be a person with an issue, and love for the earth continues without righteousness. This is the right side of the diagram, where we surrender our need to be separate from love, and form and the formless merge as one. The whole problem dissolves with the end of separation but not the love and caring for the solution. From the unification of form and the formless, the work of effectively altering climate change may continue, but the divisiveness is gone, along with the angst and discord. Here we respond by abiding within the moment, so that "I" and "the moment" are not separate or differentiated, and it is from here that a living wisdom can enter and act appropriately.

WISDOM, FAITH, AND SURRENDER

We may worry whether our love for the issue of climate change will continue after our righteousness ends. In the beginning we feel the two so inextricably connected that we may be afraid to release our anger for fear of the loss of the issue. The truth is we do not know whether we will continue to be passionate about the issue, but whatever the final product, it will be based on the wisdom of seeing clearly. Our path now becomes driven by faith and wisdom.

The truth is asking us to live without reflection or deliberation. When we deliberate on an experience, we stand back and think about it, forcing a division between the thinker and the subject being pondered, but the truth is asking us to have faith in the discerning power of awareness and to trust that love itself will act if action is necessary. The truth is welcoming us to faith, a living and abiding faith.

We can define faith as the willingness to enter the unknown without guarantees or self-control. Faith is the mind surrendering to the heart. "Faith is not being sure, but betting with your last cent."[8] It is a frequently overlooked word because it is often tied to a tightly contained and rigidly fundamental belief system that allows no room for doubt. But faith expresses itself though questions such as What or who is in control? What lies beyond my power? What is the sacred? By questioning, we doubt the established order, and this form of doubt strengthens faith. We could say we doubt our way to the truth.

In this sense faith is wide open, willing to go anywhere. The Buddha said, "Wide opened is the door of the Deathless to all who have ears to hear; let them send forth faith [*saddha*] to meet it."[9] There is a quality of adventuresomeness in faith that is willing to risk going forward. If we settle for too long, we can begin to feel fixed and determined, but faith keeps us renewed by continually exposing us to new circumstances.

Another quality that is more frequently attributed to faith is devotion. This natural openness is unguarded, appreciative, and humble. Devotedly we advance, bowing in faith to one another, knowing that no one knows the way forward. This astonishing quality of not knowing has us on bended knee in deep surrender, but instead of recoiling in fear, it is compelling us outward through gratitude.

Finally, faith expresses itself as confidence. Wisdom coalesces as a steady persistence, and faith operates out of that confidence of being. Over time wisdom develops into a certainty that is unassailable.

This is not the certainty of knowing but a general confidence of being that expresses itself through living without doubt.

The spiritual journey is all about trust. As the path develops, trust moves out from under form's volitional control into the abiding formless realm. But what then catches our fall when we eliminate trusting in our own efforts? What is the safety net for a soft landing without our exertion of influence, without having faith in our ability to power this forward? Our wisdom catches us, though faith precedes wisdom. Faith is the willingness to venture beyond what we know, and wisdom comes from having done so. Wisdom verifies that the risk was worth taking and therefore strengthens our resolve in taking further risks. Faith and wisdom reinforce each other throughout the entire pathway.

> You have faith, but it may be faith in yourself and may not extend beyond your personal empowerment. What reaches beyond your boundaries and control? Ask yourself whether the sacred is within your control. What uplifts your spirit, and how do you know it is true? What draws you back to meditation after a particularly difficult sitting? See if you can get a sense of what keeps you on your spiritual path. Is it belief or an intuitive sense beyond knowing?

A key component of wisdom is the discernment described in chapter 9, which is the pure seeing of just what is. One of the reasons it is so difficult to surrender is that we lack faith in discernment but trust our self-image. We question whether anything will be around to pick up the pieces of our dissolving image. But discernment assures us that we lose nothing when we free ourselves from the idea of self, and as our faith grows, we understand that decisions are handled very nicely from discernment. It takes faith to move further into risk, but each time, that risk is verified with deeper wisdom and greater faith.

When we resist an experience on the left side of our continuum, we trust our personal empowerment more than the unknown, and the aversive action is in opposition to faith and therefore lacks wisdom. When faith is placed in our empowerment, we count on our defenses and aggression to see us through, and we either pull back in avoidance or strike out in violence. Wisdom from the right side of the continuum bypasses "me" completely and directly surrenders control to faith.

There is a dance among faith, wisdom, and surrender that must be perfectly balanced, each feeding the other. When wisdom meets an obstruction, it surrenders all opposition, but if there is limited wisdom, the surrender will not occur. At this juncture repeated exposure of discernment to the problem usually increases wisdom sufficiently, leading to greater faith and further surrender.

I was recently having dental work and counted four hands in my mouth simultaneously. I had no idea what those hands were doing and could either worry my way through the procedure or relax more deeply into the chair. I chose the latter but noticed that I needed to *live* relaxation or I would find my way back into a defensive posture where I was trying to relax but actually worrying my way through the procedure. Living relaxation means dropping your guard and surrendering to the process without resistance.

Relaxation and surrender are the activities of faith. Surrender, as mentioned in chapter 9, is the immediate and categorical release of all tension. Surrender comes out of faith. To surrender we simply stop avoiding. Worry, doubt, control, and fear are the ways we compromise giving up our power. While I was in the dental chair, my worry was completely useless, but it appeared nevertheless. Worry was my only defense and the singular way I could establish any oversight of the procedure. Not that I had any idea of what was occurring, but worry was like a guard dog ready to bark at the slightest infringement on my safety.

The fruit of the path is a release, not a cure. We do not get over anything; we see it as unnecessary, meaningless, and untrue. The division ends, not the challenge. The dentist may strike a nerve, cancer may continue, the weather remains unpleasantly hot, and the trials of life abound, but there is no alternative created. We do not cry out in annoyance, "How could this be happening to me?" It is not happening to you, it is happening together with you. You and the irritation are arising together, never separately, and always here, always now.

> What if there were no alternatives to now? What if the mind stopped seeking other possibilities? The separated sense of you would become unemployed if it lost the ability to argue. You would become still and fade into the light of the moment. There would be no differentiation, and all would be quiet. Now test these waters and allow that to happen. See if there is any downside to quieting yourself through surrender.

THE QUIET ROAR OF THE DHARMA

There is no "where" to go; there is just "how" to go. When we prioritize the where, we will undervalue the how. The where is the searching and the how is the receiving. The how is not an intellectual question of what to do as we attempt to navigate through the moment but an opening into the wonderment of the moment that allows the discerning and surrendering necessary to permit a full engagement. The how is nondirectional and therefore allows a flexibility of responses ripe with endless possibilities. Our lives will be as busy as the importance we give the where, and busyness will strengthen our location and purpose. We will know what we are doing and why and have a solid sense of ourselves, but the sacred comes through the how. The where will confirm us as an individual, but the how will open us to the mystery.

The how is appropriate action within the unfolding moment, arising sometimes as spontaneity and sometimes as a more measured response compatible with the nuances discerned. The direction the moment takes is not our concern and is guided by forces beyond our control. Surrendering to the moment is having faith that the gover-

nance has its own way that far exceeds any manipulated response that
we could provide.

Since there is no "where" to go, all places are equally suited for
spiritual embracement. Looking beyond where we currently are into
a new location is the busy mind attempting to locate the sacred in the
where of life. Although the content may change across venues, the
fabric of the moment does not, and it is the fabric that holds the sacred. From this perspective, what we do has no effect on the formless. We can say mantras, twist our bodies into asanas, sit cross-legged
for hours, recite scriptures, or stare at mandalas. There is no activity,
spiritually defined or otherwise, that changes the proximity of the
formless. There is only wisdom, faith, and surrender, which are not
activities but a releasing of our need to be in form. That is all.

Our practices follow the "how" by opening us up to receive life
rather than try to influence it. An acronym that orients us to this receptive side of living is ROAR. Notice, as these words are defined,
that they are expressions of faith and are beautifully simple in their
pointing. They are all based on the premise that the less we bring to
any experience, the more we see what is truly there. None of these
letters suggests ambition, struggle, control, manipulation, or resistance. These words work to brighten the light of awareness and diminish the influence of self.

The first *R* of ROAR has been spoken about frequently and is
relaxation, the essence of nonresistance. Tension, the opposite of relaxation, signals that we are frightened by the current presentation of
life. Relaxing is not a doing but an undoing of that tension and strain.
Faith is required to relax, since there is no guarantee where the relaxation will take us. Relaxation is a kind of psychic free fall without a
safety net, since all boundaries and landings are created through resistance and fear. We could say that we relax our way to freedom.

Relaxation is the release of all tension in body and mind.
We may halt a deepening relaxation because we are unsure
of where this psychic release is going. Notice the limits you

place on relaxation. Name the fear you have of relaxing further and see if you can explore it thoroughly. Can you get a sense of how it operates in your life? The investigation will take you to a boundary that you currently refuse to cross. Patiently study that boundary until faith arises. Faith will feel like a readiness to cross the boundary without guarantees and will encourage a gentle crossing in your own time.

The O of ROAR is noninterfering *observation*. When we do not interfere with observation, we take the sense of self out of the awareness, and awareness becomes freestanding. Noninterfering observation is formless awareness, since the form of "me" has been eliminated. Observation works with relaxation to deepen the relaxed response. When we reach the limit of our ability to relax, observation understands the confusion and sees the boundary we refuse to cross. Active discernment holds the natural curiosity of the heart and meets that edge with a questioning investigation until there is enough wisdom and faith to let go and cross.

The A is *allowance,* the willingness to open, drop our guard, and allow everything to enter. Again we can feel the faith necessary to consent to such an opening. By removing our defensiveness, we are allowing the experience to be what it is, but how do we know it is safe? We become tense when we feel threatened, and tension is the loss of relaxation. Observation looks discerningly at the experience to determine its safety. When it decides there is no harm, it drops the tension, allowing the experience its full display.

We are getting a sense of how each of the qualities of ROAR supports the others. Observation provides the wisdom to deepen relaxation and allow greater acceptance. As acceptance expands, relaxation intensifies until a new boundary arises. Observation gently questions that boundary until we cross it in faith. This allows for increased relaxation and allowance, completing the circle.

Now we have come to the final R, which is *respond.* Our actions from the consensus paradigm mostly revolve around prior conditioning, which means we move in relationship to pleasant and unpleasant experiences. But is there a response arising within the field of the moment rather than as a reaction to the moment? If we expand beyond our self-centered perspective, this may become apparent. By allowing a full embrace of the moment rather than the circumscribed perspective of me living within the moment, we broaden the context from which actions can arise. In Buddhism this is called "clear comprehension."[10]

When all factors have equal relevance, actions arise by themselves from the whole. From the perspective of form, this looks like "I" am acting appropriately within the context of the whole, but in actuality the "I" is no more relevant than any other component of the moment. So the relative starting point on our continuum for initiating wise action would be to do what is appropriate considering all the factors present. As we move down our spiritual pathway, discerning awareness begins to uproot the isolating egoic perspective and action ascends out of formless awareness.

Relax, observe, allow, and *respond* put you in proper orientation to your spiritual pathway wherever you are and whatever you might be doing. Whenever a difficulty arises, establish your relationship to the resistance through one of these words. Use these words along with active discernment as beacons to guide, encourage, and align you to the end point of your continuum.

And so we have come down to this: there are no special spiritual places, activities, experiences, or moments. We can cry out for God as loud as we wish, and he gets no nearer than now. It is simply our belief in form that prohibits the mergence of form and formlessness. Discerning our way to the end of those beliefs is all that is necessary to know the face of God, the same face that is staring back at you in the mirror of now.

The heart is the passageway. We concede the beliefs of the mind to the unknowing mystery of the heart and love our way out of individual existence and into the realm of the formless. When appearances return, there is a smile of knowing their essence. That essence never lives in conflict with form: form and the formless dancing within the seamless whole of the heart.

A practice for the ages: Why is this thought believed?

Then the Buddha said to his monks, "Walk over the earth for the blessing of many, for the happiness of many, out of compassion for the world, for the welfare and the blessing and the happiness of all sentient beings."[11]

Notes

Abbreviations

A=Anguttara Nikaya. References are to Nyananponika Thera and Bhikkhu Bodhi, trans., *Anguttara Nikaya Anthology: An Anthology of Discourses from the Anguttara Nikaya* (Kandy, Sri Lanka: Buddhist Publication Society, 1999).

D=Digha Nikaya. Except where noted, references are to Maurice Walshe, trans., *The Long Discourses of the Buddha: A Translation of the Digha Nikaya* (Somerville, Mass.: Wisdom Publications, 1995).

Dh=Dhammapada. Except where noted, references are to Gil Fronsdal, trans., *The Dhammapada: A New Translation of the Buddhist Classic with Annotations* (Boston: Shambhala Publications, 2006).

M=Majjhima Nikaya. References are to Bhikkhu Nanamoli and Bhikkhu Bodhi, trans., *The Middle Length Discourses of the Buddha: A New Translation of the Majjhima Nikaya* (Somerville, Mass.: Wisdom Publications, 1995).

S=Samyutta Nikaya. References are to Bhikkhu Bodhi, trans., *The Connected Discourses of the Buddha: A New Translation of the Samyutta Nikaya*, 2 vols. (Somerville, Mass.: Wisdom Publications, 2000).

Sn=Sutta Nipata. References are to H. Saddhatissa, trans., *The Sutta-Nipata: A New Translation from the Pali Canon* (New York: RoutledgeCurzon, 1995).

U=Udana. References are to Nyananponika Thera and Bhikkhu Bodhi, trans., *Numerical Discourses of the Buddha: An Anthology of*

Suttas from the Anguttara Nikaya (Walnut Creek, Calif.: Altamira Press, 1999).

Introduction

1. The body of teachings expounded by the Buddha.
2. The terms *consensus* and *conventional reality* will be used throughout this book to mean the generally agreed-upon reality of separate subjects and objects that most of us believe is the true perception of life.
3. Authentic practices are continua that move us from form to the formless.

CHAPTER 1. *In Search of the Essence*

1. Mark Whittle, "Cosmology: The History and Nature of Our Universe," The Great Courses Series.
2. Ibid.
3. Greg Laden's Science Blog, http://scienceblogs.com/gregladen/2011/11/28/how-many-cells-are-there-in-th/, accessed July 10, 2013.
4. "Cellular Biology: Cell Structures and Functions," from Projects by Students for Students, http://library.thinkquest.org/12413/structures.html, accessed July 10, 2013.
5. Deepak Chopra, "One Minute Shift: The Wonder of You," Institute of Noetic Science, November 13, 2007.
6. "John Wheeler coined the term 'quantum foam' to describe the frenzy revealed by such an ultramicroscopic examination of space," quoted in Brian Greene, *The Elegant Universe* (New York: Vintage, 2000), p. 127.
7. Richard P. Feynman, "Space-Time Approach to Quantum Electrodynamics," *Physical Review* 76, no. 6: 10.
8. Vlatko Vedral, "Living in a Quantum World," *Scientific American,* June 2011.
9. Peter Tyson, "A Sense of Scale: String Theory," *Nova,* PBS, October 28, 2003.
10. Quoted in Brian Greene, *The Fabric of the Cosmos* (New York: Vintage Books, 2004), p. 8.

11. Ibid., p. 11.
12. Ibid., p. 5.
13. Ross Douthat, The Opinion Page, *New York Times,* December 22, 2009.
14. Clara Moskowitz, "Spooky Quantum Entanglement," *Live Science,* October 8, 2010.
15. Greene, *Fabric of the Cosmos,* p. 78.
16. David G. Myers, *Exploring Psychology in Modules,* 7th ed. (New York: Worth Publishers, 2007).
17. "Who Am I?", *Radiolab,* May 7, 2007.
18. Sn 1094.
19. The ego is the voice inside our minds that comments and directs us through most events. It is a clear reference and sense of "me," separate from what is not me. The ego holds the ideas and images that we define as "me" and attempts to direct our adaptations and changes so that we can make the most out of life.

CHAPTER 2. *Consensus Paradigm and Abstract Thought*

1. Manji Hazarika, "*Homo erectus/ergaster* and Out of Africa: Recent Developments in Paleoanthropology and Prehistoric Archaeology" (intensive course in biological anthropology at the Summer School of the European Anthropological Association, Prague, Czech Republic, June 16–30, 2007).
2. "Becoming Human, Part 2: Birth of Humanity," *Nova,* PBS, November 9, 2009.
3. S 56:11.
4. Amit Goswami, *The Quantum Activist,* www.quantumactivist.com.
5. As used here, *awareness* means the formless, stillness, wordless seeing, presence, or that which holds all objects and is analogous to the sacred.
6. Gospel of Thomas, 113, Coptic Version, translated by Thomas Lambdin.
7. Charles Kittel and Herbert Kroemer, *Thermal Physics,* 2nd ed. (New York: W. H. Freeman, 1980).
8. A 3:128.

9. M 140:31.
10. Bruce Rosenblum and Fred Kuttner, *Quantum Enigma* (New York: Oxford University Press, 2006), p. 4.
11. Quoted in Robert Lanza, *Biocentrism: How Life and Consciousness Are the Keys to Understanding the True Nature of the Universe* (Dallas, Tex.: BenBella Books, 2009).
12. Vlatko Vedral, "Living in a Quantum World," *Scientific American,* June 2011.
13. Sn 873–74.

CHAPTER 3. *The Divided Mind*

1. S 15:3.
2. Michael S. Gazzaniga, quoted by Benedict Carey in "Decoding the Brain's Cacophony," *New York Times,* November 1, 2011.
3. "Dan Siegel: What Makes a Healthy Mind," interview by Tami Simon, *Insights at the Edge*, podcast on www.soundstrue.com, October 6, 2009.
4. Michael S. Gazzaniga, speaking about his book *Who's in Charge?* on *The Conversation,* KUOW, Nov. 17, 2011.
5. The 1814 translation into English by the Reverend H. F. Cary is the origin for this phrase in English.
6. S 12.20.
7. Thanissaro Bhikkhu, *The Paradox of Becoming,* www.accesstoin sight.org/lib/authors/thanissaro/paradoxofbecoming.pdf.
8. Sn 744–45.
9. U 1:10.
10. A 10:107.

CHAPTER 4. *Governing Laws of the Formless Paradigm*

1. Stephen Hawking, *The Grand Design* (New York: Bantam, 2010).
2. Gospel of Thomas, 70.
3. Trauma is a different category of memory and will not be the topic of this discussion. It often requires a longer, more adaptive approach accompanied by stability of heart and professional support.
4. www.reference.com/browse/homeostasis.

5. Matt. 5:48.
6. J. Krishnamurti, "Dissolution Speech," disbanding the Order of the Star, August 3, 1929, www.jkrishnamurti.org/about-krish namurti/dissolution_speech.php.
7. *Wikipedia,* "uncertainty principle," http://en.wikipedia.org/wiki/Uncertainty_principle.
8. Richard Wolfson, *Einstein's Relativity and the Quantum Revolution,* www.thegreatcourses.com/tgc/courses/course_detail.aspx?cid=153.

CHAPTER 5. *Comparing Strategies*

1. Joel Cracraft and Michael J. Donoghue, eds., *Assembling the Tree of Life* (New York: Oxford University Press, 2005), p. 592.
2. Bill Bryson, *A Short History of Nearly Everything* (New York: Broadway Books, 2003).
3. Denial does serve a purpose in our culture because most of us are socialized to adapt our way through traumatic events. Denial allows the mind time to assimilate the stark truth that is coming through, but there is both functional and dysfunctional denial. Functional denial is building toward a readiness to allow that truth in; dysfunctional denial prolongs its resistance, creating pain for everyone involved.

CHAPTER 6. *Crossing the Divide*

1. Teachings such as the Three Characteristics of Existence: *anicca* (impermanence), *dukkha* (unsatisfactoriness), and *anatta* (no permanently abiding self).
2. M 64.
3. The sense of self will wax and wane throughout our lives, arising when there is something functional to do, but it will not be a problem unless we believe it to be who we are.
4. Sn 56.11.
5. Greene, *Fabric of the Cosmos,* pp. 62 and 77.
6. It should be noted that if our concentration is strong enough, emptiness could be experienced regardless of our motivation.
7. Greene, *Fabric of the Cosmos,* p. 11.
8. Ibid., p. 94.

CHAPTER 7. *The Buddhist Continuum*

1. God in this sense is the underlying reality of nonseparation.
2. Feeling tones are of three types: pleasant, unpleasant, or neutral. The conditioned psychic reaction to each tone is usually different. We avoid what is unpleasant, pursue what is pleasant, and bypass what is neutral. Unnoticed, these tendencies can lead to character formations that persist throughout our life.
3. I am excluding all forms of trauma in this discussion. Trauma is a special category of emotional experience that is best handled with the aid of a therapist.
4. Dan Lusthaus, *Buddhist Phenomenology* (New York: Routledge, 2002), p. 242, n. 46.
5. Peter Harvey, *An Introduction to Buddhist Ethics* (Cambridge University Press, 2000), pp. 239–40.

CHAPTER 8. *Other Continua*

1. One side note for clarity: the two ends of any spiritual continuum are actually different representations of the same thing. Like ice and steam, they are different only in appearance, but of course ice and steam are both different expressions of the same substance, in this case water. Take the continuum of form to the formless: form is the mind inducing nothing to be something through the words and images it infuses, and the formless is allowing the nothing to exist free of words. Therefore the process of moving from one side of any pathway to the other is better described as alchemy rather than transcendence. We are not really transcending anything; we are simply allowing the right side of the continuum to express its intrinsic nature, while the left side is the mentally induced nature. Anything mentally induced will have all the left-sided qualities of suffering, noise, contraction, separation, and so on, and the right side will hold all the absolute intrinsic qualities, including the end of suffering, stillness, love, contentment, and the like.
2. Chögyam Trungpa, *The Sacred Path of the Warrior* (Boston: Shambhala Publications, 1984).

CHAPTER 9. *The Discerning Power of Awareness*

1. Francesca Fremantle, *Luminous Emptiness* (Boston: Shambhala Publications, 2001), p. 198.
2. M 10.34, Satipatthana Sutta: Frames of Reference, trans. Thanissaro Bhikkhu.
3. A 3:38.
4. A Zen koan is a question, or statement, that is used in Zen practice to provoke the "great doubt" and is a test of a student's progress in Zen practice.
5. Ajahn Pasanno and Ajahn Amaro, *The Island: An Anthology of the Buddha's Teachings on Nibbana* (Northumberland, UK: Forest Sangha Publications, 2011), p. 29.

CHAPTER 10. *The Principles of Practice*

1. S 45:8.
2. M 1:25–26.
3. A 10:176.
4. M 49:23.
5. Greene, *Fabric of the Cosmos,* p. 11.
6. "With *Ignorance* as condition, *Mental Formations* arise. With Mental Formations as condition, *Consciousness* arises. With Consciousness as condition, *Mind and Matter* arises. With Mind and Matter as condition, Senses arise. With *Senses* as condition, *Contact* arises. With Contact as condition, *Feeling* arises. With Feeling as condition, *Craving* arises. With Craving as condition, *Clinging* arises. With Clinging as condition, *Becoming* arises. With Becoming as a condition, *Birth* arises. With Birth as condition, *Aging and Dying* arises." (Bhikkhu Bodhi, *In the Buddha's Words* [Somerville, Mass.: Wisdom Publications, 2005], pp. 314–16.)
7. S 44:10.
8. A 10:58.

CHAPTER 11. *The Applications of Practice*

1. In Hinduism, and in particular Jnana Yoga and Advaita Vedanta,

     neti, neti means "not this, not that" or "neither this nor that" (*neti* is the sandhi form of *na iti,* "not so").

2. The Big Bang theory is the prevailing cosmological model that explains the early development of the universe. It has the universe exploding out of nothing.

3. Sn 754–757.

4. Jiddu Krishnamurti, *Commentaries on Living,* First Series (Wheaton, Ill.: Quest Books, 1956), p. 244.

CHAPTER 12. *A Paradigm's Shift toward the Heart*

1. A 9:41.

2. A 3:128.

CHAPTER 13. *Living Nonseparation*

1. Shunryu Suzuki, *Zen Mind, Beginner's Mind* (New York: Weatherhill, 1970), p. 92.

2. U 8:3.

3. M 29:7.

4. Early Sufi masters referred to the unconditioned as the "Dazzling Dark."

5. A. F. Price and Wong Mou-lam, trans., *The Diamond Sutra and the Sutra of Hui-neng* (Boston: Shambhala Publications, 2005), p. 53.

6. Sn 755.

7. The Heart of Prajna Paramita Sutra, translated by Tang Dharma Master of the Tripitaka Hsüan-Tsang, Buddhist Text Translation Society, www.cttbusa.org/heartsutra/heartsutra.htm.

8. Mary Jean Irion, quoted in *Chocolate for a Woman's Spirit,* by Kay Allen Baugh (New York: Fireside, 1999), p. 75.

9. Mahavagga, I.5.11 in *Vinaya Texts,* trans. T. W. Rhys Davids (Delhi: Motilal Banarsidass, 1996), p. 88.

10. *Sampajañña* in Pali, which means "clear comprehension" or "clear knowing."

11. S 4:5.